TH

The Massey Lectures are co-sponsored by CBC Radio, House of Anansi Press, and Massey College in the University of Toronto. The series was created in honour of the Right Honourable Vincent Massey, former Governor General of Canada, and was inaugurated in 1961 to provide a forum on radio where major contemporary thinkers could address important issues of our time.

This book comprises the 2016 Massey Lectures, "The Return of History: Conflict, Migration, and Geopolitics in the Twenty-First Century," broadcast in November 2016 as part of CBC Radio's *Ideas* series. The producer of the series was Philip Coulter; the executive producer was Greg Kelly.

JENNIFER WELSH

Jennifer Welsh is Professor and Chair in International Relations at the European University Institute in Florence (Italy) and a Fellow of Somerville College, University of Oxford. From 2013 until 2016, she was the Special Adviser to the United Nations Secretary General on the Responsibility to Protect. She co-founded the Oxford Institute for Ethics, Law and Armed Conflict, and has taught international relations at the University of Toronto, McGill University, and the Central European University (Prague). Welsh is the author, co-author, and editor of several books and articles on international relations, the changing character of war, and Canadian foreign policy. She was born and raised in Regina, Saskatchewan, and is of Metis descent. She now lives in Italy, with her husband and two children.

At Home in the World:
Canada's Global Vision for the 21st Century

Chips & Pop:
Decoding the Nexus Generation (co-author)

Edmund Burke and International Relations

The Responsibility to Prevent: Overcoming the
Challenges of Atrocity Prevention (co-editor)

Just and Unjust Military Intervention:
European Thinkers from Vitoria to Mill (co-editor)

Humanitarian Intervention and
International Relations (editor)

THE RETURN OF HISTORY

....

*Conflict, Migration, and Geopolitics in the
Twenty-First Century*

JENNIFER WELSH

ANANSI

Hardcover edition first published in Canada in 2016 and the USA in 2016
by House of Anansi Press Inc.
This edition published in 2017 by House of Anansi Press Inc.

House of Anansi Press
www.houseofanansi.com

House of Anansi Press is committed to protecting our natural environment.
As part of our efforts, the interior of this book is printed on paper that contains
100% post-consumer recycled fibres, is acid-free, and is processed chlorine-free.

21 20 19 18 17 1 2 3 4 5

Library and Archives Canada Cataloguing in Publication

Welsh, Jennifer M. (Jennifer Mary), 1965–, author
The return of history : conflict, migration, and geopolitics
in the twenty-first century / Jennifer Welsh.

(The Massey lectures)
Previously published: 2016.
Issued in print and electronic formats.
ISBN 978-1-4870-0242-8 (softcover).—ISBN 978-1-4870-0131-5 (EPUB).—
ISBN 978-1-4870-0132-2 (Kindle)

1. History--Philosophy. 2. World politics--1989-. 3. Civilization.
4. Regression (Civilization). 5. Progress. I. Title. II. Series: CBC Massey
lectures series

D16.8.W45 2017   901   C2017-901297-5
                             C2016-901578-5

Library of Congress Control Number: 2016958330

Cover design: Alysia Shewchuk
Text design: Ingrid Paulson
Typesetting: Erin Mallory

 Canada Council   Conseil des Arts   ONTARIO ARTS COUNCIL
for the Arts   du Canada   CONSEIL DES ARTS DE L'ONTARIO

We acknowledge for their financial support of our publishing program the Canada
Council for the Arts, the Ontario Arts Council, and the Government of Canada
through the Canada Book Fund.

Printed and bound in Canada

MIX
Paper from
responsible sources
FSC® C016245

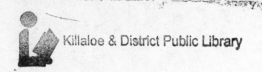

For Eleanor and Max,
and the history they will make.

CONTENTS

"History repeats itself because no one was listening the first time." — Anonymous

ONE

THE RETURN OF HISTORY

IT IS THE CONCEIT of almost every generation to think that it is living in extraordinary times. For my parents' generation, it was the trauma of the Second World War and the miracle of post-war reconstruction. For my older siblings, it was the protest movements of the late 1960s and the triumph of civil rights and women's equality. And for my generation, it was the end of the Cold War.

In the autumn of 1989, it was difficult not to believe that something monumental was occurring on the global landscape. The stirrings in Eastern Europe were not isolated accidents, but seemed part of a larger process — whose trajectory was still uncertain. I was a graduate student at the University of Oxford, and when the images of East Germans chipping away at the Berlin Wall flashed across the television screen on November 9, I jumped aboard a flight to Berlin with some of my classmates to witness, first hand, the deconstruction of an empire. When we arrived the next day, the party atmosphere along the Wall had exploded. Lufthansa flight attendants with trays were handing out canapés to those gathered, and U.S. television anchormen, fresh from their overseas journey, were hoisted on makeshift platforms to report "live from the scene." The most astute Western observer of those heady days, British journalist and writer Timothy Garton Ash, described that period in November as "the greatest street party in the history of the world."[1] And so it was. It was estimated that close to two million East Germans crossed over into West Berlin the weekend after the Wall fell — most of them to spend the welcome gift of 100 Deutschmarks they received from the West German government. I came home with my own piece of the Wall, painted with graffiti, as well as a euphoric sense of being at the centre of history.

The collapse of communist regimes was so rapid that scholars and journalists scrambled to keep up. The revolutions that had begun in Poland and Hungary, and spread to Germany, sparked upheaval in Czechoslovakia, Romania, and Bulgaria. The wave eventually spilled over into the Soviet Union itself, where suppressed nationalism in the Baltic region — Estonia, Latvia, and Lithuania — and in republics such as Armenia and Georgia, exploded into calls for independence. The deteriorating Soviet economy only heightened these nationalist sentiments and led successive constituent republics of the Soviet Union to create their own economic and legal systems. Though the genie was already out of the bottle, communist hard-liners in the Kremlin tried to reverse the changes by staging a coup against President Mikhail Gorbachev in the summer of 1991. The effort was thwarted by the president of the Russian republic, Boris Yeltsin — with the help of the army — but the communist regime in Moscow was mortally wounded. Any remaining authority it had quickly evaporated. The Soviet Union was officially disbanded on December 26, 1991, ending its reign as the world's largest and most influential communist state.

In the midst of these tumultuous events, the American political commentator Francis Fukuyama wrote a famous article entitled "The End of History." His central claim was that the demise of the confrontation between East and West in 1989 constituted much more than the end of the Cold War. It also signalled the endpoint of humanity's sociocultural and ideological evolution and the "universalization of Western liberal democracy as the final form of human government."[2] As a consequence of liberal democracy's victory, and diffusion, he predicted, we would see the waning of traditional power politics and large-scale conflict, and the path toward a more peaceful world.

A decade later, the end of the Cold War and the subsequent increase in the number of liberal democratic states was indeed accompanied by a marked decline in both interstate and ethnic wars, as well as the number of refugees and displaced persons. During the 1990s, the former superpowers collaborated on the reunification of Germany and disengaged from their proxy wars in Africa. The United States also scaled back its military presence in Europe and led the charge to expand the North Atlantic Treaty Organization (NATO) to include states that were formerly part of the Soviet bloc. Societies in Central and Eastern Europe and the Baltic region embraced democracy and were drawn into the orbit of the expanding European Union (EU) — which had begun as a free trade and customs area, but after the ratification of the Maastricht Treaty in 1993 created a common currency and strengthened political cooperation in areas such as foreign policy, justice, and immigration.

The United Nations also came out from its Cold War shadow to expand its role in international peace and security, thanks to a united Security Council. The first palpable sign of change came during the hours and days following Iraq's invasion of Kuwait in August 1990, when the Security Council — no longer paralyzed by the U.S.-Soviet standoff — acted collectively to demand Iraq's unconditional withdrawal. The unprecedented level of cooperation between the two former adversaries signalled, in the words of former U.S. Secretary of State James Baker, that "half a century after it began...the Cold War breathed its last." In January 1992, the Security Council held its first ever summit. Ambassadors and heads of state gathered to issue a statement reaffirming their commitment to the original collective security goals of the UN Charter. They also tasked then Secretary General of the UN Boutros Boutros-Ghali to come up with a list of recommendations on how to bolster the UN's capacity to resolve conflict and maintain peace in the post–Cold War era. In his subsequent report, titled *An Agenda for Peace*, Boutros-Ghali noted that the end of decades of tension between the world's superpowers had given the organization a "new source of strength" which could be harnessed to tackle new threats to international security and to develop new institutions and capacities.[3] As a result, the early 1990s saw the creation of the UN Office of the High Commissioner for Human Rights, to promote and protect human rights world-wide, and the UN Office for the Coordination of Humanitarian Affairs, to improve upon the organization's response to humanitarian and natural disasters.

For my part, I continued to revel in the glow of those magical, and predominantly peaceful, Revolutions of 1989. Democratic elections were staged in countries where one-party dictatorships had dominated for forty years. Centrally planned economies shifted almost overnight into capitalist markets, and precious consumer goods — for so long out of reach to ordinary citizens — appeared on store shelves and street corners. Everywhere, hopes were raised for a future different from what seemed to have been pre-ordained.

While the end of the Cold War offered the possibility of transcending decades of crisis diplomacy, nuclear arms buildup, and costly foreign interventions, it also promised a new beginning for those who had lived behind the Iron Curtain. I spent the summer of 1992 in Prague, teaching the ideas of Western liberalism to eager students from the former Soviet Union and communist bloc of Eastern Europe, frequenting the new bars and discos that sprang up in the Czech capital, and revelling in the workings of a new democracy led by a former dissident and playwright, Václav Havel. Looking back, it was the best summer of my life.

Not even the breakup of the former Yugoslavia, and the unleashing of violent conflict and brutal acts of ethnic cleansing, seemed to challenge the narrative of the "new world order." As a newly minted professor of international relations, I went on to analyze and teach about the structure and institutions of this emerging order, including the expanding peacekeeping role of the UN and the widening and deepening of the European Union. I also joined the chorus of believers who wondered which part of the world would next fall to the powerful sway of liberal democracy.

At the heart of Fukuyama's thesis was the audaciously optimistic idea of *progress* in history. The argument was loosely based on his reading of the nineteenth-century German philosopher Georg Wilhelm Friedrich Hegel, who saw history progressing through a series of epochs marked by the resolution of clashing ideas and propelled by technological change. Fukuyama's claim was that history (at least the history of struggle documented by many historians) would effectively end, or culminate, in the victory of liberal democracy as the guiding ideology for the modern nation-state. This victory entailed three key elements: freely elected governments, the promotion of individual rights, and the creation of a capitalist economic system with relatively modest state oversight. The ideal model, Fukuyama argued, was "liberal democracy in the political sphere combined with easy access to VCRs and stereos in the economic."[4] Once this was achieved, any other tensions or contradictions could be resolved within the context of a modern liberal democratic state.

THE ASCENDANCE OF LIBERAL DEMOCRACY

The triumph of liberal democracy was by no means a foregone conclusion. In fact, Fukuyama's model polity was the product of grand political forces and particular historical moments. Democracy itself, of course, is a very old political principle, one that is based on the deceptively simple idea of rule by the people (or *dēmos*). Its central claim is that individuals should not be powerless subjects, exposed to the whims of tyrants, but rather should have a say in creating the rules by which they are governed. In order to do so, they must also have the opportunity to participate actively in political life.

Throughout human history, this democratic imperative has been interpreted in a number of ways and by a range of political institutions. Some of these arrangements consist of methods of *direct* democracy — where all laws are created directly by a general vote of society's members — as it was practiced by small assemblies of citizens in ancient Greece more than two thousand years ago. Others are forms of *indirect* democracy; for instance, our system of elected members of a parliament, who represent the views of the people within their constituencies and make the laws on their behalf. But whether direct or indirect, rule by the *dēmos* has not always been seen as the best or most successful form of government. In fact, at various points in its historical development, democracy has been written off by its critics. The Greek philosopher

Plato decried democracy for encouraging mob rule, whereby the majority would impose its will, no matter how discriminatory or oppressive, on the minority. When the Athenians were crushed by the kings of Macedonia in the fourth century BC, democracy became a political system of ridicule rather than praise. Although there were examples of attempts to provide for broader input into political decision-making — most notably the creation and expansion of "parliaments" in England from the thirteenth century onward — for centuries political power was concentrated in the hands of largely unaccountable rulers. In sixteenth- and seventeenth-century Europe, the period that saw the origins of our modern nation-state, the most persuasive political arguments did not herald "people power" but legitimated the supreme authority of the monarch, who was answerable solely to God. After the Protestant Reformation, it was believed that only *absolute* sovereignty could counter the disorder and violence that plagued Europe and ensure the physical security of its populations.[5] Democracy, by contrast, was seen as disorderly and dangerous. James Madison, a key architect of the U.S. Constitution, deliberately avoided the term, disparaging democracies as "spectacles of turbulence and contention" and "as short in their lives as they have been violent in their deaths."[6]

It took roughly two centuries for democracy to reassert itself as an attractive and viable principle of political organization. Two key moments in its re-emergence were the American War of Independence (1775–83) and the founding of the new American republic, and the French Revolution (1789–99), during which revolutionaries fought not only to restrain the absolute power of King Louis XVI but to bring to an end the whole system of privileges for the nobility that had supported the monarchy. According to the British political theorist John Dunn, it was during this revolutionary period that the word "democracy," which was originally used as a noun to describe a system of rule, expanded to become a noun denoting a certain type of person (a "democrat"); an adjective which expressed allegiance ("democratic"); and a verb (to "democratize") which described the transformational process of adopting popular self-rule.[7]

But it was not all smooth sailing: while the protagonists of the French Revolution agreed on what they wanted to destroy, they were less united on exactly what kind of society they wanted to build.

Some, inspired by the eighteenth-century French philosopher Jean-Jacques Rousseau, believed true democracy could be realized only if rulers directly enacted the people's will — broadly understood as the will of the majority — and only if the rules of society applied equally to all. Rousseau used these two democratic ideas, consent and equality, to challenge the claim that the divine right of kings justified the law-making power and authority of the sovereign. Instead, only free, equal, and reciprocal agreements among the people could form the basis of legitimate authority in a political community and provide the source of law.[8] Legislative power thus belonged not to the ruler, but to the people and was thereafter known as *popular* sovereignty. Moreover, the state was no longer seen as part of a natural or divine order but rather as a human artifact, instituted to further the collective interests of its citizens.[9]

The potential dangers of this approach were on full and gory display when Maximilien Robespierre became the leader of the revolution in France, staging show trials and sentencing thousands of citizens to death, in a period that became known as the Terror. In the aftermath of the French Revolution, the advocates of democracy grappled with two major questions: First, who is to determine what the will of the people consists of? And second, what should happen if the will of the majority prescribes a morally unacceptable act, such as slavery or mass murder?

A second group of revolutionaries, inspired by the founding fathers of the American republic, was convinced that expressions of popular will did not on their own ensure good government. Two other ingredients were essential. First, drawing on the ideas of the English philosopher John Locke, who is widely regarded as the father of modern liberalism, they insisted that popular sovereignty had to be complemented by a set of basic rights, which would protect the minority from the arbitrary will of the majority. Second, they argued for a separation of powers among the three principal branches of government — legislative, executive, and judiciary — in order to prevent the abuse of power by any single one of them. Within this system of checks and balances, an independent judiciary was seen as a particularly vital part of the governmental architecture that would prevent tyranny of the majority. Respect for individuals, enshrined as fundamental civil and political rights, and the respect for rule of law became key cornerstones of *liberal* democracy. It is for this reason that most liberal democracies around the world now have constitutions, which act as foundational documents that clearly delineate the relationship between branches of government and set out the fundamental rights of every citizen.

The corollary to the idea of basic rights was the claim that these rights were universal — something common to all human beings. As a consequence, the revolutions of the late eighteenth century also inaugurated a process of defining and caring for "humanity" at large. A pivotal moment in this expansion of consciousness and concern was the abolition of the slave trade in Britain, which began in the 1780s and culminated in an act of British parliament in 1807. The abolitionist campaign marked the beginning of the modern humanitarian movement — one that went beyond local acts of charity to alleviating the suffering of those in far-off lands, in recognition of our common humanity.[10] The promotion of both liberty and equality in the late eighteenth century thus brought about what the British historian Jonathan Israel describes as a "revolution of the mind": it led people to radically change their way of thinking about the organization of a society, shifting away from a hierarchical model toward a more egalitarian and inclusive paradigm.[11]

Nevertheless, the democracy that emerged from this period was of a very particular kind — representative rather than direct. The term "democracy" did not connote a form of government in which the people *literally* rule — as they did in ancient Greece through citizen assemblies and juries — but rather one that selects political representatives, through elections, and entrusts them with the power to rule. James Madison argued that this political class would "refine and enlarge public views" by filtering out popular prejudice and discerning, through their wisdom and experience, the broader public interest. Furthermore, it took a century and a half for the "revolution of the mind" to translate into tangible expressions of equality, particularly in the political realm. The first form of democracy, the Athenian polis, had been profoundly hierarchical: roughly 30,000 adult males (which constituted 10 percent of the population) had political rights, while slaves, foreigners, and women had no right to vote.

The earliest liberal democracies in Europe also excluded large parts of the population from political participation. Though the ideal vision was rule by the people, limited by checks and balances, a narrow definition of the people continued to dominate politics. There were three main groups that were excluded from the *dēmos*. The first consisted of those who did not own property. Wealthy democrats, who made up a small but powerful minority, feared the consequences of enfranchising the often-impoverished majority — whose concerns could be radically different from their own. In the United Kingdom, for instance, voting rights were denied to a large segment of the British population until the early twentieth century. Gender was the second basis upon which political rights were restricted. Despite intense political activism by suffragettes from the mid-nineteenth century onward, it was only near the end of the First World War, in 1918, that women gained the right to vote in the United Kingdom and Canada. In the United States, some states took action unilaterally to extend the vote to women, but the end of sex-based restrictions on a national level did not occur until 1920, when the 19th Amendment to the U.S. Constitution was passed. In many other Western countries, voting rights were extended to women only after the Second World War.

The third and final source of exclusion was race. Though earlier expressions of humanitarianism, like the anti-slave trade movement, were allegedly based on ideals of universal human dignity, in reality they merely promoted sympathy for the "other" and not genuine equality. The slaves who preoccupied the eighteenth-century abolitionist campaign were still far from constituting "persons" with entitlements to civic or political rights. According to the American literary historian Lynn Festa, they had no real prerogatives, "except to suffer."[12] And so the denial of political participation on racial grounds continued for more than a century, and later became the focal point of the post-war civil rights movement in the United States. Despite the existence of provisions that theoretically allowed African Americans to participate in U.S. politics, the bureaucratic barriers were so high that a very small percentage could actually vote. It was only when the Voting Rights Act was passed in 1965 that African Americans were fully incorporated into the *dēmos*.

The consolidation of democracy has thus required not only one but several revolutions of the mind. Its global diffusion has also been uneven and full of setbacks. At the start of the twentieth century, there were roughly ten democracies in the world (depending on the definition being used[13]).

This number more than doubled in the years immediately following the Great War, which U.S. President Woodrow Wilson had famously described as a war "to make the world safe for democracy." But within a matter of a few years there was a period of reversal, as a result of both economic crisis (brought on by the Great Depression) and political turmoil. While new democracies in the Baltic states and Poland began to unravel, nascent democracies suffered spectacular defeats in Europe's heartland — Spain, Italy, and Germany — where fascist governments promised greater order and prosperity. Meanwhile, in Latin America, military coups overthrew democratic governments in Brazil, Uruguay, and Argentina.

It was not only a case of democratic gains being reversed. During the inter-war period the democratic ideal itself was challenged by the competing agendas of fascism and communism. In the words of the American political analyst Robert Kagan, democracy's "aura of inevitability vanished."[14] In the 1930s, the rival political systems in Mussolini's Italy, Hitler's Germany, and Stalin's Soviet Union appeared more robust and successful than that of the United States, which had retreated into isolationism, and the creaking democracies in France and Britain. "People tend to follow winners," Kagan observes, "and between the wars the democratic-capitalist countries looked weak and in retreat."[15] As a result, by 1941 there were only nine democracies in the world, causing Winston Churchill to predict a "new dark age" if Britain succumbed to Nazi Germany.

It was the decisive military defeat of fascism, and the occupation of countries such as Japan, South Korea, and Germany, that launched democracy's second big wave after 1945.[16] One of the major alternatives to democracy had been thoroughly discredited — a victory that was aided by high levels of economic growth, a burgeoning middle class, and the expansion of the welfare state in many Western societies. Indeed, the rise of market economies directly contributed to democracy's consolidation. The phenomena that facilitated economic growth — such as high education levels, ease of personal movement, the rule of law, and ready access to information — also supported broad and equal political participation. Additionally, by the 1960s, the process of decolonization and the creation of new states in the developing world, which in some cases brought about new democratic regimes, contributed to a quadrupling of the number of democracies in the world.

It was not until the 1980s, however, that democracy could claim to meet human aspirations better than its competitors."[17] In retrospect, we can see that the launch of democracy's third big wave started in the mid-1970s, with the democratization of the remaining authoritarian states in southern Europe (Greece, Spain, and Portugal), as well as a number of countries in Latin America.

But the world's reigning democracies in Western Europe and North America were still stuck in the depths of the Cold War and their ongoing competition with the communist model — spearheaded by the Soviet Union and China. In addition, their own economies were plagued by the double curse of "stagflation" (high levels of unemployment and inflation combined with low rates of economic growth). At this stage, it was still not clear that the viable alternatives to liberal democracy had been exhausted and many theorists openly mused as to whether democratization had reached its limits.[18]

It took another decade for Marxism-Leninism as an economic system to become bankrupt and for communism's political hold to crumble. The democratic revolutions in central and eastern Europe from 1989 to 1991 "turned the third wave [of democracy] into a tsunami."[19] More than half the world's population came to live under democratic rule and the number of democracies climbed to well over one hundred countries. The "pretensions" of rival systems, Fukuyama argued, were "ultimately unmasked by history."[20] *Liberal* democracy — and its combination of popular rule, protection of human rights, rule of law, and free markets — was the clear winner in the global struggle for political and economic dominance. This victory also inspired many in the West's political class to promote the liberal democratic political and economic model to the rest of world, thereby hastening what Fukuyama described as the spread of the "universal homogeneous state."

PROGRESS OR RECURRENCE?

A quarter of a century after Fukuyama's bold prognosis, where do we find ourselves? Within Western societies, many of his observations still ring true. Some have argued that all politics in liberal democracies have converged in the mushy middle, where there is a general consensus on the desirability of liberal economic policies with a basic welfare state safety net and a solid foundation of constitutionally guaranteed rights and freedoms. As the German-American political theorist Herbert Marcuse describes in his book *One-Dimensional Man*, liberalism has proven highly resilient in the political arena. Over the decades, it has developed a sophisticated capacity to integrate its critics, by offering them political representation and reforming itself at the margins — thereby keeping more radical challenges at bay. Many would claim that any fundamental critique of liberal democracy from within has become almost impossible, making the polarized positions of left and right appear antiquated. In a pre-inaugural address at the Lincoln Memorial in January 2009, former U.S. President Barack Obama famously called for a "declaration of independence...from ideology," while former British Prime Minister David Cameron once boasted that he "doesn't do 'isms.'" Policy differences across parties have become harder to detect and politics is more about "technocratic optimization."[21]

On a global scale, the "end of history" thesis also appears, on first glance, rather convincing. Democracy is still overwhelmingly the most common form of government, and its appeal to those living under alternative regimes remains widespread. Promotion of democracy and human

rights also continues to be a cornerstone — at least
on paper — of the foreign policy agendas of many
states in Europe and North America, but also in
Latin America and parts of Asia and Africa.

But if we zoom out a bit further, the picture
looks different. In fact, it seems that history has
returned.

In the Middle East, both civil and interstate wars
are raging. Indiscriminate and barbaric attacks on
civilians, the annihilation of religious and ethnic
minorities, and the starvation of populations are
a regular part of the strategic repertoire of belligerents. Rather than fostering a liberal democratic
order in the region — as George W. Bush and his
advisors sought to "kick-start" with the 2003 U.S.
invasion of Iraq — U.S. policy-makers are facing
profound governance failures in both Iraq and Syria.
Some believe the current conflict in the region constitutes the unravelling of the 1916 Sykes-Picot
agreement, by which the Middle Eastern provinces
of the crumbling Ottoman Empire were divided
into areas of British and French control, and later
evolved into independent states.[22]

In Russia, meanwhile, an authoritarian government has emerged from "free and fair elections,"
menacing its immediate and not so immediate

neighbours and brazenly recovering territories that were lost in the early 1990s with the collapse of the Soviet Union. It has also declared its intention to reinvest in its nuclear arsenal, with a specific focus on missile systems that can reach Western Europe and North America. Differences between Russia and Western states have once again hobbled the functioning of the UN Security Council, producing mutual recrimination rather than constructive diplomacy in search of common ground.

Indeed, the optimism that accompanied the rebirth of the United Nations in the early 1990s has given way to increasing frustration and despair in the face of its member states' failure to mount a collective and decisive response to situations of conflict, instability, and migration. Globally the number of displaced persons — 65.3 million in 2015 — surpasses even that of the great era of mass flight at the end of the Second World War.[23] The ramifications of the lack of collective action are most tragic in Syria. Six years on, with more than three hundred thousand Syrians dead, over six million displaced within their country, and close to five million having fled as refugees, the armed conflict rages on.

When we consider the general health of

democracy, the vital signs are equally discomforting. Nation-states that not long ago were praised for making democratic transitions — for example, Thailand or Turkey — are now exhibiting symptoms of a backslide into authoritarianism. Even the liberal democracies of Europe and North America are lumbering under significant levels of unemployment, slow growth, and increasing wealth inequality, as well as rising intolerance toward immigrants and refugees. In January 2016, Denmark's government illustrated the depths to which European states have descended, passing a bill that allows Danish police officers to search refugees upon their arrival and seize their valuable assets to pay for their accommodation. But perhaps the most symbolic action of all was taken by the leader of Hungary's populist party, Viktor Orbán, who had been a central figure in Hungary's peaceful transformation from communism a quarter of a century before. In the autumn of 2015, he invested 100 million euros to erect a razor-wire fence along his country's border with Serbia to deter the flow of migrants. As Garton Ash sorrowfully noted: "Europe used to be known as the continent where walls come down and is now the one where they are going up again."[24]

Of course, some might argue — much as Fukuyama himself has done — that when observing broad historical trends, we shouldn't become fixated on short-term phenomena or bumps in the road. The hallmark of a durable political system is its long-term sustainability, not its performance in any given decade.[25]

Despite the fallout from the tumultuous 2008 financial crisis, over the past forty years there has been an overall increase in economic output — on all continents. This growth is largely due to the liberalization of trade and investment, and the penetration of market forces in former communist countries. A similar story could be told in the political sphere, where there was an almost four-fold expansion in the number of electoral democracies between the mid-1970s and 2010. This increase can only partly be explained by the revolutions in Eastern Europe in 1989; it also results from a larger trend that began in Latin America, and which subsequently spread to sub-Saharan Africa and Asia.

Seen from this vantage point, what we witness in the Middle East is not the refutation of the "end of history" thesis, but rather evidence of its midway point. At this stage in liberal democracy's journey, conflicts occur either within states that are still "historical," (i.e., not liberal democratic) and thus in transition — such as Iraq — or between historical states and those that are "post-historical." While these conflicts should trouble us, the argument goes, they should not make us doubt the ultimate endpoint.

What I want to suggest, however, is that we cannot bank on this optimistic reasoning — or the linear thinking that underlines it. The negative political and economic trends we are experiencing a quarter of a century after the end of the Cold War are starting to feel less like "transitions" on the path toward a post-historical world, and more like the return of history.

DEMOCRACY IN CRISIS AT HOME AND ABROAD

The past ten years have seen a consistent decline in the number, as well as the quality, of democracies, when considered through measures such as the integrity of elections, freedom of expression, or freedom of the press.[26] More troubling, according to the political advocacy organization Freedom House, is that the acceptance of democracy as the world's dominant form of government is under greater threat now than at any point in the past twenty-five years. Autocratic regimes openly flout democratic values and consolidated democracies show a lack of confidence and capacity. The American political scientist Larry Diamond goes as far as to characterize these trends as evidence of a "democratic recession." The number of democracies worldwide began to decline a decade ago and has now flat-lined, the result of either overt coups or the incremental decay of democratic values and institutions. Not only is there evidence of corruption and abuse of power, but oppressive governments have also experimented with new techniques of censorship — thanks to technology — and new legal strategies to deny space to opposition groups or civil society.[27]

Five years ago, during the Arab Spring, we held our breath at the momentous sight of the huge rallies against the country's oppressive regime in Cairo's Tahrir Square. Today we see an Egypt where press freedom is curtailed and political opposition figures are imprisoned and executed. To date, only Tunisia — where the Arab Spring began — has managed to consolidate democracy, yet its progress remains fragile and is under constant attack. In fact, journalists have reported that the country turns out the largest percentage per capita of recruits to the so-called Islamic State.[28] Similarly, a decade ago African states were praised for moving toward multi-party elections and constitutions limiting the role of the executive; today many leaders of these same states — such as Burundi and the Democratic Republic of the Congo — are asking to overrule the constitutional provisions on presidential term limits and stifle any viable opposition to their continued hold on power.

All of these developments indicate that while democratic government — defined in minimalist terms as free and fair elections — still dominates the global political landscape, the two other critical elements that make up *liberal* democracy — respect for human rights and the rule of law — are in much shorter supply. Two decades ago, the author and CNN host Fareed Zakaria warned of the rise of "illiberal democracy," a form of government offering the promise of popular legitimacy but without the robust checks on the concentration or abuse of executive power, or on the violation of individual rights — particularly freedom of speech and association.[29] By focusing only on how governments are selected (i.e., whether through the ballot-box or not), he contended, we downplay the more fundamental issue of what goals and policies those governments are pursuing. "If a democracy does not preserve liberty and law," he wrote, the fact "that it is a democracy is a small consolation."[30] Today illiberal democracies are not only trampling on the rights of their own citizens, but frequently engaging in, or sponsoring, acts that threaten the security and well-being of populations in other societies.

But the malaise cuts deeper, to encompass liberal democracy as well. Across many advanced liberal democracies, levels of trust in political institutions are at an historic low and populist parties are enjoying unprecedented levels of influence and electoral success. These parties have moved from the margins of national politics to its very centre, thereby framing the public debate and normalizing nationalistic and xenophobic rhetoric. Whether it be Marine Le Pen's Front National in France, Geert Wilders's Freedom Party in the Netherlands, or the U.K. Independence Party, the anti-immigration and anti-globalization mantras of populist parties constitute a powerful challenge to both the legitimacy of Western governments and the international institutions they have created. The most recent illustration of the rise of populism was the stunning victory for the "Leave" side in the British referendum on membership in the European Union, which managed to galvanize the support of (primarily) English working-class voters who believed that mainstream parties and bureaucratic elites had been ignoring their concerns. Right-wing populism also shaped the race for the White House in 2016, with the meteoric rise and victory of the Republican candidate, Donald Trump.

Populist politicians have successfully seized upon two core ideas associated with democracy. The first is the idea of popular sovereignty. In a true democracy, they chorus, it is the people who are in control. But through the processes of bureaucratization and globalization, they argue, the people have been stripped of their governing power and decision-making has shifted to so-called experts and distant elites in international organizations. The public utterances of almost every populist politician today include the refrain "Take back control." On the day after the referendum in the United Kingdom on the European Union, Nigel Farage declared that the result had been a victory for "real people, ordinary people, decent people."

The other democratic ideal co-opted by the populists is fairness. As the eminent American political scientist Sidney Verba explains, democracy requires two forms of equality. The first is equal participation in politics, or what he calls "equal political voice." This is achieved not merely through universal suffrage, but also through freedom of speech and the press, equal standing under the law, and the equal right to organize politically. But equal voice is only one part of the equation; democracy also requires equal *consideration* of citizens' interests. In short, all voices need to be heard by government.[31] Otherwise, the decisions of legislators will not be perceived as fair or legitimate. Today's liberal democracies, populist politicians insist, have neglected the interests of ordinary working people and catered to the preferences of wealthy elites.

And they have a point. Since the end of the Cold War, the spread of prosperity has been, to put it mildly, less than equitable. While global income inequality has decreased over the past two decades — thanks to the rise of highly populated countries like China, India, and Indonesia — inequality *within* societies has been markedly increasing since the 1980s, particularly in highly developed countries. Indeed, the gap between rich and poor in most OECD countries is at its highest level in thirty years, and the share of national income appropriated by top income earners has dramatically expanded. At the end of 2014, the wealthiest 10 percent of the population in OECD countries earned almost ten times more than the poorest 10 percent (by contrast, in the 1980s, the ratio was 7:1).[32] Furthermore, the very top of the pyramid — the so-called 1 percent — has acquired an ever-greater share of national income over the past three decades.

If we use an alternative measure, the French economist Thomas Piketty's idea of *wealth* inequality — that is, disparities not only in the level of salaries, but also in capital assets accumulated over the years — the division between rich and poor in advanced liberal democracies is even starker. For much of the post-1945 period, economists were optimistic that economic growth and the diffusion of knowledge and skills would prevent wealth from becoming concentrated in fewer and fewer hands. But the current slowdown in economic growth in many developed economies, accompanied by unemployment and a decline in real wages, means that the efforts of many to increase their skills and qualifications are not necessarily translating into greater economic equality. As a result, Piketty predicts, it is inherited wealth — and not the income we earn in the workplace over a lifetime — that will be decisive in determining our economic well-being, much as it was in the eighteenth and nineteenth centuries.[33] The challenge to the idea of equality of opportunity, and to the possibility of social mobility, could not be starker.

Turning to the international stage, the performance of liberal democracy — in terms of resolving conflicts, building peace, and promoting humanitarian values — is equally dismal. We see history returning in the form of massive numbers of displaced war refugees and increasingly lethal tactics employed against civilian populations.[34] Despite fewer wars being waged overall today, between 2008 and 2015 the number of conflict deaths increased threefold, given the intensification of violence and the erosion of respect for principles of international humanitarian law (IHL). In 2014 alone, the number reached just over 125,000 — the highest level in two decades.[35] Established after 1945 to prevent the future waging of "total war" — particularly against civilian populations — IHL consists of a series of restrictions to ensure that the logic of military necessity is balanced with considerations for human life during armed conflict. More specifically, it requires all parties to a conflict to distinguish between civilians (and civilian objects such as schools) and military objects, to grant safe and unimpeded access to those offering humanitarian assistance, and to respect the protected status of medical facilities.

The violence experienced by civilians in recent armed conflicts is reaching levels not seen since the Second World War, and there is a race to the bottom in terms of the restraint exercised by conflict parties.[36] Today's conflicts involve a much greater use of explosive weapons in populated areas; regular attacks on schools, markets, hospitals, and medical personnel; targeting of critical civilian infrastructure (including water facilities); and the denial of access to civilian-populated areas to humanitarian convoys that carry life-saving supplies. This scale of civilian harm is not the tragic but inevitable consequence of what happens in the "fog of war"; rather, it is the result of conscious choices made by warring sides — some of which are supported by Western governments. The images of emaciated and starving children in Madaya, Syria, at the start of January 2016 prompted many Western countries to increase pressure on both the Syrian government and rebel forces to come to the negotiating table. But the plight of these civilians was only the

tip of the iceberg: between 2014 and 2016 the estimated number of those living under daily siege in
Syria was between 450,000 and 650,000.

HISTORY RETURNS, WITH A TWIST

These phenomena of the past five years do not constitute mere bumps on the road, or transitional
moments, in the eventual triumph of the West's
liberal democratic model. Instead, they pose fundamental challenges to its sustainability and raise difficult but legitimate questions about the decisions
its leaders have taken. They also call into question
the peaceful future that was promised by the end
of the Cold War and the "end of history" thesis.
Above all, they should prompt us to revisit the courageous struggles of the past that helped to establish our own liberal democracies, and the decisions
and compromises that were made — both nation-
ally and internationally — to ensure that inequality would be contained and managed, difference
would be respected, wars would be limited, and
power put in the service of collective rather than
narrow objectives.

In the following chapters, I will address different

dimensions of history's return in the twenty-first century. In the next chapter, The Return of Barbarism, I will examine how the strategies and tactics of both state and non-state armed actors are flouting established principles of international humanitarian law and putting civilian lives at greater and greater risk. In Chapter Three, The Return of Mass Flight, I will analyze the unprecedented nature of today's migration challenge and show how new walls are being erected within and beyond Europe. Chapter Four, The Return of Cold War, will discuss how Russian President Vladimir Putin's revival of geopolitics and his particular brand of "sovereign democracy" are challenging the West in ways reminiscent of the Cold War standoff. And in the final chapter, The Return of Inequality, I will examine history's return within Western liberal democracies themselves. I will argue that the dramatic increase in economic inequality and its attack on the value of fairness is, in many ways, the greatest threat to the sustainability of our stability and prosperity.

In coming full circle back to Fukuyama's depiction of the "end of history," it is worth remembering that his claim was not wholly triumphalist. At times, it even carried an air of melancholy. In the post-historical era, he predicted that the epic struggles that marked history, and that had fostered so much courage and idealism in past generations, would be overtaken by bureaucratic tinkering and ever more sophisticated forms of consumerism. Once all the big questions of politics are settled, notes the American historian Walter Russell Mead, humanity starts to look a lot like the nihilistic "last man" described by the philosopher Friedrich Nietzsche: "a narcissistic consumer with no greater aspirations beyond the next trip to the mall"[37] (or in the case of many, the online shopping site).

What we have today, however, is only a partial version of this story. On the one hand, a liberal democratic core co-exists with societies that are still very much in the depths of history. And as Russell Mead observes, those who have seemingly transcended history are incapable of understanding the motives and of countering the strategies of those nations "where the sun of history still shines."[38] In a phone call with U.S. President Barack Obama in the immediate aftermath of Russia's annexation of Crimea in 2014, German Chancellor Angela Merkel was rumoured to have said that Vladimir Putin was "living in a different world." But he is very much part of our planet and our century, where geopolitics and revisions of territory are once again "live" practices. On the other hand, as I will show, history is both banging against the door of liberal democracies — in the form of those fleeing violence and poverty — and threatening to destabilize them from within, through extreme inequality and angry populist politics, as well as through foreign-inspired acts of terrorism in Western cities.

Running through the following chapters are three main themes. First, if history is returning, it is doing so with a modern twist. History never fully repeats itself. So while ISIS uses swords to behead its enemies, an act that is reminiscent of the barbarism of the Middle Ages, so too does it use social media to recruit fighters and disseminate images of its crimes. While the pictures of migrants and asylum seekers walking for days to reach borders or crossing the sea in dilapidated boats remind us of earlier episodes of mass flight, they are also using smartphones and social networking to gain quicker or more accurate information about how to evade border controls or what conditions might be like in destination countries. And just as President Putin uses tanks and artillery to attack Ukraine, so too does he wage his battle in cyberspace through elaborate efforts at disinformation at home and assaults on the information technology infrastructure of his "enemies."

My second theme has to do with the use of history in the present. While the end of the Cold War seemed to usher in a period in which people all over the world sought to transcend their history, today's global system contains pockets of those who wish actively to return to it. One prominent example is Putin himself, whose dramatic intervention in Crimea and subsequent amassing of troops on the frontier with Ukraine harkened back to an imperial Russia that treated borders as fluid and neighbours as subservient to Russian interests. His actions also confounded European leaders' belief that Russia privileged mutual engagement and interdependence with the West over confrontation, and rattled their confidence in the continuation of a stable post–Cold War order. Indeed, for years Western military strategies had been dominated by the deployment of military operations *abroad*, and not by the maintenance of a formidable defence force at home. But in response to Putin's moves in Ukraine, European armies are once again training for war in their own neighbourhood.

The jihadists in contemporary Syria and Iraq are also nostalgic, seeking to redraw the map of the Middle East and re-create the caliphate ruled by their eighth-century hero, Harun al-Rashid (conveniently downplaying the fact that the rule of this caliph was marked by toleration of Shiite and religious minorities).[39] Elsewhere, in states that are classified as peaceful, such as India, history is fuelling a conservative backlash against modern-ization, marked by dangerous hatred of minori-ties and restrictions on the freedom of women. In keeping the past alive, today's users of history are not straightforwardly reclaiming what they had or what they lost. Instead, argues the British nov-elist and journalist Aatish Taseer, they are creat-ing something radically new and destabilizing.[40]

Although there are cracks in the foundation of contemporary Western liberal democracy, many insist that there is still no viable alternative to it. All the potential candidates — monarchy, fas-cism, socialism, and various forms of totalitarian-ism — have been discredited. We live in societies without genuine opposition, where even to imag-ine an alternative economic and political system seems futile. Even those who deny freedom and engage in brutal tactics against their political oppo-nents often co-opt the language of democracy. So while "we are not there yet," the argument goes, we should remember that Fukuyama's proposition was ultimately a normative one, about the contagious desirability of liberal democracy. And in this realm of ideas, he may be justified in claiming victory. As he wrote in 2014: "Russia and the Ayatollahs' Iran pay homage to democratic ideals even as they trample them in practice."[41]

But ideals become static and stale. If the foundations that underpin them are not understood by each new generation, it will lead to a waning of commitment to their realization. And therefore my third and final theme is that the return of history should encourage us all to remember that our own liberal democratic society was not inevitable — that it required sacrifice, compromise and leadership — and that we must all, as individuals, take a more active role in its preservation and growth.

After all, it has been autocracy, not democracy, which has been the longest-running form of politics in human history. And we know from past experience that liberal democratic advances can be reversed. In 1848 — a year referred to as the "Springtime of the Peoples" — liberal revolutions swept across Italy, France, Germany, and the Austrian Empire, throwing some kings and princes out of their palaces and threatening many others with political oblivion. But their gains were short-lived and monarchs staged an effective counter-revolution. The defeat of the revolutionaries was a product of both internal and external factors: fragmentation within the liberal movement itself, the military might of autocratic powers determined to crush the revolution (particularly Russia and Prussia), and the neutral stance taken by Britain and France who, as Robert Kagan has pointed out, were "more concerned with preserving peace among the great powers than with providing assistance to fellow liberals."42

It was the resolve of particular countries that helped to revive liberal democracy at the turn of the twentieth century, and again after the fascist challenge during the Second World War. But as with every episode in liberal democracy's evolution, there was also a role for courageous individuals.

Though judged to be the "natural" result of the bankruptcy of the communist system and the magnetic pull of the West, the Revolutions of 1989 required *individual* imagination and bravery — on the part of both the protesters and the politicians whose positions of power would soon be toppled. When one man (or woman) in Prague chose to lift a key ring out of his pocket and shake it in the air, he modelled a simple act that would be replicated by 300,000 people, thereby creating the sound of a revolution.[43] In May of 1989, when the reform-minded Hungarian Prime Minister Miklós Németh announced that his government would cease to finance the security barrier — an electrified wire fence — between his country and Austria, he was offering East Germans an indirect route to freedom, while simultaneously punching the first hole in the Iron Curtain and testing Moscow's resolve. And when Soviet leader Mikhail Gorbachev made the conscious decision in October of 1989 *not* to support repression in East Germany (where authorities had mobilized police and military forces to crush peaceful demonstrations and prepared hospitals for a possible flood of victims[44]), and to instead privilege the reform of the Soviet Union through improved economic ties with West Germany, he was enabling a revolution that could not be contained — despite his belief that it would somehow stop at his own borders.

The simplistic plotlines that now, almost thirty years later, recount the events of 1989 — that communism was destined to collapse because it was no match for the West, or that Ronald Reagan's June 1987 call to Gorbachev to "tear down this wall" was

the spark that ignited an inevitable process — need
to be recast with greater sensitivity to the interplay
between tectonic forces, the actions of individual
agents, and sheer accident.

We now know, thanks to *Newsweek* correspon-
dent Michael Meyer, that two individuals in particular made vital decisions on November 9 that,
unwittingly, led to the opening of the Wall.[45]
The first was the official spokesman for the East
German Politburo, who at the regular daily brief-
ing was charged with announcing the decision to
allow each East German the right to hold a pass-
port. Just before 7 p.m., when pressed by reporters as to when this new ruling would come into
effect, the spokesman — who had been on holidays
when the decision was made — was taken by surprise. In his confusion, he stated, "Immediately."
This news, captured live on television, was interpreted by East Germans (against the intentions of
the regime) as giving the green light to leave the
country. And so they flocked to the various cross-
ings to the West. At one such crossing, Checkpoint
Charlie, another individual — an East German border guard — made the second fateful decision, with
unintended consequences. As he nervously watched
the crowds mobilizing at the Wall's checkpoints, he

frantically tried to reach his superiors for orders. Just after 11 p.m., after several unanswered phone calls, he shrugged his shoulders and gave the order to "Open up." The rest, as they say, is history.

Grand narratives, like the "end of history" thesis, do not take individual agency seriously enough. They also tend to overlook the fact that some historical developments were often unpredicted or regarded as impossible (even if in retrospect they might have seemed inevitable). The crumbling of the Berlin Wall and German reunification are two examples. Another is the fall of the Roman Empire. If we continue to muddle along, lulled by the conviction that our model is best, that current challenges will ultimately not defeat us, and that everyone else in the world "wants what we want," we will not be prepared to respond to an unforeseen shock or an emerging sign of decay.

Liberal democracy has overcome many crises in its relatively short history. But its capacity to do so has lulled both the rulers and the ruled in Western societies into a state of complacency.[46] Our relative success in the past has created blind spots that now threaten to take us into a decade or more of great political, as well as economic, turmoil. History is back, with a vengeance.

TWO

THE RETURN OF BARBARISM

IN THE SUMMER OF 2014, the so-called Islamic State of Iraq and Syria (ISIS), locally known as Daesh, waged a violent campaign against civilian populations in Ninewa province in northern Iraq, home to many of the country's ethnic and religious minorities. As ISIS advanced on cities, towns, and villages, it systematically wiped out centuries-old communities and traditions, deliberately destroying shrines, temples, and churches, forcing residents to convert to Islam at gunpoint, executing community and religious leaders in public squares, kidnapping women and subjecting them to sexual enslavement, and coercing young boys to fight for them. While the exact number of dead is still unknown, 800,000 people were forcibly displaced.

The wrath of ISIS was particularly focused on the Yazidi community — a Kurdish-speaking minority whose religion derives from ancient Persian faith and contains elements of both Christianity and Islam. Islamic State's English-language magazine, *Dabiq*, condemned the Yazidi as "devil worshippers" and proclaimed that their polytheistic religion had to be eradicated, given it could not coexist alongside ISIS's puritanical interpretation of Islam. Unlike other Christian and Jewish minorities, who were given the option of paying a tax (the *jizya*) to avoid conversion or death, the Yazidi were made the object of an explicit campaign of ethnic cleansing.

During the first week of August, roughly 40,000 Yazidis who managed to leave their homes before the onslaught became trapped along a craggy ridge on the top of Mount Sinjar, encircled by ISIS fighters and facing dehydration and starvation. United Nations human rights officials recalled desperate phone calls from stranded Yazidi mothers, threatening to kill themselves and their daughters if the international community failed to come to their rescue, for fear of capture and sexual enslavement by Islamic State. The then U.S. President Barack Obama eventually authorized protective air strikes on August 7, claiming in a televised address to the nation that he would not allow a genocidal massacre on his watch. On August 14, Syrian Kurdish forces, supported by U.S. air power, established an evacuation route that enabled the Yazidis to flee from Mount Sinjar. But many died on the mountain, and the majority who escaped have faced continued upheaval and insecurity.[1]

The systematic and brutal violence perpetrated by Islamic State against the Yazidi, along with other minorities in Iraq and Syria, is a far cry from the progressive picture of the Middle East painted by so many commentators in the winter of 2011, during the early stages of the so-called Arab Spring. Sparked by a symbolic act of individual courage—vegetable seller Mohammed Bouazizi's decision to set himself on fire in front of a provincial government building in protest of police corruption—non-violent demonstrations across Tunisia succeeded in forcing the departure of the long-serving president, Zine al-Abidine Ben Ali. The domino effect of the popular uprisings in Egypt, Bahrain, Yemen, and then Syria, which drew millions into mass action for the first time, seemed to confirm the Middle East as the next successful site of the spread of liberal democracy that Fukuyama had predicted.

Half a decade on, however, the democratic surge inspired by these acts of civil resistance has seemingly reversed, leading not only to the continuation of previous patterns of corruption and the reinstallation of updated versions of autocratic regimes but also to a new wave of government crackdowns, civil war, and bloody sectarian violence. The depths of the turmoil, and the ease with which terrorist organizations have taken advantage of the power vacuum to establish new franchises, has led some to nostalgically wish for the "good old days" of the Middle East's authoritarian order. The number of deaths from terrorist attacks in the year 2014—32,685—shattered all previous records and is nine times higher than it was at the beginning of the twenty-first century. These deaths were also concentrated in just five (non-Western) countries, with Iraq topping the list.[2]

Others, however, see this current period of instability as proof of the "no pain, no gain" thesis—namely, that political transition is a bumpy affair, with inevitable setbacks, and that democratic evolution entails a certain level of suffering. As political scientist Sheri Berman argues, many revolutions, including those in France in 1789 and Russia in 1917, have had a vicious "undertow," plunging their societies into waves of violence and counter-violence. According to this view, the fault lies not in the democratic model, or in the population's "immaturity" and inability to embrace it. Rather, it can be found in the previous system's pathologies and divisive strategies of rule and its tendency to leave behind pent-up distrust and animosity. "Even failed democratic experiments," she writes, "are usually critical positive stages in the political development of countries, eras in which they get started on rooting out the antidemocratic social, cultural, and economic legacies of the past."[3]

There are three problems with this *longue durée* view of political development. The first is that it assumes that violent upheaval, euphemistically described as a "setback," is serving one greater purpose: the eventual triumph of liberal democracy. In reality, however, the violence enables (and forecloses) all kinds of dynamics that were not necessarily inevitable and whose trajectory is difficult to predict. In Syria and Iraq, for example, it has crowded out non-violent forms of activism and motivated many ordinary people to align with extremist organizations out of concern for day-to-day survival. The civil war in Syria grew out of a peaceful protest, inspired by the Arab

Spring, which called for political reform and an end to police brutality. Even in the midst of the war that subsequently engulfed the entire country, the Syrian Nonviolence Movement continued to operate — in spite of kidnappings, detention, and death — by documenting human rights violations and publishing pamphlets and magazines, but also doing all it could to maintain elements of "normal" life. During the short-lived ceasefire in March 2016, hundreds of Syrians took to the streets in peaceful protest once more, demonstrating their commitment to a future without violence.

Second, the "no pain, no gain" thesis suggests that the particularly lethal sectarian violence seen in the Middle East was to a large extent preordained, as opposed to a phenomenon that was aided and abetted not only by local actors but by follies of Western policy as well. The U.S.-led invasion of Iraq in 2003, designed to contain the threat posed by Saddam Hussein's alleged accumulation of weapons of mass destruction, was initially declared a victory — symbolized by former President George W. Bush's famous "Mission Accomplished" speech from the aircraft carrier USS *Abraham Lincoln* — but soon descended into armed insurgency, renewed combat, and ultimately sectarian violence. The public inquiry to identify lessons from the Iraq conflict, which was initiated by the British government in 2009 and published its findings in July 2016, not only concluded that the United States and United Kingdom had chosen to intervene in Iraq prematurely on the basis of flawed intelligence, but also presented a damning critique of woefully inadequate post-war planning. Sir John Chilcot, chair of the two-year investigation, firmly rejected the argument that the potential for chaos in Iraq could only be seen in hindsight. Many of the difficulties encountered after the coalition's "successful" military campaign—internal strife, regional instability, and the growth of violent extremism—"had been, or could have been, foreseen."[4]

And third, the macro-level perspective of the political developmentalists obscures what is specific about both our current period and the regions in which democratization is on the back foot. In particular, it does not help us to understand what is arguably the greatest symptom, and greatest beneficiary, of the pushback against the protest movements of the Arab Spring—namely, the Islamic State. When the United States finally withdrew its troops from Iraq in 2011, it believed it had dealt a sufficiently lethal blow to local insurgents and violent extremists to prevent their re-emergence. Just over three years later, however, ISIS had taken control of vast swathes of territory in Iraq and Syria (including Iraq's second-largest city, Mosul); was subjecting conquered populations to brutal forms of repression, including public stonings, amputations, and crucifixions; was raping women and girls and forcing them into sexual slavery; had coercively recruited and enlisted children between the ages of eight and sixteen into its ranks; and had replaced al-Qaeda as the world's pre-eminent jihadist group.

DEFYING HUMANITY'S LAW

The widespread and systematic attacks directed against civilian populations by ISIS have been characterized by the United Nations High Commissioner for Human Rights as acts that could constitute "crimes against humanity."[5] Over the past 150 years, and in the past three decades in particular, governments worldwide have invested considerable effort and political capital into strengthening the international legal framework governing war by promoting the protection of civilians and the principle of "distinction" — which requires parties in a conflict to at all times distinguish between combatants and civilians, and to direct attacks only at combatants — ensuring unfettered access to humanitarian assistance, and establishing courts to address the most serious violations of international humanitarian and human rights law. These advances have been supported by all kinds of governments, both democratic and not so democratic. But liberal democracies have been particularly active both in the diffusion of these rules of engagement and in insisting on their implementation in specific cases. More importantly, as I hinted in Chapter One, the laws of war grow out of an older movement in favour of humanity that was crucial to the very creation of the liberal democratic model.

The debate as to whether war can or should be regulated has a long pedigree in history. Across all religions and cultures, the view has persisted in some circles that the right to kill in war is unlimited, and that pillage, rape, torture, and imprisonment are simply part of war's repertoire. Various political leaders, and their military subordinates, have either embraced such violence as essential to an ethic of war or found strong reasons to argue for its application as an exceptional necessity. In 1864, during the American Civil War, Union General William Tecumseh Sherman famously ordered the bombardment of the city of Atlanta and forcibly removed its remaining occupants. General Sherman — who is credited with the claim that "war is hell" — argued that it was both necessary and legitimate to attack not only enemy combatants, but also enemy civilians who were engaged in the broader war effort (for example, arms and food production). By expanding the battlefield to include civilian infrastructure, he believed, the Union would undermine civilian morale on the Confederate side and bring about a more rapid victory.

Co-existing with this perspective, however, has been another, less powerful, yet remarkably resistant approach — what the humanitarian advocate Hugo Slim calls the "ethic of restraint"[6] — which calls for clear boundaries around who can be killed in war and by what means. From this perspective suffering is a profound problem in war and not simply an inevitable consequence of it.

Versions of this approach can be found in a variety of religious and secular traditions. But it is perhaps most obvious in the so-called Just War tradition, which found its most important early expression in the work of St. Augustine, a theologian of the late fourth century, who was writing at the time of the fall of the Roman Empire. Augustine faced the challenge of reconciling Christians' proscriptions against killing, which dominate much of their scripture, with their active participation in the Roman state after the conversion of Emperor Constantine to Christianity. Whereas the ancient Roman view of war justified any degree of violence against enemies believed to be a threat to the existence of the Roman state, Augustine argued that the employment of force through war could only be justified as a punitive measure in response to a specific unjust act. If force was deployed in the name of a just cause, and declared by an authorized body (which for most of the Middle Ages meant the Christian emperor or the pope), it would effectively become a judicial act. Soldiers in this enterprise were therefore not wanton killers, but agents of the law.[7]

The problem with this penal approach to war, of course, is that both sides could claim to be fighting on the side of justice. Confronted with the prospect of further punishment if their side lost, combatants thus fought on to a bitter and brutal end. In the mid-eighteenth century, the Swiss jurist and philosopher Emmerich de Vattel addressed this lack of protection for the "losers" in war by arguing that pronouncements about justice should focus not on war's *causes* but rather on its *conduct*. In the world of sovereign independent states that was emerging out of the remnants of a united Christendom, rulers could no longer set themselves up as judges over one another. Instead, belligerents had to forge a consensus on the common rules for *how* to fight — applicable to both sides equally. The laws of war thus developed rules for how to protect enemy prisoners, observe truce flags, and outlaw torture.

Our modern articulation of the law of armed conflict, and of humanitarian action, takes its cue from this agnostic approach to war's causes. In 1862, the Swiss financier and entrepreneur Henri Dunant wrote his famous *Souvenir de Solférino*, an eyewitness account of the epic 1859 confrontation between the forces of the Austrian Emperor Franz Joseph on the one side, and the French army under Napoleon III and the Sardinian army under Victor Emmanuel II on the other. The battle was a crucial episode in the larger nationalist struggle to unify Italy, which had been divided among France, Austria, Spain, and various Italian city-states, and was the last major battle in which armies operated under the personal command of their monarchs.

Dunant described in vivid detail the carnage he found the day after the Battle of Solferino, which challenged the romantic way in which European writers and poets had previously written about war, and facilitated a deeper consideration of its senseless aftermath. As the Yale historian John Fabian Witt has noted, Dunant focused moral attention "on the casualties of combat, diverting our gaze from the passions and convictions and projects that brought men to the field in the first place." Indeed, Dunant was implicitly suggesting that no causes were so great as to warrant such wanton death and destruction.[8]

The following year, Dunant succeeded in his mission to create relief societies to care for wounded soldiers — what became the International Committee of the Red Cross — giving birth to our modern form of humanitarianism. While in earlier times villagers and religious orders had informally cared for individuals that were wounded or impoverished in wartime, Dunant's project created formal, state-sanctioned humanitarian action, which rested on the idea of a trusted neutral third party that the warring parties would recognize. The purpose

of that action was to resolve the issue of suffering during war, regardless of the partisan attach-
ments of those who were in distress. In 1864, a
diplomatic conference in Geneva — the First Geneva
Convention — marked a significant departure in the
regulation of war, by committing twelve European
states to recognizing the neutrality and immunity of ambulances and military hospitals and to
take care of wounded and sick soldiers. The First
Geneva Convention was followed by the Hague
Conventions of 1899 and 1907, which — among
other things — attempted to regulate the use of particularly destructive weapons and offer protections
to prisoners of war.

If the regulation of war was initially focused on
the plight of soldiers and prisoners of war, Geneva-
based law and practice, together with organizations delivering humanitarian assistance, began
to address the suffering of non-combatants as well.
This move was particularly influenced by the First
World War, during which forced displacement,
massacre, starvation, and disease were experienced
by non-combatants on all sides. After the war's
end, non-combatants became even more prominent subjects in both the ethics and the practice of
war. In addition, they took on the particular label

that we take for granted today. Prior to 1914 various terms were used to describe them, such as unarmed inhabitants, non-combatants, the enemy population, or the occupied population. In the 1920s, the Red Cross and other humanitarian organizations began to use the term "civilians," in order to distinguish this population from military personnel. They also expanded their operations, providing medical attention, sanitation, food, and shelter for war-affected *civilian* populations.[9]

In focusing on civilian suffering, these organizations were drawing on an earlier body of national law, the American Lieber Code of 1863, which had been created to regulate the conduct of the Union during the American Civil War (and which was later translated by European jurists for use in the 1870–71 Franco-Prussian War). The elements of the Code were penned by Francis Lieber, a former Prussian military officer who fought against Napoleon, and gave explicit attention to the protection of non-combatants and their property. While Lieber prohibited unnecessary cruelty, wanton violence, rape, and pillage of the non-combatant population, he also articulated what has become known as the "principle of military necessity." In Witt's magisterial study of the Code and its use in the Civil War, he demonstrates how the rationale of military necessity reflects a deeper view about suffering in war — one that differs from Dunant's more generic account. For Lieber, not all suffering was the same; some of it was in the service of a higher political goal, including, in historical perspective, the rescue of Western civilization from "barbarians." In short, war could in some cases work to ultimately *reduce* suffering.[10]

This was a different account of the relationship between war's ends and means. The philosophy was not, in Witt's words, "a one-size-fits-all reduction of suffering," but rather one that emphasized the need for a series of contextual judgements about what level and mode of violence was justified at different points in a particular contest. If military necessity warranted, armies could, for example, force civilians to suffer the effects of siege warfare or bombard historical monuments or cultural institutions. Variations on this logic were in evidence in key episodes during the Second World War, when governments on the Allied side chose to firebomb German cities (killing thousands of civilians) or when the U.S. government weighed the damage that would ensue from dropping the atomic bomb on cities in Japan against the prospect of shortening the war in the Pacific and avoiding the deployment of more Allied ground troops.

These two views of suffering in war — that it is to be minimized at all cost or that it is to be balanced against the ultimate aims of the war — both find expression in the Geneva Conventions of 1949 and their Additional Protocols of 1977, the body of law that is most influential for national militaries today. In short, our contemporary laws of war attempt to strike a balance between military necessity and humanitarian considerations, wherever and whenever they collide. The very name that we use to describe it — international humanitarian law — gives credence to this dual heritage. On the one hand, it is true that the principle of distinction has been codified in the Additional Protocols I and II. On the other hand, Lieber's idea of military necessity is also built into the Geneva Conventions, as part of the legal justification for particular attacks on legitimate military targets — even if such attacks have adverse consequences for civilians.

The delicate balance that modern IHL represents requires vigilance on the part of national armed forces and the various organizations that try to hold them accountable for their conduct during war. Without it, the mutual interest that warring parties have in respecting the laws of rightful conduct in war — laws that apply to *both* sides — can quickly erode into unregulated killing. Since 1945, the governments of Western liberal democracies have been at the forefront of efforts to disseminate IHL and encourage ratification of the relevant treaties. In addition, the armed forces of Western states have invested extensively in training other national militaries on how to comply with their requirements. This by no means suggests that Western states have consistently complied with IHL; their violations of the laws of war, whether by French forces during the Battle of Algiers or by American forces at My Lai during the Vietnam War, have been legendary. But there is strong evidence that liberal democratic states have gone the furthest in actually implementing the legal commitments they signed onto, by drafting Codes of Conduct for their land, air, and naval forces; designing rules of engagement for particular campaigns that respect the principles of distinction and proportionality; and acting to hold violators to account.

Where adherence to the laws of war is particularly difficult is in the context of civil conflict. Indeed, the legal frameworks that regulate international armed conflicts (wars between states) and non-international armed conflicts (wars within states) are not identical — despite the advances made with the Additional Protocols. One of the biggest differences is the obligation relating to treatment of prisoners of war, which are non-existent in a civil war context. More generally, in civil conflicts warring parties are rarely evenly matched, arguably reducing the power of the "mutual restraint" argument. In a situation of asymmetry, the stronger side may be much less worried about retaliation for an excessive use of force. On the other hand, the weaker side may believe it has to use extraordinary means to defeat its more powerful enemy, including spreading terror in the local population.

The other challenge to attempts at regulating civil conflict is that some of the warring parties are not representing or controlled by a government, and are thus much more difficult to hold accountable. Following the signing of Additional Protocol II in 1977, non-state armed groups fighting in a civil war incurred obligations to comply with the Geneva Conventions — particularly so-called Common Article 3, which calls upon belligerents to refrain from using violence against those taking no active part in an armed conflict (i.e., civilians). Individual members of non-state armed groups can also be prosecuted by the International Criminal Court or other international tribunals for grave violations of international humanitarian law. But in practice it has been extremely difficult to encourage non-state armed groups to comply with the laws of war or to apprehend their members for alleged international crimes. An even more complicated question is whether non-state armed groups that control territory have obligations to protect populations under their remit — beyond the negative obligations *not* to commit atrocity crimes. Thus far, the international community has been reluctant to suggest that they do, for fear that such a move would also entail recognizing armed groups as "state-like" entities, with legitimate authority over a territory and population.

The difficulties and dilemmas associated with enforcing international humanitarian law in civil conflicts have been tragically illustrated in both Iraq and Syria, particularly in the areas dominated by ISIS. In fact, far from trying to conceal or downplay their criminal acts — so as to prevent punishment or prosecution — members of ISIS glorify the horrors that they inflict on their captive populations, by hanging their bodies on electricity poles

in full view of local civilians or showcasing beheadings on social media.

MEDIEVAL MONSTERS?

Throughout the rise and spectacular spread of
Islamic State across Iraq, and later into Syria, many
Western commentators have likened its barbaric
war and occupation tactics to a throwback from the
Middle Ages. During a House of Commons debate
in December 2015, in which British MPs deliberated
on whether the United Kingdom should expand its
air strikes from Iraq into Syria, former U.K. Prime
Minister David Cameron described adherents to
ISIS as "medieval monsters" who "enslave Yazidis,
throw gay people off buildings, behead aid workers
and force children to marry before they are even
ten years old." With the succession of videos showcasing murder and cruelty — each more gruesome
than the last — ISIS seeks not only to deter the
enemy, through the fear of falling into the hands
of those who practice barbarism, but also to entice
more fighters into its ranks. History has returned,
so it seems, in a particularly twisted form.

Looking back, of course, the West itself is no

stranger to forced conversions, public beheadings, or the wanton destruction of religious monuments and graveyards. Doctrinal war between different branches of Christianity is an integral part of Western civilization's early history and formed the backdrop of the development of the laws of war. Starting in the second half of the sixteenth century, after the Protestant Reformation challenged the dominance of the Roman Catholic Church, European societies were plunged into a series of religious battles. They began with the French civil war and culminated in the tumultuous Thirty Years' War (1618–48) between Protestant and Catholic states, which then morphed into a more general battle among Europe's great powers. Whereas previously religion had been a key source of internal stability, and served as the motor of extra-European wars and conquests, during the Thirty Years' War a fractured Christianity began to turn in on itself — in ways not unlike the contemporary conflicts between branches of Islam in the Middle East.

The British historian Mark Greengrass has vividly described the barbarism and "carnivals of death" that marked intra-Christian conflict during this period, including the butchering of the pope's guards on the steps of St. Peter's Basilica in 1527 during

Charles V's Sack of Rome. But one of the most notorious episodes was the St. Bartholomew's Day Massacre of 1572, when Admiral de Coligny, a key leader of the French Calvinist Protestants (otherwise known as the Huguenots), was killed and thrown out of his window. His death sparked a wave of anti-Huguenot violence throughout Paris, in which the bodies of the dead—including many women and children—were collected in carts and thrown into the Seine. The religious violence and wars of the late sixteenth and early seventeenth centuries also prevented Europe's dynastic rulers from uniting against the rising power of the age—namely the Ottoman Empire. Indeed, it is telling that England's Queen Elizabeth I was less worried about Islam than she was about Catholic Spain.

The radical ideology espoused by Islamic State today not only incites religious violence but also adopts the language of millenarianism that is reminiscent of earlier religious prophecies about the end of the world. It mandates that its members are following the "true" path of Allah and setting the stage for an apocalyptic battle between coalition forces and the "armies of Rome" on Middle Eastern soil, at the Syrian city of Dabiq. When the severed head of aid worker Peter Kassig was showcased in an ISIS video in November 2014, the executioner declared that he was "burying the first American crusader in Dabiq, eagerly waiting for the remainder of [Western] armies to arrive."

The particular brand of jihadism that marks ISIS derives from Salafism, a branch of Sunni Islam that advocates strict adherence to the law and social structures existing in the earliest days of Islam. It takes its name from the Arabic *al salaf al salih*, meaning the "pious forefathers." These forefathers include the Prophet Muhammad, as well as the first "caliphs" — or successors — who led Muslims following Muhammad's death in 632 AD and whom the Salafis revere as a model for all aspects of daily life. As a result, in the territory that ISIS controls, all laws and decrees — including what to eat and drink, and who to talk to — claim to honour and replicate "the Prophetic methodology."[11] According to Princeton University's Bernard Haykel, an authority on Islamic State's theology, its followers also believe that their practices of slavery, beheadings, and public crucifixions are faithfully reproducing the norms of war that marked Muhammad's conquests in the first half of the seventh century. ISIS fighters, he claims, "are smack in the middle of the medieval tradition and are bringing it wholesale into the present day."[12]

One of the initial weaknesses in Western leaders' response to Islamic State after 2010 was the failure to understand the nature and role of the religious ideology that underpins it. The theological justifications for its actions were treated as a mere medieval "disguise." In our liberal democratic model, where the principle of secularism has led to a tolerance of religious diversity or, increasingly, the retreat of religion into the private sphere, it was difficult to believe that religion could *matter* so profoundly, not just to a group's tactics but to its core strategy. And so Western analysts and policymakers searched for the more concrete political motives that must lurk beneath. The West eventually found those underlying objectives in earlier generations of al-Qaeda, when Osama Bin Laden announced his goals of securing the U.S. withdrawal of its forces from Saudi Arabia and the end of support for dictatorships in Muslim lands. But the Islamic State, with its apocalyptic vision, seemed to put nothing remotely recognizable on the negotiating table as it continued to seize territory in Iraq and Syria.

TWENTY-FIRST-CENTURY RELIGIOUS WARRIORS

Part of the mystery of ISIS is its hybrid quality: both medieval and modern, both diffuse and territorially rooted. Like al-Qaeda before it, the organization operates in the West through a diverse set of autonomous and decentralized cells. The British journalist James Meek describes this nebulous and mobile network as "somewhere between a franchise and an ethos," with no fixed address or command-and-control centre. Thus the attacks on Paris's bars and music halls or on the transportation hubs in Brussels were not so much directly ordered by Islamic State as inspired by it.[13]

In the Middle East, on the other hand, ISIS is more state-like, with an identifiable infrastructure, including a training centre in Raqqa and a clear plan to build a territorial base. Its initial military strategy was designed to capture key supply routes, electrical infrastructure, and lucrative oil fields—all stepping stones to expanding its control over territory, making itself financially self-sufficient, and deepening others' dependence on it for energy supplies.

When Islamic State seized Mosul, Iraq's second-largest city, in June of 2014, its ambitions to conquer territory and govern became more than just metaphor: from a pulpit in the city's Great Mosque, Abu Bakr al-Baghdadi, the self-proclaimed leader of ISIS, declared himself the next caliph, successor to Muhammad, and invited Muslims from around the world to come and pledge obedience. A stream of jihadists subsequently flowed into Syria and Iraq, despite Western efforts to restrict it. What distinguished the ISIS claim to territory, however, was that it crossed established boundaries. Unlike other terrorist groups — such as the Irish Republican Army in Northern Ireland, the Basque separatists in Spain, or the Tamil Tigers in Sri Lanka — which have sought to carve out land from within an existing state, often through secession, ISIS's goals are more expansionist. It seeks to radically alter the map of the region by eradicating two existing states (Syria and Iraq) and creating one unified caliphate.

Consequently, whereas al-Qaeda has continually shifted location and morphed in form, partly by retreating underground, the ambition of the Islamic State forecloses this option. It cannot continue its caliphate without authority over a piece of land. "Take away its command of territory," writes the Canadian journalist Graeme Wood, "and all those oaths of allegiance are no longer binding." The holding of territory is combined with a very modern state-building project, complete with administrative, financial, and legal structures. Some ISIS videos, when not showcasing gruesome executions, feature images of "ordinary" civilians going about their business in the caliphate — visiting schools, markets, and dental clinics. These scenes of everyday life help to feed the narrative that Islamic State–held territory is an island of peace in a region of chaos.

But the significance of the well-ordered caliphate goes beyond its status as a governing entity that offers protection or as a place where Sharia law (the religious legal system governing the members of the Islamic faith) can be enforced. It is also what Wood describes as a "vehicle for salvation," as adherents to Islamic State believe that Muslims cannot live a fully Islamic life, no matter how devout their daily practices, unless they pledge their allegiance to a caliph.[14] Travelling to the territory that ISIS controls thus becomes part of an individual's spiritual redemption.

ISIS has conveniently used this theological dictum to recruit the significant number of bodies it has needed to wage conventional battles and maintain its geographic foothold. Guerilla-style warfare or ad-hoc terrorist acts are insufficient to reach its territorial goals. It also needs, and thrives upon, traditional forms of military victory over regional armies and the Western states that support them. The conquest of the Iraqi city of Ramadi in May 2015 clearly illustrated how Islamic State commanders skilfully executed a complex battle plan that evaded both detection and airstrikes. They managed to out-smart not only their larger opponent, the Iraqi Security Forces, but also the much-lauded U.S.-trained Special Operations force known as Golden Division, which had been fighting for months to defend the city. During their attack on Ramadi, ISIS fighters also demonstrated the lethal consequences of their capture of Western military equipment: they converted U.S. military armoured vehicles — which had been designed to protect their inhabitants from small-arms fire — into mobile mega bombs with a force equal to that of the Oklahoma City bombing, destroying the defensive perimeter of the Iraqi Security Forces as well as a number of multi-storey buildings.[15]

These displays of military prowess provided some of the core content for ISIS's virtual propaganda machine, which is used primarily to recruit foreign fighters. In fact, it is no exaggeration to say that modern technology is the fuel for the ISIS fire. Compared with other terrorist or extremist groups, the Islamic State is more sophisticated and more present in cyberspace, especially in social media. While in the past organizations such as al-Qaeda used the Internet primarily to communicate between terror cells, Islamic State has embraced it for a whole host of purposes, including self-promotion, radicalization and recruitment, fundraising, and even intimidation. Al-Hayat, the ISIS media centre, generates close to forty pieces of media each day (more than many national television networks), including photo essays, articles, and audio programs — all in multiple languages. The organization not only floods Twitter with an estimated 50,000 Tweets daily, but has proven cannily adept at ensuring that its carefully stage-managed execution videos access the widest possible audience, by latching them onto popular Twitter hashtags, such as the hashtag used for the 2014 World Cup in Brazil.

Islamic State is also an early adopter of cutting-edge messaging applications, such as the Germany-based "Telegram," which create safe channels of communication and make it more difficult both to detect and to counter propaganda messages.

The Telegrams disseminated from Al-Hayat have enabled followers to share training manuals and advice on how to obtain weapons or build bombs, and to engage in either small group or lone wolf–style attacks. In this way, Islamic State has benefitted from the modern preoccupation with privacy, heightened by Edward Snowden's revelations about the extensive social media monitoring by U.S. and European intelligence agencies. In the wake of the Snowden affair, technology companies have rushed to honour their commitment to safeguard customer privacy. But by making encryption software freely and cheaply available, tech giants have also allowed ISIS to conceal its activities.

A final illustration of the hybrid character of ISIS is its use of modern methods of birth control to perpetuate the systematic rape of female captives under its control. The leadership of Islamic State maintains that its practices of sexual enslavement are closely aligned with those of the original Prophet Muhammad — not to mention a powerful recruitment tool. Because an obscure ruling in medieval Islamic law stipulates that a man must ensure the woman he takes as a sexual slave is not pregnant before he has intercourse with her, today's ISIS recruits provide their slaves with either the birth control pill or injectable contraception (such as Depo-Provera). This enables women to be passed on from one ISIS fighter to the next, without any unwanted pregnancies.

One middle-aged woman, who was tasked with "chaperoning" a group of young female Yazidis during their trips to the local hospital to receive their regular shots of Depo-Provera, describes how the girls were bought and sold by ISIS commanders and recruits. In one tragic case she was asked to escort her own teenage daughter, who was raped by multiple fighters. According to the findings of a UN-based clinic in northern Iraq, the practice appears to be succeeding in its perverse aims: of the more than 700 rape victims that sought treatment at the clinic, only 5 percent reported pregnancies, which is well below the 20- to 25-percent fertility rate for young women in any given month.[16]

THE FOREIGN TERRORIST FIGHTER

The promise of an endless supply of sexual slaves has been one of the key planks in Islamic State's promotional materials. But if the content of its propaganda frequently looks medieval, its form is profoundly contemporary and directed at a peculiarly modern target: would-be Western recruits. The background music to its slick promotional videos is designed to resonate with Western youth culture, and the scenes often bear an eerie similarity to popular Western video games, such as *Call of Duty* and *Grand Theft Auto*. The proof of the power of these recruitment tools can be found in the numbers: at the end of 2015 the United Nations estimated that violent extremists such as Islamic State had recruited more than 30,000 foreign fighters from more than one hundred countries to travel to Syria and Iraq, as well as to Libya, Yemen, and Afghanistan.[17] What sets these warriors apart from mercenaries, both past and present, is that they are not simply roving guns for hire: they provide their services (largely) for free. Recruiters appeal to those whose identity is tied to a transnational, rather than local, community — in this case, the brotherhood of heroes who avenge the Muslim Ummah — and convince their target audience that this community is facing an existential threat. In short, the reward for risk-taking is spiritual rather than material.[18]

History is replete with examples of the foreign fighter, lured by the prospect of heroism and attracted to the grandeur of a bigger cause. Prominent instances include the Mexican Civil War of the 1830s, during which foreign recruits from the United States helped to roll back a potential military dictatorship, or Afghanistan following the Soviet invasion in 1979, when fighters from across the Middle East were recruited to support the mujahideen in their battle to save religion from communism. Given that the stakes for foreign fighters are often different from those of local actors, history also shows that the former are more devoted to battle and engage in more lethal forms of violence — making it harder to defeat the warring side that they support. It is therefore not surprising that conflicts involving foreign fighters are often longer in duration and feature higher casualty rates.

One of the most famous cases, with certain parallels today, is the Spanish Civil War (1936–39), during which close to 40,000 foreigners fought on the side of the fledgling Second Spanish Republic (supported by the Soviet Union) against Franco's fascists (who enjoyed the backing of both Hitler and Mussolini). The trials and tribulations of the International Brigades — military units made up of volunteer foreign fighters — were immortalized in George Orwell's book *Homage to Catalonia* and have since served as inspiration for subsequent generations of student radicals and guerilla fighters worldwide. Then, as now, young men (and to a lesser extent women) travelled great distances to fight in a foreign conflict out of a mixture of idealism and disaffection. Then, as now, their raw potential was mobilized by skilled recruiters — in the case of the International Brigades, through a global network of communist parties. And then, as now, governments attempted to prevent the departure of their nationals to fight in foreign conflicts, with little success, and regarded them with suspicion when they returned home.

The young and embattled Spanish Republic held out the promise of a new and more progressive form of democracy, if only it could defeat both the fascist rebellion and the remnants of aristocracy and elitism. And in the context of the 1930s, when communism was not the prime enemy of the West — as it was subsequently during the Cold War — the image of a fragile democracy beating back fascism was a powerful magnet for younger generations who not only were infatuated with noble political causes in foreign lands, but also sought an alternative to economic hardship at home. In Canada, where 1,600 men and women volunteered to fight for the Mackenzie-Papineau Battalion on the side of the Republicans, the particularly grim conditions of the Great Depression produced a pool of poor and unemployed, many of whom were radicalized while "riding the rails" in search of work. In his book *Renegades: Canadians in the Spanish Civil War*, Michael Petrou describes how the Spanish Civil War served as a canvas upon which the idealists could project their aspirations and the disenchanted could wage their ideological battles. For Norman Bethune, the famous Canadian doctor who pioneered the mobile blood transfusion unit for use by the Republican forces in the civil war, anti fascism was a reaction to the poverty and political crackdowns he had witnessed in Western societies in the 1930s.

The authoritative voices who study the recruitment of foreign fighters in Europe today point to trends that, on the surface at least, look familiar. The French scholar Olivier Roy describes the radicalization of second-generation Muslims in Europe as part of a youth revolt against society, articulated as an Islamic narrative of jihad and strategically manipulated by Islamic State to achieve its larger goals. Roy has found that the trait common to those who have travelled to Iraq or Syria, and then returned home to participate in acts of terrorism on European streets, is not a psychiatric deformity — as some might expect — but frustration and resentment against their own society. "It is the psychological state of suffering that is key," he writes, "a discrepancy between expectations and social outcomes."[19] This is what makes young radicals open to the image of heroism and notoriety that ISIS offers.

But here is where the parallels with previous foreign fighters begin to break down. Some of those who travelled to Syria between 2011 and 2016 had an explicitly political agenda, born out of the promise of the Arab Spring: the defeat of Syrian President Bashar al-Assad's authoritarian regime and the creation of a moderate and democratic government. They sought to support the rebel opposition and groups such as the Free Syrian Army. Like many in the International Brigades of the 1930s, their goal is the spread of democracy and the enhancement of civil liberties. The more worrying majority of travellers, however, are better described as foreign *terrorist* fighters, whose political agenda or cause is difficult to locate. Instead, their primary motivation, as Roy puts it, is the "fascination for a narrative": to join the fight to bring about the apocalyptic standoff between the followers of Muhammad and the infidel West. And unlike previous foreign fighters, who both backed and became enmeshed with local allies, today's travelling jihadis rarely identify with the local Arab populations they are theoretically meant to support.

If political aims play little or no part, the role of religion is even more ambiguous. In contrast to Islamic State adherents in the Middle East itself, where a particularly strict interpretation of Islam is central to their goals and behaviour, the religious beliefs of European-based jihadists are only recently acquired. Contemporary research on radicalization shows that very few foreign terrorist fighters, or participants in ISIS-sponsored terrorism in Europe, were previously active in religious activities or regular attendees at the local mosque. Many, in fact, have a history as petty criminals involved in theft or drug dealing. The religious dimension of their profile only seems to matter at a later stage of the process of radicalization, by providing what Roy calls a "framework for personal transformation." Jihad, for them, is the only real "grand cause" in the global marketplace.

This particular relationship to religion accounts for the fact that very few jihadis speak about paradise, and those that do frame it in nihilistic terms — revenge or suicide — rather than in terms of building a better society, as it is discussed in religious texts. These features of the modern foreign terrorist fighter also help to explain why, according to experts on radicalization, so many of the policy tools employed to counter their rise in Western democracies have had such limited effect. The close monitoring of mosques, for example, has brought law enforcement agencies little concrete information that can help foil terrorist plots, and imams have had very limited influence over the process of radicalization. Similarly, calls to "reform Islam" appear to have had little effect, as those who are radicalized are fundamentally disinterested in what Islam *actually* means or entails. Yet, at the same time, to consider Islam only through the prism of fighting terrorism will validate the narrative of persecution and revenge that feeds the process of radicalization.

THE ROOTS AND BRANCHES OF ISLAMIC STATE

The appeal of Islamic State has also been enhanced by its ability to harness the anger that has accompanied foreign — and largely Western — intervention in the Middle East. Far from being a throwback to the Middle Ages, ISIS is therefore a very modern creation — a product of the interventions undertaken by the United States, with the support of its key allies, in the early part of our new century, most notably the 2003 war and occupation of Iraq. Much like Fukuyama, who believed the global victory of liberal democracy was assured, the Bush administration assumed that a short war in the Middle East would bring Western-style progress: out of the "creative destruction" sparked by the military defeat of Saddam Hussein would emerge parties, elections, liberal constitutions, and capitalist markets.

The destructive part of that prophecy certainly came to pass. But the pieces are still strewn across the Middle East. Indeed, it is not difficult to draw a very straight line between the aftermath of the U.S.-led invasion of Iraq in 2003 and the creation of Islamic State as a breakaway faction of al-Qaeda.

During the early post-war years of American and British occupation, Abu Musab Zarqawi, the former leader of al-Qaeda in Iraq, launched a campaign to deliberately provoke a confrontation between the two main branches of Islam — Shia and Sunni — through a series of devastating attacks on Shia religious ceremonies and institutions. His goal of fostering polarization ultimately ran afoul of the more seasoned al-Qaeda leadership, who believed these violent tactics would alienate the group from the local support base it needed to operate. In 2013, the organization split. In the meantime, Zarqawi's strategy of sectarianism was unwittingly assisted by the U.S. occupying authority, whose de-Ba'athification policy (designed to rid Iraq's civil service of former members of Saddam Hussein's Ba'ath Party) led to the mass dismissal of Sunnis from key positions in the military, police, and social services — including 30,000 public servants and 400,000 soldiers. The Chilcot inquiry into Britain's role in the Iraq War described the decision to dismantle Saddam's security apparatus as one of the greatest mistakes of the post-war period, as it instantly created a pool of unemployed and disaffected who subsequently fed the insurgency.[20]

U.S. forces also led a series of attacks against Sunni-populated areas and the subsequent capture and imprisonment of Sunni prisoners, some of whom were subjected to torture. After the infamous detention and torture practices at the Abu Ghraib prison came to light, Sunni detainees were transferred to Camp Bucca. It was here that one particular detainee — now known as Abu Bakr-al Baghdadi — forged connections with a group of former Ba'athist officers who had been imprisoned in Abu Ghraib. Baghdadi later became the leader of Islamic State, and his network of former inmates have been among his closest advisors. The experience of Sunni detainees at the hands of the U.S. military has thus cast a long shadow. As the Middle East scholar Adam Hanieh observes, it "not only further entrenched the country's emerging sectarian divisions, but also, in a concrete sense, actually forged the Islamic State itself."[21]

But while the origins of ISIS lie in the specific context of the post-2003 invasion of Iraq, its spread in the Middle East had much to do with the reversals of the 2011 Arab Spring and the failure of democracy to take hold. Two phenomena combined to create the "ecosystem" in which Islamic State flourished: first, the disillusionment that followed the failure to change autocratic regimes; and second, the fear and sectarian violence that insecure rulers across the region *deliberately* fostered to try to maintain their hold on power — particularly Syria's President Bashar al-Assad. While throughout the civil war Assad has tried to paint a simple picture — either support my regime or support the terrorists — in reality he and other members of his regime have actively collaborated with members of ISIS and spared the organization from the aerial attacks to which the government has regularly subjected the Syrian population.

Meanwhile, the United States is still recovering from the shame of Abu Ghraib, still debating whether and how to close the Guantanamo Bay detention centre, and still debating the rightness or wrongness of torture. Was this the enlightened leadership that Fukuyama predicted for America at the end of the Cold War? The over-stretch in Iraq has also scarred political and military elites in the United States, as well as in the United Kingdom, both of which now have a deep-seated fear of prolonged military engagements and an unwillingness to enforce their own "red lines." This has left the field open not only to Islamic State, but also to those governments that dabble in their own forms of barbarism.

THE STATE AS PERPETRATOR

While today's nation-states like to point the finger at non-state armed groups as the primary perpetrators of barbarism, today's greatest violators of international humanitarian law are national governments. As UN Secretary General Ban Ki-moon stated in his report for the first ever World Humanitarian Summit held in May 2016: "Flouting the most basic rules governing the conduct of war has become contagious, creating further risks to reinterpret and blur their application... When States disrespect or undermine international humanitarian and human rights law, including through expansive interpretations, other States and non-State actors regard this as an invitation to do the same."

Part of the reason for the increasing temptation to bypass international humanitarian law — especially its prohibitions on targeting non-combatants — is the long-standing suspicion that not all civilians can be considered innocent, given the multiple roles that civilians can play in directly or indirectly supporting the war effort. This power of civilian support was evident at least as early as WWII, when citizens did everything from sewing wounded soldiers' pajamas to working in munitions factories. Such forms of engagement gave rise to the argument that certain groups of civilians should not be immune from attack, given what Hugo Slim calls the "ambiguity of [their] non-combatant identity." In many contemporary wars, civilians are not "simple two-dimensional caricatures," Slim writes, that "suffer violence and receive aid."[22] In many wars, civilian populations actively assist one or another side of the conflict, whether voluntarily or through coercion. In addition, today's battlefield is becoming less distinct, with fighting taking place in civilian population centres, and civilians becoming increasingly involved in activities more closely resembling warfighting—whether it be, for example, by damaging military objects of the "enemy side," sabotaging the transmission of information, or providing targeting intelligence.[23] The conflict in Gaza between Palestinians and Israelis is a prominent example, along with the ongoing war in Syria.

In the early hours of the morning of August 21, 2013, families in the Damascus suburbs of Ghouta rushed to the basements of their apartment buildings, as they had many times before, to avoid aerial bombardment. But on this day they were tragically exposed to Sarin nerve gas (a chemical agent twenty times more deadly than cyanide), which was launched through surface-to-surface rockets. Using witness statements, GPS information, and satellite imagery, the organization Human Rights Watch confirmed four sites in Zamalka, a district about six kilometres east of the centre of the Syrian capital of Damascus, where at least eight rockets struck — some of them close to local mosques. A few hours later, Muadhamiya, a town about twenty kilometres to the west of Zamalka, was also struck by rockets containing Sarin.[24] Within hours, dozens of videos were uploaded online displaying large numbers of distressed and visibly sick adults and children with no external signs of injury. In some of the most graphic footage, dozens of bodies, including many small children and babies, were laid out in rows on the floors of clinics and mosques, and on the streets of Muadhamiya, Zamalka, and nearby areas.

In their subsequent report to Ban Ki-moon,[25] UN weapons inspectors drew on testimony from over fifty exposed survivors who had experienced shortness of breath, disorientation, blurred vision, nausea, vomiting, and loss of consciousness. They were the lucky ones. There is debate over the numbers that died, owing to the chaos resulting from the large number of casualties, the lack of any large hospitals in the affected areas, and the information war that has characterized the Syrian conflict. The Violations Documentation Center (VDC), an activist-run site cited by the United

Nations that uses internationally accepted norms to verify deaths, lists at least 588 fatalities, including 135 women and 108 children. (For its part, a preliminary U.S. government assessment determined that 1,429 people had been killed, including 426 children.) When presenting the UN report in mid-September, Ban Ki-moon declared that it detailed the "most significant confirmed use of chemical weapons against civilians since Saddam Hussein used them in Halabja in 1988."[26]

The UN inspection mission was not asked to ascertain who was behind the attack. However, by examining the debris field and impact area, the inspectors found "sufficient evidence" to calculate azimuths, or angular measurements, that allow the rockets' trajectories to be determined "with a sufficient degree of accuracy." When plotted on a map, the trajectories converge on a site with a large military base that is home to the Syrian Republican Guard 104th Brigade. The Human Rights Watch assessment claimed that the 330mm rockets used in the strikes were "of a type not listed in standard, specialised, international or declassified reference materials," but which had been documented in a number of other attacks on opposition-held areas in the months leading up to the attack. The organization also said these rockets would be compatible with the 333mm Falaq-2 launcher produced by Iran, which the Syrian government is known to possess.

American and French intelligence assessments, released within two weeks of the attacks, went further, concluding with "high confidence" that Syrian government forces had used Sarin gas on opposition areas. The French report noted that "the launch zone for the rockets was held by the regime while the strike zone was held by the rebels," and that at the time Syrian government commanders feared a wider attack on Damascus from the opposition. It also observed that the section of the Syrian military responsible for filling munitions with chemical agents — Branch 450 of the Syrian Scientific Studies and Research Centre (CERS) — was staffed only by members of the president's Alawite sect and was "distinguished by a high level of loyalty to the regime."[27]

President Assad and other Syrian officials were quick to deny their perpetration of the rocket attacks, and called on Washington and Paris to present incontrovertible proof. Russia also challenged Western countries to publish their evidence, with President Vladimir Putin describing claims that the Syrian government was responsible as "utter nonsense."[28] For decades Moscow has regarded Syria as its most important ally in the Middle East, given the latter's strategic location (bordering the Mediterranean, Israel, Lebanon, Turkey, Jordan, and Iraq), its hosting of the only Russian military base outside of Russia, and its heavy reliance on the import of Russian weapons. In addition, tens of thousands of Russians live in Syria, thereby creating crucial commercial and cultural ties as well. When faced with international condemnation of its key friend in the Middle East, it is perhaps not surprising that Russian officials insisted that the UN report was "distorted" and "one-sided" and that it was in fact rebels in the Damascus suburb that had inflicted the pain on its population, hoping to provoke international military intervention.

That intervention was not forthcoming, despite President Obama's claims the previous summer that the use of chemical weapons was a barbaric act that crossed America's "red lines" and would change the U.S. government's calculations regarding the use of force. In a brilliant stroke of diplomacy, Russian Foreign Minister Sergey Lavrov floated a proposal whereby Syria would agree to place its chemical weapons under international control and dismantle them, while the United States would agree not to conduct a military strike on the country. In mid-September, the Syrian government played out its part of the script by sending a letter to Ban Ki-moon, announcing Syria's accession to the Chemical Weapons Convention. Lavrov and U.S. Secretary of State John Kerry then hammered out a detailed plan for the accounting, inspection, control, and elimination of Syria's chemical weapons, later approved by the UN Security Council.

The plan obliged Syria to provide a full declaration of its stockpile, unfettered access to all chemical weapons sites in the country, and a schedule for shipping agents out of the country. On May 1, 2014, it was reported that Syria had missed its self-imposed deadline to remove all of its chemical weapons from the country (set for the end of April), and that approximately 8 percent of the stockpile, containing mostly Sarin precursor chemicals, remained in Damascus. Meanwhile, the Organisation for the Prohibition of Chemical Weapons — the body responsible for facilitating compliance with the Russian-American plan — was asked to investigate the use of chlorine gas in rebel-held areas in early April (a fact which it eventually confirmed).

In March 2015, the UN Security Council adopted a resolution condemning the use of chlorine as a weapon in Syria's civil war and threatening coercive action under the UN Charter if chemical arms were used again.

The very existence of the modern-day Chemical Weapons Convention is testimony to the international community's belief that certain weapons and tactics of war are so destructive, and so indiscriminate, that they shock humanity's collective conscience. During the First World War, Canada's military premiere on the world stage occurred in a battle involving chlorine gas. While most consider the battle at Vimy Ridge in 1917 as Canada's first great war-fighting moment, the country's history of war actually began two years earlier when battalions of the 1st Canadian Division (which had been hastily assembled in the summer of 1914) helped hold the line against the Germans in the Second Battle of Ypres. On April 22, 1915, the Germans released 168 tons of chlorine gas, filling the trenches and forcing Allied troops to climb out into enemy fire. Over 6,000 French and colonial soldiers died within minutes, through a flooding of the lungs some have described as a sensation similar to drowning — but on dry land. The survivors

fled en masse, leaving a huge four-mile opening
in the defences and transforming the village of St.
Julien (which had been comfortably in the rear of
the 1st Canadian Division) into the new front line.
As one observer at the time recounted:

> One cannot blame them that they broke and fled.
> In the gathering dark of that awful night they
> fought with the terror, running blindly in the
> gas-cloud, and dropping with breasts heaving in
> agony and the slow poison of suffocation man-
> tling their dark faces. Hundreds of them fell and
> died; others lay helpless, froth upon their ago-
> nized lips and their racked bodies powerfully
> sick, with tearing nausea at short intervals. They
> too would die later — a slow and lingering death
> of agony unspeakable.[29]

German troops were unprepared for the staggering effects of the gas attacks and failed to fill the
gap immediately. The Canadians took advantage
of the delay, urinated into their handkerchiefs to
counter the effects of the chemicals, and for forty-
eight hours held part of the line against further
attacks until reinforcements appeared.

In the wake of the German gas attacks, other

belligerents, including Great Britain, Russia, the United States, and Italy, raced to develop and deploy this lethal but highly effective weapon of war. It is estimated that 1.3 million casualties died from the use of gas during the First World War. And while chemical weapons were primarily designed for deployment on the battlefield, civilians in nearby towns (who did not have access to protective gas masks) were often their indirect victims. At Versailles, in the treaty bringing an end to the Great War, state parties agreed to outlaw the use of asphyxiating, poisonous, and other gases. The subsequent Geneva Protocol (upon which our modern convention is based) repeats this prohibition and extends it to bacteriological methods of warfare, with the preamble to the treaty declaring that the use of such weapons "has been justly condemned by the general opinion of the civilized world."

The taboo on the use of chemical weapons has largely been respected in the last century, not least in the Second World War — during which both sides developed the capability but were deterred from using it due to the threat of in-kind retaliation. Moreover, the Chemical Weapons Convention, which came into force in 1993 and now has 191 signatories, extends the earlier prohibition on the production and stockpiling of chemical agents as well. This seemingly strong global consensus is what makes the documented use of chemical agents in Syria in 2013 so conspicuous and so ominous. It is also crucial to note that this case involved attacks not only (or even primarily) on combatants, but also on civilian populations in urban centres. The conflicts that mark our contemporary landscape are taking a particularly lethal toll on civilians, with a remarkably meek response — thereby threatening to erode hard-won advances in international humanitarian law.

CONTEMPORARY CHALLENGES TO INTERNATIONAL HUMANITARIAN LAW

In recent years — a period in which the lethality of civil conflict for civilians has intensified — warring parties have driven a bulldozer through every ambiguity or opening in international humanitarian law in order to roll back their obligations to protect civilians. This is true not only for ruthless conductors of armed conflict like Bashar al-Assad, but also for liberal democracies when they are at war. The practice of U.S. drone strikes in Pakistan,

Yemen, and Afghanistan during the first term of the Obama presidency drew on the questionable assumption that all "fighting-aged males" in a certain vicinity were combatants, unless there was specific evidence to the contrary. This permissive approach to defining targets not only ran against the spirit of the Additional Protocol to the Geneva Conventions, but also challenged the core normative advance made during the twentieth century to explicitly protect civilians.

And when liberal democracies are not directly challenging core norms themselves, they are permitting — or even worse, actively assisting — others to do so. In a third of today's civil wars, third-party actors from the outside are supporting one or more of the parties to the conflict.[30] Some have gone as far as to use force in support of entities responsible for widespread and systematic violations that could constitute atrocity crimes. Others have either supplied the weapons used to commit these crimes, turned a blind eye to their trade and transportation, or used their political influence to shield perpetrators. For example, far too little has been done to ensure full respect for international humanitarian law during the conflict in Yemen (which began in 2014), despite the ties that exist between the parties to the conflict and important regional and global powers, such as Iran, Saudi Arabia, the United States, and the United Kingdom. Some of these countries are state parties to the Arms Trade Treaty — an agreement that explicitly seeks to control arms flows to actors that may use them in ways that breach international humanitarian law.

All of these cases of violations of the laws of war are creating a gap between the public's knowledge and expectation of IHL, which is at an all-time high, and the actual reality of compliance with the law in today's conflict. As the ICRC's legal advisor Helen Durham has warned, we must not allow this gap to develop into a vicious cycle — where not respecting the law becomes the "new normal." Public cynicism about the behaviour of warring parties, she suggests, "can all too easily be used as a smokescreen for states and armed groups to claim the law is failing. They may then seek to justify their violations as inevitable and realistic behaviour in armed conflict."[31]

To avoid going backwards to a history of total war, today's liberal democracies need to do better. They cannot assume the battle for restraint has been won. As the heirs to the eighteenth-century practice of humanitarianism, they need to see civilian suffering in war, and the erosion of the principle of civilian distinction in particular, as a warning sign. It should spark the re-evaluation of their own military conduct, and those of their so-called allies. It should also motivate them to redouble their efforts to consolidate legal and normative advances, and consistently condemn violations when they occur.

The ethic of restraint needs to be promoted in the hardest cases, even when we might suspect that civilians are not passive victims and are actively plotting against one side. As Slim eloquently articulates it, "civilian" is not a moral label that we grant others "only when we feel they are neutral…it is an identity primarily based on our enemy's humanity."[32] If we give up on the latter, then we are letting military necessity rule and abandoning the delicate balance at the heart of international humanitarian law. We should have no illusions about what could follow.

HISTORY RETURNS

As the Syrian war inched closer to its fifth anniversary in February 2016, a particularly haunting image was projected through television and social media: the hollowed-out faces of starving civilians in Madaya, a town of 40,000 people northwest of the capital, Damascus. The town had been under siege since the previous summer, cut off by forces of both the Syrian government and Hezbollah, its Lebanese ally. It was peppered with landmines and surrounded by mountains covered in snow, so any effort to supply food aid had become too perilous for humanitarian agencies, leaving residents without access to food, water, or electricity for weeks at a time. Accounts circulated of desperate parents feeding stray cats and dogs to their children, or wives boiling grass to feed their husbands.

At the height of the crisis, 20,000 people faced the risk of death from starvation, bringing an already overwhelmed medical system to the point of collapse. The director of operations for *Médecins Sans Frontières* (MSF), Brice de le Vigne, described doctors facing empty pharmacy shelves and growing lines of starving and sick patients, leading them to resort to feeding severely malnourished children with medical syrup — the only source of sugar and energy. The town had become, in his words, an "open-air prison," with no way in or out given the bullet and landmine injuries inflicted upon those who tried to leave.

In truth, however, there were more Madayas out of the public spotlight, in many parts of Syria. The United Nations estimated that 400,000 people were living under siege in the winter of 2016, as the Syrian regime and its allies fought for previously rebel-held areas and exerted pressure on rebel groups in the north of the country. In a game of like-for-like brutality, civilian suffering and starvation had become a strategic goal and institutionalized weapon used by all parties in the conflict. In short, not only was the principle of distinction being violated but so too was the fundamental norm of providing access to humanitarian assistance. The then U.S. ambassador to the United Nations, Samantha Power, said that the disturbing pictures of civilians at Madaya brought back memories of the Second World War.

And so they did. After Nazi Germany invaded the Soviet Union in June 1941, German armies had by early September approached Leningrad from the west and south while their Finnish allies approached to the north down the Karelian Isthmus. Leningrad's entire able-bodied population was mobilized to build anti-tank fortifications along the city's perimeter in support of the city's 200,000 Red Army defenders. Leningrad's defences soon stabilized, but by early November its 2.5 million civilians had been almost completely encircled, with all vital rail and supply lines to the Soviet interior cut off. In October, police began reporting the appearance of emaciated corpses on the streets. Deaths quadrupled in December, peaking in January and February at 100,000 per month. By the end of what was even by Russian standards a savage winter — on some days temperatures dropped to -30°C or below — cold and hunger had taken somewhere around half a million lives.

The following two winters were less deadly, thanks to there being fewer mouths left to feed and to food deliveries across Lake Ladoga, the inland sea to Leningrad's east, whose shores the Red Army continued to hold. Mortality nonetheless remained high, taking the total death toll to somewhere between 700,000 and 800,000. But it is the stories of the conditions to which civilians were reduced that linger as the more vivid symbol of how barbarous war can be.[33] Pet owners swapped cats in order to avoid eating their own, and there wasn't a dog to be seen. People searched desperately for substitute food, including cotton-seed cake (usually burned in ships' boilers), "macaroni" made from flaxseed for cattle, "meat jelly" produced from boiling bones and calf skins, "yeast soup" from fermented sawdust, joiner's glue boiled and jellified, cough mixture and cold cream — anything that contained calories. Some even licked the dried paste off the wallpaper and rumours of cannibalism abounded.

This is what history looks like, and we must never forget it. This is what the laws of war were designed to prevent, and we must always question arguments about how "other" goals justify their violation. Indeed, if our own liberal democratic model is to survive the changing nature of contemporary conflict, we must do more than just question.

THREE

THE RETURN OF MASS FLIGHT

IN THE EARLY HOURS of September 2, 2015, Alan Kurdi, a three-year-old Syrian boy of Kurdish ethnicity, washed up on the shore near the lively Turkish resort town of Bodrum. Early morning joggers spotted the boy and reported their grim finding to local police. A photograph of Alan's lifeless body, clad in a red T-shirt and navy trousers, soon made global headlines and instantly became an iconic symbol of the swiftly intensifying migration crisis.

According to a journalist and friend of the family, Alan and his family — father Abdullah, mother Rehanna, and older brother Ghalib — had fled the suburbs of Damascus in 2012, under the daily threat of bombardment, for the northern city of

Kobanî near the Turkish border. But bloody clashes between Kurdish forces and ISIS forced them to relocate again to Turkey, where they remained for three years, waiting to obtain visas to travel to Canada. Alan's father — who was unable to work legally — was forced into exploitative jobs on the black market. At one point the family was reduced to sleeping in a factory washroom because they had nowhere else to live.[1]

Abdullah's sister Tima, a hairdresser who had been living in Vancouver for the past twenty-five years, tried to sponsor the asylum claim of her other brother Mohammed and his family, which would have paved the way for Abdullah's family as well. Canadian authorities later reported that the application was returned as incomplete "as it did not meet regulatory requirements for proof of refugee status recognition."[2] Since the Kurdi family had fled to Turkey, which was deemed a safe country, Canadian law made it almost impossible for them to qualify for asylum. Having given up hope that they could obtain an asylum visa from Canada, the family reluctantly decided to try to claim asylum in Europe by travelling to the Greek island of Kos. Tima managed to pull together CAN$5,800 for Alan and his family to make their ill-fated journey.[3]

Abdullah would later tell the press that initially the water had been calm when they set out in the dark early morning hours of that September morning. The four-kilometre crossing normally takes about half an hour. But with twelve passengers and a captain on board, the dingy was overloaded. Upon encountering turbulent water, the captain panicked and after five minutes jumped overboard to swim back to shore, leaving Abdullah in control of the vessel.

"I took over and started steering," Abdullah told reporters a day after the event. "The waves were so high and the boat flipped. I took my wife and my kids in my arms, and I realized they were all dead."[4] He would later describe how he tried his best to keep the boys' heads above water as the waves pushed them down.

The photograph of Alan had a huge impact around the world. Politicians in the West were pressured to consider more generous asylum policies for refugees from Syria, Iraq, and Afghanistan, who were fleeing war and persecution. In Canada the reverberations had an added dimension: after it was reported that Kurdi's family had been trying to reach Canada, refugee and asylum policy became a prominent issue in the 2015 Canadian federal election. The Conservative government lifted some of the legal obstacles to asylum-seeking, but the controversy surrounding Alan's death also helped shape the new Liberal government's agenda when it came to power after the October 2015 election. The new prime minister, Justin Trudeau, pledged to welcome 25,000 Syrian refugees, the first of whom he personally greeted at Toronto's Pearson International Airport in early December.

In late November, nearly three months after Alan's death, Canadian immigration officials reversed their earlier decision to reject seven of his relatives (Alan's uncle Mohammed and his wife and five children) to live with Tima in Vancouver. Alan's father was extended the same offer of asylum, but he chose a different path: after being taken in by the president of Iraqi Kurdistan, Abdullah began working to help refugees locally. He abandoned all thoughts of reaching Canada, but later stated: "Losing my family opened the door to many other families, and I'm not angry at the Canadian people."[5]

THE RETURN OF THE REFUGEE

Alan's story is one part of a global crisis of forced displacement brought on by protracted conflicts in countries such as Syria, Iraq, Afghanistan, Eritrea, and Somalia, and by the more recent spread of ISIS strongholds in the Middle East. The total number of displaced people in the world today has reached a record 65 million. War and persecution have driven more people from their homes than at any point in recorded history.[6] Of this number, 40.8 million are internally displaced persons, or IDPs — forced to flee but remaining within the confines of their country — but almost 25 million have moved across one or more international borders. And in the year 2015 alone, more than 5,000 died en route to finding safety. Approximately 3,700 deaths occurred on the Mediterranean Sea.[7]

Calls to solve the worst migration crisis in the post-war period have become an almost daily feature of European media reports. Solutions are hotly contested and often obscured by claims that refugee flows are pushing Western societies to the breaking point. The spectre of mass flight is also raising awkward questions about the alleged triumph of the liberal democratic model, particularly the promise of decreased conflict and more stable societies. Many of today's migrants come from war-torn countries in the Middle East, where the seeming promise of the Arab Spring has been snuffed out by either a return of authoritarianism or the outbreak of civil war.

History is full of stories of the great re-mapping of populations through migration, both within and across borders. The makeup of modern China, for example, is the product of huge transfers of people across thousands of kilometres — often as a result of the Communist Party's warped ideological ambitions, such as the Cultural Revolution's forceful attempt to empty Chinese cities of bourgeois and capitalist factions.[8]

Canada's own economic, social, and political development was profoundly shaped by waves of immigrants from around the world. In this case, mass migration was encouraged rather than forced, as it carried the promise of economic advancement for both the migrant, who was seeking work and greater prosperity, and the receiving country, which needed quick population growth to develop its resources and economy. One of the most important periods of population growth was from the 1870s up until the First World War, when Canada saw a huge influx of Europeans to the western prairies, where they would settle agricultural land and create new urban centres. In the 1890s, Canadian Minister of the Interior Sir Clifton Sifton was particularly focused on bringing "sturdy" Hungarians, Romanians, and Ukrainians — who faced unemployment and overpopulation in their own countries — to settle what would become Alberta, Saskatchewan, and Manitoba.

While economic opportunity has frequently been a driver of migration, the most dramatic and concentrated episodes have been fuelled by persecution and war. The term "asylum" originated in ancient Greece and literally means "what cannot be seized." Temples frequently constituted a sacred place of refuge, where the gods could protect the persecuted and oppressed. As the Greek form of political organization — the "poleis," or city-state — developed and diffused, diplomatic treaties were created both among the polis and between Greek city-states and other peoples, and began to include the recognition of the right of asylum.[9]

The practice of granting protection to the persecuted also appears to have featured in ancient Rome, centred on temples honouring the god Asylaeus. In fact, some legends suggest that Romulus — one of the twin brothers who founded Rome in the eighth century BC—erected an altar to Asylaeus, patron god of fugitives and exiles, in order to offer sanctuary to those fleeing punishment for breaking the law. Asylum also figures prominently in all three of the monotheistic religions of Judaism, Christianity, and Islam, imposing a duty of hospitality and protection to strangers. As a religious command, it thus features in many holy texts and is designed to offer refuge to all those in distress, whether innocent or guilty.[10]

When the Roman Empire later adopted the Christian faith, through Emperor Constantine's conversion in the fourth century, the power of the Church gave the right of asylum further territorial expression. This was initially manifest in the creation of separate spheres of jurisdiction between civil and religious powers, and the establishment of church premises and land as inviolable places of refuge. In the Middle Ages, when the unified *res publica christiana* gave way to a system of separate sovereignties, asylum morphed from a territorial prerogative of the Church into a right granted by a sovereign political authority.

The first modern case of expulsion and the granting of asylum occurred in the context of Europe's

religious wars and the Reformation. In 1685, after
the revocation of the Edict of Nantes — which had
previously offered legal guarantees to those prac-
ticing the Protestant religion — French Huguenots
were faced with forced conversion to Catholicism or
displacement, and over the following decades more
than a quarter of a million left Catholic France for
refuge abroad. As refugee scholar Emma Haddad
posits, this case of forced displacement hints at
many of the characteristics common to the contemporary cases of mass flight, most notably the phenomenon of individuals fleeing the consequences of
the actions of a government against its own people.
It was also in reference to this religious minority
of French Protestants that the term "refugee" was
first coined.[11] Of those who left France, between
40,000 to 50,000 settled in England and — despite
incidents of xenophobia and violence — were by
and large welcomed as skilled contributors to the
national economy.

By the late eighteenth century the nature of
asylum had moved beyond a sovereign right — to
grant or not to grant refuge — to become an expression of a sovereign duty toward humanity.[12] This
move harkened back to the religious conception of
asylum, which called for hospitality toward and

protection of strangers. But the *legal* duty to provide asylum was first enshrined by France after the French Revolution, in its 1793 constitution, as part of a broader effort to protect populations from political persecution. Article 120, which states that the French people *"donne asile aux étrangers bannis de leur patrie pour la cause de la liberté"* (must offer asylum to those who have been banished from their home countries for taking up the cause of liberty), continues to be used as a reference by states when formulating principles of asylum in their constitutions.

During the twentieth century, flight from persecution also gave rise to large population movements that galvanized the international community. One famous case came in the wake of the Soviet Union's repression of the Hungarian democratic uprising in 1956, which caused an exodus of about 200,000 people, or 2 percent of the total Hungarian population. Most of these refugees — approximately 180,000 — initially fled to Austria on trucks, trains, or by foot, but its government immediately and successfully called on other European states to both provide financial assistance and share in the task of refugee resettlement.[13] As a result, most of the refugees were resettled very quickly in a large number of states. The response to the Hungarian crisis set the standard for future global responses to mass flight. Those sharing in the burden included Canada, which was one of only two countries (the other was Venezuela) that accepted Hungarian migrants without quotas. In less than a year, 37,000 refugees were admitted to Canada, some travelling on ships chartered by the government. The intake included most of the professors, technicians, and graduate students from the Sopron School of Forestry in Hungary, who transplanted their campus to the University of British Columbia and gradually helped build a new faculty of forestry on the west coast of Canada.

It is in the context of war, however, that the duty of providing asylum has most frequently been enacted. The First World War displaced millions of civilians across Europe, Russia, and the Ottoman Empire, either as a result of enemy occupation of territory or through the coercive deportation of populations believed to be disloyal or threatening. One particularly notable episode was the mass flight of 1.5 million Belgians when the German army invaded their country in the early months of the Great War, killing more than 6,000 civilians and destroying homes and property.

During the autumn of 1914, between 200,000 and 250,000 Belgian asylum seekers made it to British shores, in concentrated waves. The southern port of Folkestone, England, for example, received 16,000 desperate Belgians in one single day. The warm welcome initially shown to these refugees — including local middle-class women arriving to serve tea at reception centres — stemmed in large part from Britain's *casus belli* for joining the fight against the Kaiser: to defend Belgium, and European values such as democracy, from German aggression and autocracy.[14] Moreover, given that in 1914 Britain was part of the war but not yet seeing any significant fighting, the mission to "Look after a Belgian" provided ordinary citizens with a way of doing their part for the war effort. This sense of empathy was coupled with the quick realization that highly skilled and hard-working Belgian refugees made a significant contribution to Britain's expanding war economy. It is telling, for example, that the mystery writer Agatha Christie modelled her famous fictional detective, the wise and industrious Hercule Poirot, on a Belgian refugee that she had met in her hometown of Torquay. As time went on, however, a pattern that has become familiar took hold: initial feelings of empathy and obligation turned to resentment, particularly when Belgians living in purpose-built villages had running water and electricity, while many of their British neighbours did not.

But it was the Second World War that sparked the most pronounced and geographically dispersed example of conflict-related migration, with asylum seekers originating in multiple countries and crossing more than one international border. With the defeat of the Axis Powers in Europe, a flood of refugees flowed out of the eastern part of the continent, including approximately twelve million ethnic Germans who were expelled after the end of Nazi rule, 200,000 Jews fleeing from renewed persecution in eastern Europe, and the more than one million wartime displaced that were still on the move in central Europe. The end of colonial rule and the creation of new states in the developing world compounded these historic levels of mass flight. The partition of India in 1947, for example, was accompanied by widespread communal violence that led to the displacement of between ten and twelve million people. And in 1948, the establishment of the state of Israel prompted 700,000 Palestinians to flee to neighbouring countries and territories, inaugurating one of the world's longest-lasting refugee crises.[15]

It was against this backdrop that our current legal regime for refugees was established. In 1943, the Allied powers created the United Nations Relief and Rehabilitation Administration to deal with the scores of war-displaced people across Europe, Africa, and the Far East. In 1946, this body gave way to the International Refugee Organization (IRO), the first agency to deal comprehensively with refugees in war-torn Europe. Though the IRO successfully repatriated or resettled more than a million people during its five years of operation, the emerging Cold War divisions between the superpowers meant that the organization could work only in areas controlled by the Western armies of occupation and did not evolve to address the new challenge of refugees fleeing communist regimes in Europe. Nonetheless, many member states of the United Nations argued that some kind of organization was essential to overseeing and coordinating global refugee issues.

In December 1950, following heated debates over the proper remit of such a body, a resolution was passed founding the United Nations High Commissioner for Refugees (UNHCR) as a subsidiary organ of the General Assembly. The organization was originally intended to operate for only three years, starting in January 1951, as a compromise to those states that did not see the need for a permanent entity and viewed refugee situations as a temporary problem.[16] UNHCR was given a mandate to "provide, on a non-political and humanitarian basis, international protection to refugees and to seek permanent solutions for them," a mandate which would subsequently be broadened by a number of UN resolutions. A few months later, in July 1951, the UN approved the Convention relating to the Status of Refugees — also known as the Refugee Convention — which built on the 1948 Universal Declaration of Human Rights (Article 14) by affirming the right of persons to seek asylum from persecution in other countries, defining who can claim refugee status, and setting out both the rights of individuals who are granted asylum and the responsibilities of nations that grant asylum.

The core of the Refugee Convention is the principle of *non-refoulement*, which forbids countries from turning away refugees whose life or freedom would be threatened if they were forced to return to their home country. It thus requires states to process an individual asylum applicant upon arrival in order to determine whether he has a genuine need for international protection. If the answer is no, then deportation proceedings can begin. If the answer is yes, the applicant is granted refugee status that: a) gives him the right to stay; and b) activates the state government's duty to integrate him into his new society and political community — usually through a process of naturalization. While the scope of the Convention was initially limited to European refugees from before 1951, a 1967 Protocol later removed these geographical and time limitations. (At the time of writing, 145 states are party to the Convention and 146 states are party to the Protocol.)

UNHCR was originally intended as a small and low-budget organization that would oversee implementation of the Convention and play an exclusively legal and advisory role. But in the 1960s, as new conflicts triggered massive refugee movements in Africa, UNHCR was transformed from a body almost solely focused on Europe to one that was spending about two-thirds of its budget on its operations in Africa.[17]

The denouement of the Vietnam War presented another challenge for UNHCR and the international community. The fall of Saigon in 1975 caused an outflow of hundreds of thousands of people (some estimates put the total number as high as

1.5 million) who crossed the waters to other Southeast Asian states such as Malaysia, Singapore, Thailand, the Philippines, and Hong Kong. By the end of 1978, many had drowned in their effort to reach safety — leading the press to call the refugees "boat people" — while others were living in makeshift camps where local populations were growing increasingly resentful of their presence. The wars that Vietnam subsequently initiated with Cambodia and China in 1978 further increased the number of people trying to leave Indochina.

As images of the drowned refugees went around the world, causing a global outcry — much like the photo of Alan Kurdi did in 2015 — the UNHCR managed to secure an agreement, which remained in place throughout the 1980s, that allowed the refugees to land and disembark in Southeast Asian countries. In exchange, all those who were granted refugee status were settled in third countries, mostly the United States (which accepted 823,000 refugees in total), Canada and Australia (137,000 each), France (96,000), and Britain (16,000),[18] where they went on to make significant social and economic contributions. More generally, the response to the displacement of civilians during the Vietnam War demonstrated the capacity of the international community to *collectively* address what its members deemed a global problem.

In the 1980s, the UNHCR evolved again, by not only providing legal assistance to those seeking asylum but also delivering material assistance to millions of refugees in camps and protracted conflict situations throughout the developing world. In 1991, the fall of Yugoslavia saw Europe become, once again, the centre of UNHCR's focus of operations. The brutal ethnic conflicts that followed the Croatian War of Independence (1991–95) and the Bosnian War (1992–95) displaced close to four million people, with approximately 600,000 to 800,000 permanently settling in other European countries (roughly half went to Germany) and between 10,000 to 15,000 ending up in the U.S., Canada, and Australia.[19] Within a decade a second crisis erupted when fighting broke out between the forces of the Federal Republic of Yugoslavia and Albanians who were demanding independence. Following NATO airstrikes in March 1999, more than half a million people fled Kosovo into neighbouring Macedonia in the space of just two weeks. By the end of April 1999 half of the residents of Kosovo were refugees or internally displaced people.

At the time, European governments, led by Germany, established refugee camps in Kosovo and Macedonia. NATO troops initially took the lead in establishing shelters and providing food, and then turned the operation of the refugee camps over to UNHCR and other relief agencies. There were calls for each member state of the European Union to accept a quota or share of the refugees, but — in a preview of what was to come — most European states opposed such a burden-sharing scheme. When the Kosovo War ended in 1999, more than 200,000 Serbs and other non-Albanian minorities fled to Serbia, giving the country the largest refugee population in Europe.

The UNHCR is now a permanent global organization with an annual budget of around U.S.$3.5 billion and more than 7,000 staff in over 125 countries. The gradual expansion of its remit over the years — to provide both protection and assistance to refugees, stateless persons, and other displaced people — speaks to the reality that mass flight is a perpetual challenge, not a temporary crisis, and a core feature of a more globalized world.

MEASURING THE SIZE OF THE CHALLENGE

Today's spectre of mass flight, however, is quantitatively different from what the world has encountered in the past. In the Middle East, it reflects the aftermath of the 2003 Iraq War, the unfinished Arab Spring, and subsequent conflicts in Syria and Libya; in other parts of Central Asia and Africa, it stems from long-standing conflicts — as in Afghanistan and Somalia — as well as the breakdown of governance and security. From 2011 to 2015, global forced displacement increased by more than 50 percent, from 42.5 to 65.3 million people. In 2015 alone, more than 12 million people were newly displaced due to conflict or persecution — meaning that an average of 34,000 individuals *per day*, or twenty-four every minute, were fleeing their homes to seek protection and security elsewhere.[20]

To understand the magnitude of the movement, consider the numbers in a different way. If the total population of displaced persons today constituted a nation, it would be larger than the United Kingdom, France, and Italy, and significantly larger than Canada. One in every 113 human beings is now either a refugee, internally displaced, or seeking asylum. More than half of them are children, many of whom are unaccompanied or separated from their parents. Furthermore, the prospects of returning home for many migrants have evaporated: by the end of 2015, the number of refugees considered to be in a protracted situation, with no immediate prospect for further movement or resettlement, was 6.7 million.[21]

The current crisis is not only unprecedented in size, but also in the variety of host countries to which migrants are travelling and the diversity of nationalities on the move. If you were reading or listening to Western media, you would likely have the impression that Europe is at the centre of the contemporary refugee crisis. But this is only partly true. The top five host countries for refugees in 2015 were all outside of Europe — places where the capacity to protect is weak or overstretched.[22] Turkey was at the top of the list, with 2.5 million refugees. Its neighbour Lebanon was the largest per-capita host country, with a ratio of 183 refugees per 1,000 inhabitants. The demographic makeup of these two countries has been profoundly affected by migration, but so too has almost every sector of their societies: the labour market, public finance, health care, education, infrastructure, traffic control, and waste management. In 2014 Lebanon's then Minister of Education Elias Bou Saab compared the refugee crisis to a natural disaster like a hurricane or earthquake, but in this case, "the earthquake is not a one time event, but has been ongoing for four years."

The main contributor to today's crisis of mass flight is the civil war in Syria. By the end of 2015, it was the world's biggest producer of refugees, with 4.9 million Syrian refugees residing in 120 countries. While the vast majority are hosted by neighbouring states, the ultimate destination of many of those who are on the move is Europe.

In 2015, more than one million migrants crossed into Europe and close to 950,000 lodged asylum applications. This "grand march to Europe," as one UNHCR official has called it, resulted from a number of factors, including the intensification of the smuggling trade and the open-door policy of Germany (which received roughly one-third of Europe's asylum claims in 2015), under the leadership of Chancellor Angela Merkel. But above all, the spike in mass flight reflects a loss of hope among refugees. Many fled their countries believing their displacement would be temporary, but after years of living in makeshift camps (or worse), the reality of protracted conflict in their home countries (particularly Syria, Iraq, and Afghanistan) led them to continue on, hopefully to claim asylum in Europe.

Like the Kurdi family, an increasing number of those marching toward Europe have sought to make their journey by crossing the Mediterranean Sea — given that it is shorter, and allegedly safer, than overland alternatives through North Africa. But by 2016, the Mediterranean Sea had become one of the deadliest "borders" in the world, and Western countries, particularly in Europe, were in the midst of a politically charged debate about insiders and outsiders that was dominating election results and the direction of public policy. Concern about the movement of people, both into and within Europe, was an especially pivotal point of debate during the 2016 British referendum on membership of the European Union. One of the key actors on the Brexit side — the UK Independence Party — staged a press conference in which its leader, Nigel Farage, spoke in front of a huge placard featuring a long queue of migrants and refugees and a bolded title: "Breaking Point." Though politicians from mainstream parties in Britain roundly condemned the poster as at best scaremongering and at worst inciting racial hatred, the sentiment that Britain had taken in too many "foreigners" was widespread and one of the motives behind the high numbers who voted Leave.

NEW WALLS IN EUROPE

Following the Second World War, the last time the world faced a migration crisis of this scale, countries pulled together to forge the United Nations Charter, the Universal Declaration of Human Rights, and the Refugee Convention. This time, however, bold leadership has been in short supply.

On the one hand, there have been remarkable displays of political courage, most notably by German Chancellor Angela Merkel, who insisted that an open-door policy was Germany's humanitarian duty. She took to publicly chastising East European politicians, particularly Hungarian Prime Minister Viktor Orbán, for erecting barriers on their southern borders and failing to learn the lessons from their own years behind the Iron Curtain. "The refugees won't be stopped if we just build fences," she remarked in the autumn of 2015, "and I've lived behind a fence for long enough" (a reference to her own formative years in East Germany).

In the face of criticism from members of her own political party and falling poll ratings, Merkel continued to emphasize that the right to asylum was a crucial part of German Basic Law and a direct reflection of efforts to address the Nazi legacy.

Scores of ordinary citizens also became actively involved in the provision of aid to refugees. Those living on one of the key frontlines — the Greek islands that have become the landing point for thousands of migrants — have worked tirelessly to provide a warm welcome, despite the country's own severe economic crisis which left the Greek government unable to adequately provide for many of its *own* citizens. In recognition of their empathy and self-sacrifice, a prominent group of academics from some of the world's leading universities — including Oxford and Harvard — nominated the residents of the Greek islands of Lesbos, Kos, Chíos, Samos, Rhodes, and Leros for the Nobel Peace Prize. In Germany, Refugees Welcome, a grassroots organization billed as the "Airbnb for refugees," was overwhelmed with offers of accommodation once Chancellor Merkel announced Germany's open-door policy. And in Canada, both local churches and private citizen initiatives have raised money to sponsor the resettlement of refugee families from Syria. By banding together to "adopt" families, ordinary citizens have proven able to achieve more than the Canadian government could on its own — thereby increasing the total number of refugees that could be admitted into the country. This model garnered international attention and interest, with a feature article in the *New York Times* marvelling at the "angry mob of do-gooders" in Canada who were impatient to welcome displaced Syrians.[23]

On the other hand, there has also been opposition to liberal asylum policies and to local refugee processing and reception centres. The German newspaper *Die Zeit* reported more than two hundred instances of refugee hostel attacks in Germany in 2015, in which approximately one hundred people were injured. And despite Angela Merkel's promise in September 2015 that German police would investigate and prosecute those responsible "with all means available," only four of the attacks resulted in convictions.[24] An even more troubling trend is the rise of lethal attacks, including one incident in early 2016 when a hand grenade (which failed to go off) was thrown into an asylum centre in Villingen-Schwenningen in southern Germany, which at the time housed more than two hundred people.

European views surrounding refugee policy have hardened, revealing a darker side of contemporary liberal democracy. In a Eurobarometer poll from November 2015, immigration was named as the most important issue facing the European Union by citizens of every EU country (apart from Portugal, where it was the second-most prominent issue). A staggering 58 percent of Europeans named immigration as one of their top two concerns.[25] This configuration of attitudes has occurred against a background of hotly contested debates about the nature, triggers, and solutions to the pressures on Europe's frontiers. The immediate future of the current wave of mass flight is uncertain. Arguably, we should stop conceiving of it as a temporary crisis — which connotes something short and sharp — and begin to acknowledge it as the "new normal." And it is a normal we have had our own hand in creating. The protracted conflicts in the Middle East, which the international community has been unable to resolve, combined with the territorial gains of ISIS, which is terrorizing populations under its control, will continue to produce thousands of migrants seeking protection.

More broadly, we are living through an era of profound state failure in countries where institutions are corrupt, ineffective, or — in some cases — non-existent, and where governments cannot provide basic security, let alone public services, for their populations. These are the parts of the world that Fukuyama believed would remain mired in "history," until they embraced the benefits of liberal democracy. But as decades of efforts to promote democracy from abroad have illustrated, the structural challenges facing countries in crisis cannot be eliminated overnight by transplanting political and economic models from the West. And many citizens of these states, who continue to live with economic hardship, weak rule of law, and, in the worst cases, political violence and conflict, are acutely aware — given modern communications and technology — that there are more peaceful and prosperous alternatives elsewhere. Democracies in the West have come to have a magnetic pull on their aspirations.

Rather than witnessing the spread of stable liberal democracies worldwide, which develop the capacity to provide for the security and economic needs of citizens, we are seeing the large-scale movement of populations to zones of peace and prosperity. There is little doubt that refugees will continue to seek safe haven in Europe and that some will persevere in their efforts to reach the continent. One of the EU's favoured responses has been to increase aid to camps in those countries experiencing the greatest influx of migrants and refugees. But in recent years, countries such as Jordan and Lebanon have adopted measures to stop the flow of new arrivals almost completely and taken steps to revoke the permission to stay of those already in the country. This leaves Turkey as the only haven at the Syrian border — a fact that has been seized upon by the European Union. In late 2015, Turkey and the EU struck a deal in which the former effectively became Europe's "bouncer," by helping to prevent irregular migration in exchange for financial assistance and the reopening of negotiations on Turkish membership to the EU. In the spring of 2016, a more far-reaching agreement stipulated that asylum seekers arriving in Europe can be sent back to Turkey — the latter having been deemed a safe country — under the condition that for every migrant returned, Europe would resettle a recognized Syrian refugee currently living in Turkey.[26]

In addition to these measures, Europe has been forced to intensify its search-and-rescue efforts in the Mediterranean, which is now aptly described as "Europe's graveyard." In direct response to the 2013 Lampedusa migrant shipwreck, in which an estimated 360 migrants from Libya died in one crossing, Italy instigated Operation Mare Nostrum, which succeeded in rescuing 150,810 migrants (as well as arresting 330 alleged smugglers) in the year in which it was operative.[27] In 2015, the Italian program was replaced by the European Union's Operation Sophia, a military mission primarily designed to combat illegal smuggling on the south-central Mediterranean, but which has also engaged in search and rescue. According to the EU, more than 35,000 lives have been saved as of April 2017, and approximately 400 illegal boats neutralized.

While the mission was deemed largely successful, many point out that it is treating only the symptoms of mass flight and not the deeper causes, and that smugglers are simply adjusting their tactics in response.[28] The numbers appear to vindicate that critique: in a period of just three days in May 2016, 700 migrants died trying to cross the Mediterranean in rubber dinghies. In a cruel twist of fate, rescuers from the non-governmental organization Sea-Watch attached fluorescent life jackets to the corpses floating in the water, so that a nearby Italian naval ship could locate them more easily. "It was strange," recalled one member of the rescue team, "as we usually use life jackets to save people."[29]

Despite repeated calls from Chancellor Merkel and other European politicians to reach a common solution to a common challenge, European states have been unable to agree on how to address the crisis facing their continent. In theory, the European Union has the capacity, and the resources, to mount a more robust and collective response to the Grand March. It also has a wider interest in doing so: tackling the refugee crisis could help the EU undertake reforms that are long overdue — such as strengthening its external border and enhancing its common foreign and security policy — and thus reinvigorate the Union in the wake of the Euro crisis.

Yet European politicians have so far failed to design clearer and safer passages or to implement proposals to share the burden of asylum seekers more equitably. When confronted with a serious test of its common resolve, the members of the EU failed miserably. The impact of this disunity has been devastating. European countries have not only fallen short of meeting the humanitarian and medical needs of refugees, by tolerating the continuation of squalid conditions for many of those who arrive, but their efforts to deter migration have only increased the demand for smuggling networks and pushed people toward more dangerous travel routes. In a damning report called *Obstacle Course to Europe,* the humanitarian organization *Médecins Sans Frontières* claims that the year 2015 will be remembered as the year in which Europe "catastrophically failed in its responsibility" to protect thousands of people.[30]

A quarter of a century after the end of the Cold War, is this what a coalition of victorious liberal democracies looks like?

A TWENTY-FIRST-CENTURY REFUGEE CRISIS...

One of the key differences between today's surge in migration, and those of earlier decades, is the evolution in the motivations for mass flight. Our current legal and policy framework for refugees is based on the experience of the victims of Nazi Germany during the Second World War. The ideal/ typical refugee is someone who has no choice but to leave her home country due to life-threatening danger — usually as a result of persecution on the

basis of political opinion or membership in a religious, ethnic or other vulnerable social group. The
inherent assumption is that what distinguishes refugees from other migrants is that their departure is
forced. They are *pushed* out of their country rather
than *pulled* to other countries by the promise of a
better life. This image and the rules that support
it ascribe very little initiative or choice to refugees.
Instead, they are seen as being tossed around by
forces beyond their control.

Since the end of the Second World War, however,
the drivers of displacement have both changed and
diversified, and a sharp dichotomy between forced
and voluntary migration has become increasingly
hard to maintain. A minority of today's refugees
continue to be driven by individual persecution on
the basis of race, religion, ethnicity, or political convictions. But a fast-growing segment is displaced
by other phenomena, ranging from civil war, gen-
eralized violence, food insecurity, natural disasters,
and environmental change. While the refugee reg-
ulations and policies of some countries have taken
these developments into account by broadening the
grounds on which people can claim asylum, most
notably to include those fleeing situations of gen-
eralized violence and victims of persecution based

on gender or sexuality, there has not been a thorough overhaul of the original refugee framework. The terms remain largely the same as when they were established in 1951.

Two other contemporary problems challenge the ideal/typical profile of the refugee. First, today's population of refugees has become intricately intertwined with other migratory streams that have emerged over the past few decades, particularly economic migrants who are escaping poverty and unemployment. In order to stem the flow of those in the economic category, many Western governments have placed restrictions on migration—but in so doing have also limited the legal options for refugees seeking asylum in other countries. As a result, asylum seekers have been forced to use clandestine or illegal (and increasingly criminalized) migration routes, which situate them in the same population stream as irregular economic migrants. These "mixed flows," as they are sometimes called, make it difficult and costly for receiving states to differentiate between refugees and other migrants,[31] thereby giving populist politicians all the raw material they need to question the motives of those seeking admission to Western countries.

In addition, while Western rules are designed to address a simple scenario, there is frequently a complex interaction between the push-and-pull factors of mass flight. Today's refugees are driven by a combination of motivations — not just the need to escape from violence and human rights violations, but also the search for employment and higher living standards. This not only adds to the challenge of distinguishing between refugees and economic migrants, but calls into question the "clean" categories used in law and policy-making. Are they refugees or are they migrants? The answer to that question matters deeply for the treatment of the individuals who arrive on our shores: if they are deemed refugees, governments have a legal duty to keep them until their claim for asylum is fully processed; if they are identified as economic migrants, they can be returned to their home countries. The reality for many of those on the move, however, lies somewhere in between.

Even within the category of those regarded as asylum seekers, the picture is not as clear as it used to be. Historically, the role of states and organizations tasked with assisting those fleeing war and persecution was to provide a "first country" of refuge. But many of those who manage to make it to Europe's shores today, like refugees in the past, have exhibited extraordinary initiative. It stands to reason, therefore, that they have clear preferences regarding where they want to go to build a new life — based on, for example, the presence of family members or networks of fellow nationals, the language and employment opportunities in the destination country, and the relative difficulty of gaining refugee status. As a result, some do not apply for asylum in the first safe country they access. Thousands of the refugees that have reached the Greek islands, for example, have their hopes set on countries farther afield, such as Germany or Sweden.

This particular pattern of migration has been used as evidence for the claim that these are not "real refugees" but economic migrants or "welfare seekers." But we need to ask ourselves: would we be any different? Wouldn't we want the best opportunities for ourselves and our children? Alan Kurdi's family spent years in Turkey — a safe third country — but without any sustainable livelihood. The movement of refugees beyond the safe first country has also created a dilemma for organizations with a mandate to assist and protect refugees. In a world of scarce resources, where does the responsibility of an organization like UNHCR begin and end? Should it insist on asylum claims in the first country of arrival or should it facilitate safe passage to third countries as well?

A second distinguishing feature of contemporary migration is its reliance on new technology. The revolution in information and communication technologies has also transformed the nature of mass flight. The ease of access to the Internet and social networking and messaging applications, facilitated by the increasing ubiquity and affordability of smartphones, has radically changed how refugees undertake and experience their journey and informed their ultimate destinations. Such tools allow for easier, quicker, and more accurate information exchange among (prospective) asylum seekers about everything from how to evade border controls to what the conditions are like in destination countries. In an article in *Wired Magazine*, Alessandra Ram explains how, "apps of every kind help find a place to sleep, translate foreign languages, offer guidance on what to pack, and help manage money. Almost every need is met with mobile."[32] Those travelling by boat often use WhatsApp to update their location on Google Maps, not only alerting the authorities to their location should trouble arise

but also allowing those on the move to avoid exor-
bitantly high call rates. For Hassan, a twenty-seven-
year-old Syrian refugee who travelled through ten
countries to get to Great Britain, technology saved
his life when the nine-metre dinghy he took from
Turkey to Lesbos sank. By holding his smartphone
above the water, he was still able to text a friend who
then alerted the Turkish coast guard and ensured
the group's rescue.[33]

But for many in receiving countries, scenes
of migrants arriving on their shores with mobile
phones challenges their image of the "huddled
masses." It raises suspicions about how "needy" they
really are. When people flee from violence and persecution, they are forced to make quick decisions
about what to take with them. For those who left
post-war Europe, it was a photograph, a small family heirloom, or a university diploma. But this is
twenty-first century mass flight: the most valuable possession is a smartphone. It is the only tool
that enables refugees to both find safe passage and
maintain a lifeline back to their loved ones.

The smartphone has empowered not only those
en route to Europe but also those living in refugee
camps. A survey among the population of Zaatari,
a Syrian refugee camp in Jordan, found that over

80 percent of young people had a smartphone and that more than 50 percent used the Internet more than once a day.[34] Recognizing the empowering potential of Internet access for vulnerable refugees, Mark Zuckerberg of Facebook pledged in September 2015 to bring Internet connectivity to all refugee camps, telling a UN forum that "Internet access is an important enabler of human rights."

Another way in which technology has changed the nature of mass flight is by providing novel ways to assist refugees more effectively and efficiently. In addition to matching refugees with available accommodation, smartphone apps have been developed to assist refugees in finding their way around their new towns and cities, navigating the bureaucracy of registering for asylum, and accessing basic services including health care. Technological advances have also made the saving of lives at sea more effective. With European border agencies tasked with patrolling the roughly 2.5 million square kilometres of the Mediterranean Sea, the Migrant Offshore Aid Station (MOAS) — a humanitarian project based in Malta — uses two remote-piloted aircraft, otherwise known as drones, to scour the sea and locate refugees in distress. The Schiebel S-100 Camcopters, which can fly for up to six hours and provide a live video stream, has played a pivotal role in enabling MOAS to save more than 10,000 lives.[35]

Technological advances, however, are "dual use." They not only provide opportunities for refugees and those who help them; they have also assisted those who seek to capitalize on their desperation. For example, Arabic-language Facebook groups have become the most popular way for smugglers to advertise their services. In addition, governments are leveraging new technology to enhance the effectiveness of border controls. It's no coincidence that the development and expansion of biometric identification technologies (which rely on fingerprints, facial scans, and iris scans) have intensified in the past few years: in the wake of the refugee crisis, security concerns have arisen concerning the difficulty of screening refugees for potential terrorist links. Indeed, the U.S. government has declared it is developing new technologies for precisely this purpose.

The final difference between our contemporary wave of mass flight and those of earlier periods relates to the way in which refugees move across borders. The nature of travel in the twenty-first century has created a particularly incongruous situation for refugees. On the one hand, we live in an increasingly globalized world in which the means of travel have for many of us become highly "democratized." Now there are more, faster, cheaper, and safer connections between cities than ever before. The explosion of budget air travel in particular has brought long-distance travelling within reach of the lower-middle classes in many parts of the world. It has also opened up travel routes for refugees, as the expansion of Turkish Airlines into markets such as Somalia clearly shows.

On the other hand, Western governments have intensified their efforts to keep unwanted immigration (including asylum migration) at bay. These policies go beyond stepping up the patrol of their own physical border areas through sophisticated techniques of biometric identification. They also involve the externalization of migration control beyond their borders, through efforts to patrol the open seas and repatriate migrants before they have ever set foot on national territory, and through policies that outsource migration control to airlines, private security firms, and transit countries.[36]

Ironically, these developments have forced today's asylum seekers to use distinctly pre-modern modes of travel to bypass restrictions: walking across borders to evade checkpoints or crossing the open sea in rickety dinghies. It is worth pointing out that in the 1970s, Vietnamese refugees were forced to travel by boat because the communist regime had made it illegal to *leave* the country, making air travel out of the country impossible. The current refugees who try to access Europe by boat do so because they believe there are no legal ways to *enter* the continent. Western policies have unwittingly contributed to the carnage in the Mediterranean Sea. They have also fostered the development of the criminal industry of people smugglers worth billions of euros.

. . . OR A TWENTY-FIRST-CENTURY SECURITY THREAT?

With the significant decline in military threats to most Western states since the end of the Cold War, academic and popular conceptions of security have been broadened. Migration generally, and refugee flows in particular, have increasingly been depicted by the governments and electorates of Western countries as potential threats to national security.

One implication of this "securitization" of asylum

seekers is the tendency to reframe the responsibility to tackle refugee situations as a matter of peace and security and to focus on the immediate causes of displacement. It is perhaps no surprise, then, that in the autumn of 2015, when European Union countries moved into the second phase of Operation Sophia, which was designed to disrupt the flow of migrants from the Libyan coast, they requested authorization from the United Nations Security Council, the body charged with maintaining international peace and security. The Council mandated member states to "use all necessary measures" (code words for coercion) to confront vessels on the high seas suspected of being used for human smuggling or trafficking.

The logic of securitization extends from causes into consequences, by emphasizing the destabilizing effects that the presence of refugees can have on the security, communal cohesion, and national identity of neighbouring states. One recent example is the efforts by the Kenyan government to close down Dadaab, the largest refugee camp in the world, because it feared the population of Somali refugees had become a recruiting ground for terrorists. These fears have also spread to Western countries, most notably the United States, where the idea that the inflow of migrants and refugees (particularly those who are Muslim or Arab) could threaten national security has legitimized increasingly restrictive border and asylum policies.

These kinds of measures were given additional impetus by the 2015 attacks on bars and nightclubs in Paris, and the alleged use of the Greek asylum route by the perpetrators of those acts — a connection that has never been definitively proven. The scandal that erupted over widespread sexual harassment in Cologne and other European cities on New Year's Eve 2015, some of which was thought to be the responsibility of groups of young male asylum seekers from the Middle East and North Africa, added to the general sense of unease and insecurity among populations of EU countries. The fact that young single men are strongly overrepresented in overall refugee flows leads some to predict an increase in sexual harassment, crime, and terrorist attacks.

These incidents have also contributed to an unprecedented surge in support for populist far-right political parties running on anti-immigration platforms across the Western world. In France, the Front National led by Marine Le Pen captured the largest number of votes in the first round of regional elections in December 2015. More dramatically, in the spring of 2016, Norbert Hofer, the leader of Austria's far-right Freedom Party, rode to prominence by magnifying fears about immigration. The party dominated the first round of voting and was only narrowly defeated in the second round by a coalition backing the Green Party candidate.

In many other parts of Europe, including liberal-leaning Scandinavia and the Netherlands, anti-immigration parties are seeing their popularity soar and their influence in coalition governments increase, dealing fatal blows to the centrist parties that have dominated European politics for the past seventy years. Those political leaders such as Merkel, who have tried to strike a more welcoming tone toward refugees, have been subjected to intense criticism — from both populist parties at home and other European countries. Some have gone as far as to blame the German chancellor's open-door policy for sparking the British public's decision to leave the European Union.

The winning formula behind these populist party advances — the mobilization of mistrust and fear against a clear scapegoat (the refugee), combined with the identification of an easy solution

(the closing of borders) — is eroding the traditional ideological divisions between left and right
and eliminating the possibility of a viable middle ground.[37] This politics of fear harkens back to
a simpler past, when nation-states were (supposedly) more homogeneous and self-sufficient, and
calls for a strong nationalist agenda that will put
"us" back in control. What is particularly worrying
for European liberal democracy is that mainstream
parties have co-opted part of that agenda, thereby
compromising the values that laid the foundation of
the European Union out of the ashes of the Second
World War — namely, trust and interdependence
among the nation-states of Europe.

Closer to home, the perceived threats posed
by refugees also dominated the race for the
Republican nomination in the run-up to the 2016
U.S. presidential election. Donald Trump's infamous call to ban all Muslim immigrants to the
United States — "They're not coming to this country if I'm president" — was designed to build an
image of a commander-in-chief who could protect Americans from their enemies and has left
an indelible mark on the nature of the debate
over who and how many should "get in" to the
United States. Although President Trump has

encountered numerous obstacles to the implementation of his so-called Muslim ban, he
continues to depict migrants and refugees as
"criminals" and security threats.

The securitization of refugees and asylum seekers has led Western governments to move away
from welcoming migrants into their societies and
focus their energies instead on how to keep them
at bay. Governments have buckled under strong
incentives to shirk the duty of non-refoulement
and to resist efforts at integration. They have also
placed great emphasis on the problem of fairness
in processing asylum requests, suggesting that
those with the means to make it to Western countries are not necessarily those in most acute need
of international protection. Given the costs and
difficulties associated with the journey, it is often
argued that the relatively well-off, the young, and
the able-bodied are disproportionally represented
in the refugee flows that reach Europe.

These frustrations with the historical approach
to receiving refugees — as outlined in the Refugee
Convention — have led some states, including
Canada, to prefer an alternative approach: the
organized movement of pre-selected refugees,
which would lead to permanent settlement. The

benefit of resettlement, as compared to processing arrivals, is that governments exercise greater
control over who "gets in." They can effectively
screen and select those deemed most worthy of
international protection, rather than those who
were healthy, young, and rich enough to make it
to the destination country. This option is more
palatable for electorates worried about "queue
jumpers," or about taking in refugees who are
security risks.

Despite the attractiveness of this option, worldwide refugee resettlement numbers are a drop in
the ocean. Currently, resettlement placements are
available for only approximately 1 percent of the
world's refugee population.[38] In addition, resettlement has been an especially unpopular option for
European countries, given that it does not reduce
the number of asylum applicants and thus merely
puts additional pressure on the system. While some
argue that increasing the number of resettlement
places available in Western countries would significantly reduce the burden of irregular asylum seekers arriving at the border, it is not clear that those
who are targeted for resettlement and those who
risk the dangerous journey to reach the West are
part of the same group.

Giving governments the freedom to essentially pick and choose which refugees are accepted also comes with its own hazards. Some resettlement governments are suspected of "creaming off" economically useful refugees, while leaving the more vulnerable populations in camps. This has been the critique levelled at Australia's resettlement program, which has been used as a rationale for a restrictive border control regime. Furthermore, discussions about which refugees are most amenable to integration can mask problematic racial, national, or gender stereotypes in the selection process, giving some national or religious groups preference at the expense of others. Canada's choice to include only women, families, and gay men in the Syrian resettlement campaign — because these groups were seen to pose a lower security risk or, in the case of gay men, be at risk of persecution — is one example of a policy that could be considered stigmatizing. But so too are the calls by several European leaders, as well as U.S. Republican politicians, to admit only Christian refugees.

Many Western countries are investing heavily in trying to prevent the arrival of asylum seekers, and/or in making the process of claiming asylum once arrived exceedingly difficult. While borders can never be sealed completely, there are some indications that restrictive migration and asylum policies do have a modest deterrent effect.[39] The cost of this approach, however, is not only financial. Tightening borders affects the very identity of a liberal democratic society, denying international protection to many who are in genuine need. Liberal democracies have been at the vanguard of creating international mechanisms to promote and protect human rights — including the right to asylum. And at the core of this "rights revolution," as the Canadian author and academic Michael Ignatieff has called it,[40] is the idea that rights are universal and unconditional: they belong to all human beings, regardless of nationality or place of birth. Liberalism is also associated with ideas of free trade and free movement; by closing borders to refugees and asylum seekers, Western liberal democracies seem to be privileging the free flow of goods and services over the free flow of people.

There is one further negative consequence of the West's recourse to restrictive asylum and refugee policy: it provides violent extremists, such as members of ISIS, with more ammunition for their propaganda war. When liberal democracies close their doors to desperate, stateless people, it serves the strategic interest of extremist groups by bolstering their narrative of hate against the West.[41]

CHANGING THE SCRIPT

In order to respond more effectively and more humanely to twenty-first-century mass flight, Western liberal democracies need to become bolder and more creative about fulfilling their duty to protect. This requires three ingredients: policy innovation, to respond to the nature of contemporary migration; a shift in mindset from viewing refugees as a *cost* to appreciating how they can contribute their talents and skills; and a reactivation of our moral consideration for those seeking a better life.

As a first step, governments could more actively explore alternatives to both traditional naturalization policies and organized resettlement schemes. One option is to offer special "humanitarian" visas to refugees in transit countries such as Lebanon, Jordan, and Turkey. These have the double benefit of improving the safe passage of refugees by helping them to avoid resorting to smugglers or embarking on a perilous journey, as well as the security of destination countries by checking traveller identities before they reach Western countries in large numbers.[42] Another option is to offer forms of temporary protection to refugees, while leaving open the possibility of ultimate repatriation to their place of origin. When the Refugee Convention was drafted after the Second World War, displacement was often caused by the redrawing of national boundaries (particularly in relation to Germany, Poland, and the Balkan countries), and was therefore expected to be permanent. That is why the preferred solution was permanent settlement and integration within the newly drawn borders of their place of residence. However, in the 1980s, when approximately half of the world's refugees were living in Africa, UNHCR and other UN agencies encouraged repatriation back to the country of origin once a conflict had abated or ended — given concerns over burdening poor host countries with the presence of large migrant populations. Around the same time, the United States introduced a system of temporary protection in which nationals of designated countries *already in the country* were automatically eligible for protection status, without leading to permanent resident status.

Even though the European Union has a policy on temporary protection, it has not activated this measure in the current crisis. This could stem from the fact that the flow of Syrian refugees has continued over several years: there is no end in sight to the conflict and a low probability of large-scale repatriation in the medium term. Another reason, perhaps, is moral hazard: allowing temporary protection might result in even more applicants. A final concern is that once on European soil, refugees would have multiple avenues to contest a request to repatriate (whereas if they are living in a refugee camp and that camp closes, they have little choice but to comply).

Governments could also explore the possibility of giving resettled refugees a kind of dual status: the right to re-establish themselves in their home countries while also retaining their right of residence in the country of asylum. "Revolving" or "part-time" refugees may be more likely to take up voluntary return options if the risks of return are managed and if there are incentives to contribute to the rebuilding of their country of origin. These transnational solutions have been pursued by millions of people without formal assistance programs; many more might opt for them if they were properly supported by asylum countries and the broader international community.[43]

One of the biggest obstacles to crafting more creative solutions lies within contemporary liberal democracies themselves: democratically elected politicians are focused on a short time frame. Their DNA is hard-wired to address public opinion about real-time crises, rather than devising long-term responses to endemic challenges. This is one of the reasons why it is so difficult to activate a public discussion about either the deep structural causes that are driving mass flight — such as protracted conflict and state failure — or the demographic trends of aging populations in Western societies, which argue for open rather than closed borders.

In order to "change the script" on mass flight, the citizens of Western liberal democracies need to recognize, in the words of the Turkish-American philosopher Seyla Benhabib, that "'the other' is not elsewhere."[44] She is right at our borders, asking to come in, or is already trying to make a life among us.

Three particular shifts in mindset are needed. The first requires us to revisit the long-standing debate within liberal democracies about how the rights and interests of those who are members of our political community should be weighed against the interests of those who are outside it. In political theory, this debate is broadly between communitarians and cosmopolitans. Communitarians believe that our primary obligations are toward others within our national society and that as democratic communities we have the right to collectively regulate who comes in and who goes out. Cosmopolitan liberals, by contrast, emphasize the rights of individuals, wherever they may reside. They assert that borders are morally irrelevant and that denying refugees political membership and keeping them stateless constitutes a violation of human rights. A commitment to liberal principles of equality and freedom thus demands a policy of open borders.[45]

Most moral philosophers recognize that we have at least some ethical duties toward outsiders and would agree that those fleeing violence and persecution are among the most deserving of our concern. Therefore the main point of contention is about precisely how strong and extensive this claim ought to be.

One way of resolving this debate is to weigh the obligation to aid refugees against the costs to the receiving society. But what exactly counts as reasonable or unreasonable costs? On one end of the spectrum is the American ecologist and philosopher Garrett Hardin, who uses the metaphor of "lifeboat ethics" to emphasize the limited capacity of rich and developed countries (the "lifeboats") to take in people who are metaphorically swimming in the surrounding waters. Governments of the West have a moral duty *not* to let in more people if it means surpassing or even approaching the limits of what the country can reasonably sustain.[46] On the other end of the spectrum is the Australian moral philosopher Peter Singer, who argues that unless the cost to our quality of life is greater than the gain to theirs, there are no reasonable moral grounds to exclude those in need. Singer famously used the example of coming across a small child in a shallow pond whose life can be saved at the cost of ruining an expensive pair of shoes: choosing to let the child drown is morally analogous to refusing to let in refugees by pointing at the economic costs of hosting them.[47]

These arguments, and the many positions in between, are mirrored in today's political debate about refugee policy. But our notion of "costs" needs to be re-evaluated in a world where the interests and values of an increasing number of people are intertwined, and where the very real prospect of significant population decline in many Western liberal democracies calls for greater openness toward refugees and asylum seekers.

The second shift is to rethink how we see the twenty-first-century refugee. Too often Western publics view statelessness, and migration, as the result of failure. And we pity. But if our current world is one in which *one in every hundred people is displaced,* how can it be "their fault" or "someone else's problem"? As the Russian-American wartime reporter and author Anna Badkhen tells us, failure today "is of a planetary scale. It belongs to all of us."[48] And those who embark on the other side of the Mediterranean, hoping to reach "us," are closer than they seem. Standing on the southern shore of Sicily in the summer of 2015, I might not have (quite) seen them, but I could certainly feel them — especially the souls of those lying at the bottom of the sea in front of me.

In reimagining the refugee, we also need to have the courage to consider whether the legal definition, designed for the post–World War II period, is still fit for today's purpose. Back then, refugee status was limited to individuals who could prove they had a "well-founded fear of persecution for reasons of race, religion, nationality, membership of a particular social group or political opinion." But as I have outlined, the drivers of displacement today are not always captured by

this definition. It excludes those fleeing general-
ized violence, environmental change, food insecurity, or extreme economic deprivation. Are
"survival migrants,"[49] as one analyst has called
them, any less deserving of protection? While
there are pragmatic reasons to worry about a
formal change to the legal definition of a refugee — including the concern that the terms might
become even more restrictive — we need to re-
examine the ethos that underpins the current
legal framework.

The 1951 definition was based on the special
claim of those who are politically persecuted: they
seek permanent membership status in another
political community, given the breaking of the
bond of protection between them and their government. Their special status thus stems from the
fact that their needs *by definition* cannot be met
in their country of origin because of an oppressive government — unlike, for example, victims of
a famine who can be brought food or victims of war
who can be brought peace. But this privileging of
civil and political rights needs to be questioned in
our modern age, when refugee streams are intrin-
sically entangled with the search for physical and
economic security and when the root causes of

displacement cannot necessarily be located in a single country. Indeed, it has become painfully obvious that the solutions to the refugee crisis cannot be imagined or designed within the confines of a sovereign state framework alone.

The third and related shift is to get out of our national straightjackets and recognize that, as the saying goes, we are all in this together. As long as war, persecution, and the breakdown in governance are part of the human condition — and history suggests this is so — we are all ultimately at risk of being forced "on the move." If faced with the kind of instability and fear that daily haunts citizens of Syria, many of us would likely resort to their strategies for survival. Part of what was so haunting about the pictures of Alan Kurdi was that he could have been the child of any one of us.

The reality of interconnectedness suggests that we should opt for what Benhabib calls "porous" rather than completely open borders.[50] As democratic societies, we do have a right to set our norms of membership. But we also need to recognize that those so often affected by these norms — the stateless who are kept at bay — have little to no say in how they are drafted. Democratic leaders, supported by a democratic citizenry, must therefore continually reflect on the impact of their exclusionary practices and correct for them. These "democratic iterations," as Benhabib calls them, are both a political and moral obligation.

The recognition of our collective vulnerability, and responsibility, also suggests that we should worry as much about the "sin of omission" — failing to play our part in sharing the burden of mass flight — as we should about the "sin of commission" — turning asylum seekers away at the border. The magnitude, duration, and ongoing impact of twenty-first-century mass flight calls for a global response — one that acknowledges that the responsibility for refugee protection and settlement cannot continue to be allocated on the basis of proximity or the "first safe country" where an individual refugee lands. Asylum is a global public good from which all countries, and all individuals, benefit.

The duty to provide asylum is as old as history itself. So too is the phenomenon of mass flight. But liberal democracies have a particularly intimate relationship with migrants and refugees: our response to episodes of political persecution and armed conflict outside our borders has helped to define who we are. Today we face a crisis of forced displacement on a scale never seen before. Yet our political systems are failing to meet the challenge, and narratives of fear are crowding out our humanitarian obligations. As Western governments continually fail to exercise their collective responsibilities, the liberal democratic model is increasingly tarnished. This opens up a space for those who position themselves as alternatives or rivals to the West.

FOUR

THE RETURN OF COLD WAR

ON THE AFTERNOON OF February 22, 2014, anti-government protesters took to the streets of the Ukrainian capital of Kiev. You could smell the scent of revolution. Earlier that day, the country's parliament had voted to eject reigning President Viktor Yanukovych from power, following three months of protests and clashes over his last-minute refusal to sign an economic association agreement with the European Union and to accept, instead, a generous economic package from Russia. Rumours abounded that the former president had fled the city for the Russian-speaking east of the country. Security forces abandoned Yanukovych's lavish residence on the outskirts of Kiev, enabling ordinary citizens to roam freely around its vast gardens, which included

a golf course and private zoo (complete with kan-
garoos and ostriches). Meanwhile, protesters rode
atop trucks in the central avenues and squares of
the city, their raised hands displaying the famous
peace sign, celebrating what they believed would be
the dawn of a new era in Ukraine's political future.

But only a few hours later, in a city roughly 500
miles away, more fateful decisions were underway
which would lead Ukraine down a more uncertain
and violent path. In Moscow, where Yanukovych's
downfall was viewed as an illegitimate coup d'état,
Russian officials refused to recognize the interim
government that was formed in Kiev. During an all-
night meeting in the Kremlin with representatives
from the defence ministry and Special Services,
Russian President Vladimir Putin devised a plan
to rescue Ukraine's deposed president. As the talks
broke up, he also ordered his officials to initiate a
mission to absorb Crimea — the southern peninsula
that had been transferred by the Soviet Union to its
then-socialist Ukrainian neighbour in 1954 — back
into the Russian motherland.

The plan was devised and executed with light-
ning speed. Surprise military drills were conducted both on Russia's border with Ukraine
and on its Black Sea base on the peninsula. On

February 27 and 28, armed men in masks and unmarked uniforms — later referred to as the "little green men" — seized key airports and regional government buildings, including the parliament in Simferopol (Crimea's administrative centre). In the days that followed, gunmen surrounded the regional parliament, while the legislature voted in a new government comprised of pro-Russian representatives. This body quickly issued a Declaration of Independence of the Autonomous Republic of Crimea and called for a referendum on the territory's future status. Meanwhile, the Russian parliament authorized Putin to deploy troops to Ukraine, if deemed necessary.

The facts on the ground, however, suggested an invasion was already underway. On March 1, four Russian ships docked at the Crimean port of Sevastopol and Spetsnaz Special Forces brigades began to arrive. Soon Russian-plated vehicles were blocking roads, Russian troops were seizing natural gas facilities and storming air bases, and the Russian fleet was trapping Ukrainian warships. When the referendum was held on March 16, it was denounced by Ukraine, the European Union, and the United States as illegal, given the speed with which it was organized, its violation of the territorial integrity of Ukraine, and the occupation of Crimea by Russian soldiers at the time of the vote. Nonetheless, officials reported that 97 percent of Crimeans cast their ballots to join the Russian Federation (making the territory's declaration of independence extremely short-lived). Two days later, President Putin appeared on a huge stage in front of the Kremlin to announce that Crimea and the key city Sevastopol were "returning to their native harbour." This was swiftly followed by legislation formalizing the annexation of the Crimean peninsula, thereby integrating it into the Russian Federation and transforming it into a forward-operating base for the Russian army and navy.

Russia's daring intervention in Ukraine was widely condemned throughout the Western world, and beyond, as a violation of the accepted principles of international law regulating the use of force and a brazen challenge to the territorial status quo. Article 2.4 of the UN Charter effectively outlaws aggression, famously declaring that all member states "shall refrain in their international relations from the threat or use of force against the territorial integrity or political independence of any state."

Russian officials, including the country's diplomats, were well aware of the potential damage

that charges of illegality could create — both repu-
tationally and materially — and thus made a series
of attempts to legitimize the Kremlin's moves on
the Crimean Peninsula. Russia began by arguing
that its military action was in fact in accordance
with the provisions of the UN Charter, as it was
defending Russian speakers in the Crimea who
were vulnerable to attack following the ouster of
the Ukrainian president. Given that concrete evidence of systematic persecution of Russian speakers
was lacking and that efforts to dispatch independent
observers to the region were blocked, another rationale was forwarded — namely, that Russian actions
were a response to a request for military assistance by Viktor Yanukovych, the democratically
elected leader of Ukraine. In an emergency session
of the Security Council, during which Western and
Russian officials traded accusations, Moscow's permanent representative to the UN, Vitaly Churkin,
proclaimed that Ukraine was "in the grip of outright terror and violence driven by the West." He
then held up a signed letter from Yanukovych,
dated March 1, requesting help to "restore law and
order."[1] When the merits of this argument also
proved doubtful, Kremlin officials retreated behind
the claim that Russia itself had never used military

force; rather, it was the local Ukrainian militia that had stormed the bases and ports in Crimea.

The majority of member states of the UN was not convinced by Russia's justifications. A General Assembly Resolution on March 27, 2014, approved by 100 states (with eleven negative votes and fifty-eight abstentions) called on parties to "desist and refrain from actions aimed at the partial or total disruption of the national unity and territorial integrity of Ukraine." The scheduled meeting of the G8 — the group of industrialized countries that expanded from the G7 to include Russia after the end of the Cold War — was abruptly cancelled, and international economic sanctions were slapped upon Russia.

COLD WAR ECHOES

For those of us who lived through, or studied, the Cold War, the Russian intervention in Crimea was eerily reminiscent, both in word and deed, of decades of strategic and ideological competition between the United States and the USSR. The international system from the late 1940s to the late 1980s was described by scholars as bipolar — meaning that two states, or "poles," dominated all others across the key dimensions of power (political, military, economic, and cultural) and established two rival spheres of influence. In this case, most Western and capitalist states fell under the influence of the U.S., while most communist states fell under the influence of the USSR. These two superpowers then competed for the support of "unclaimed" areas and endeavoured to undermine each other's hegemony, wherever and whenever they could.

In this polarized and competitive context, both the United States and the Soviet Union frequently intervened in their respective spheres, claiming to be rescuing persecuted nationals abroad or responding to a request for assistance from governments under threat. In all cases, the sovereignty and territorial integrity of the target states were severely compromised and made subordinate to a higher goal — whether that be the need to maintain "socialist solidarity" (as was the case with the Soviet invasion of Czechoslovakia in 1968) or "collective self-defence" against the introduction of an "alien ideology" into the Western hemisphere (as was the case with the United States' intervention in the Dominican Republic in 1965).[2]

But the intervention that arguably had the greatest impact on the trajectory of the Cold War, and its aftermath, was the December 1979 Soviet invasion of Afghanistan, a country that had become the focal point of superpower competition because of its strategic position en route to both the Persian Gulf and Indian Ocean. In fact, Russia's interest and intervention in Afghanistan had a long history, stretching back to the nineteenth-century competition — or "Great Game," as historians refer to it — between the Russian and British empires in Central Asia. In 1979, however, Moscow's objective was to keep Afghanistan friendly to the Soviet Union by shoring up a fledgling Marxist government that only a year before had managed to oust the country's increasingly pro-Western president. The new pro-Soviet regime in Kabul was now confronting an increasingly powerful insurgency from the mujahideen: Islamic warriors who fought under the control of tribal leaders. Though comprised of many different ethnic groups — including Pashtun, Uzbek, and Tajik — the mujahideen were united in their opposition to "godless" communism and the spectre of foreign occupation, and were bolstered in their cause by foreign fighters from across the Arab world.

In June 1979, the Soviets responded to pleas from the regime for military assistance by sending a detachment of tanks and personnel (arriving without combat gear and disguised as technical specialists) to guard the government in Kabul and secure key airfields. Only six months later, it was clear that a more robust presence was required: in addition to the growing insurgency, internal fighting and coups between competing factions had erupted within the Afghan government. On Christmas Eve, heavily armed elements of a Soviet airborne brigade were airlifted into Kabul — later supported by ground forces that had entered Afghanistan from the north. On December 27, troops dressed in Afghan uniforms occupied major governmental, military, and media buildings in Kabul, including the Presidential Palace. During the assault on the palace, Afghan President Hafizullah Amin was killed, bringing his short-lived presidency to an end and elevating to power his rival socialist, Babrak Karmal.

While the dispatch of Soviet troops was designed to prop up a faltering client state, the intervention did not bring the stability it had promised. On the contrary, it exacerbated nationalistic and anti-Soviet feeling that had been growing in Afghanistan, thus strengthening the insurgency, and drew the USSR further and further into direct combat. Soviet armour columns were soon fanning out across the country, occupying major population centres, airbases, and strategic lines of communication. But the mujahideen continued to move with relative freedom throughout the countryside and employed clever guerilla tactics, such as sabotaging powerlines and pipelines and ambushing Soviet and Afghan troops. A stalemate ensued, and the Soviets continued to invest blood and treasure in a cause that was beginning to look unwinnable. In 1989, after nine years of grinding conflict — with 15,000 of its troops killed and over 500,000 injured — the Soviet Union withdrew its forces, leading many to describe the war in Afghanistan as Moscow's Vietnam.

The extent and size of the Soviet campaign (with more than 80,000 troops deployed in the first months alone) shocked U.S. officials in Washington. Indeed, the intervention marked the only time the Soviet Union invaded a country outside the Eastern bloc — the buffer zone of "friendly" socialist states that Stalin had created after the Second World War in Central and Eastern Europe — and reignited suspicions about the nature and geopolitical designs of the regime in Moscow. The administration of U.S. President Jimmy Carter had been closely watching the Soviet military buildup from the outset. Until those fateful days in December, it had calculated that the Soviets would not invade, based on the assumption that Moscow would conclude that the costs of invasion were simply too high. This miscalculation would lead many opponents of the president, especially on the Republican side, to condemn his approach to U.S.-Soviet relations as "wishful thinking."

The invasion also brought an abrupt halt to the process of détente — the easing of tensions between the superpowers that had been so favoured by the dovish President Carter. Détente had actually started in 1969, under the Nixon administration, with the first round of bilateral conferences and corresponding treaties between Moscow and Washington known as the Strategic Arms Limitation Talks (SALT). SALT was designed to tackle a key driver of Cold War rivalry, namely the escalating nuclear arms race. One of the first casualties of the Soviet invasion was the so-called SALT II negotiations, which Carter suspended on January 2, 1980. This move was quickly followed by the recalling of the U.S. ambassador from Moscow. In his subsequent State of the Union address, President Carter described the intervention in Afghanistan as "the greatest threat to peace since the Second World War" and set in motion a variety of retaliatory policies, including economic sanctions; embargoes on the sale of U.S. grain, corn, and soybeans; and a boycott of the 1980 Moscow Olympics. The events of December 1979 also profoundly affected the White House's foreign policy in the Middle East. Prior to the Soviet intervention, the U.S. had shown only a peripheral interest in Afghanistan; afterwards it became obsessed with undermining Moscow's influence in the country and containing further possible Soviet expansion toward the Persian Gulf. In a move that would have long-lasting repercussions, Washington intensified its efforts to arm the mujahideen rebels through a CIA program code-named Operation Cyclone — one of the longest and most expensive covert operations ever undertaken by the United States.

Superpower relations entered a new and increasingly dangerous phase, one which, according to Cold War historian Melvyn Leffler, was "more ominously hostile than at any time since the Cuban Missile Crisis of 1962."[3] In 1980, Jimmy Carter lost the presidential election to Ronald Reagan,

who ran on an anti-détente platform and promised a more vigorous anti-communist foreign policy. Under President Reagan, American support
for the Afghan mujahideen evolved to become
a centrepiece of U.S. foreign policy. The Reagan
Doctrine provided military and financial backing
to anti-communist resistance movements not only
in Afghanistan, but also in Africa, Latin America,
and Asia. The goal was no longer just to contain the
extent of Soviet influence — the policy that had been
pursued by presidents as far back as Truman and
Eisenhower — but to engage in so-called roll-back
by reversing communist gains and installing governments friendly to the West. Reagan also vowed
to bring down what he called the "evil empire" with
a new round of defence spending, with a particular
focus on nuclear weapons. The Republican president soon announced plans to deploy long-range
nuclear weapons in the heart of Europe and to construct a missile defence shield (colloquially known
as "Star Wars") to protect the United States from
Soviet nuclear strikes.

Many factors combined to bring about the dissolution of the Soviet empire and the collapse of
the USSR. But one that is often cited is the strain
placed on the Soviet economy by its efforts both

to continue waging a costly war in Afghanistan and to keep up with the West in the arms race. The Soviet defeat in Afghanistan also shattered the image of the Red Army as an invincible force and gave non-Russian republics in the USSR confidence that that their own quest for independence might not be countered with military force from the centre. All of these developments, combined with the very different leadership style and objectives of Mikhail Gorbachev—who had taken charge of the Kremlin in the spring of 1985—created the possibility for profound change within the Soviet Union and beyond.

Though Gorbachev was a committed reformer, his goal remained the success of Soviet Union as a *socialist* state. His policies of *perestroika*—restructuring—and *glasnost*—openness—were designed to fix both a stagnating economy, particularly through technological modernization, and a creaking political system by proposing multi-candidate elections and the appointment of non-Communist Party members to government. He did not wish for, nor work toward, the dissolution of the USSR—though this is what famously transpired in 1991, making Gorbachev the eighth and last leader of the Soviet Union.

Boris Yeltsin, who served as the new president of the Russian Republic until the end of the 1990s, ushered in a freer and more open society, including a free media and robust political opposition and criticism. He also fully embraced free market capitalism by eliminating price controls from the previous Soviet era, privatizing state-owned assets (particularly in the natural resources sector), and allowing for ownership of private property. Russia seemed well on its way to Western-style liberal democracy, with help from its old nemesis the United States, which eagerly sent experts and advisors to assist in the transformation. The West was also able to incorporate Yeltsin and his cadre of diplomats in the creation of a new security order for Europe, built around a reunited Germany and further agreements between Russia and the United States to reduce their stockpiles of nuclear weapons.

But the optimism was short-lived. Russia's liberal democracy had a sputtering start and never really got lift-off. Yeltsin's tenure as president was coloured by corruption, crime, and a virtual collapse of the Russian economy. By the late 1990s, the country's gross domestic product was half of what it had been at the start of the decade. While the so-called oligarchs became extraordinarily wealthy through their acquisition of former state-owned assets, ordinary Russians fell deeper into poverty: inflation was rampant, living costs sky-rocketed, and tax collection was too weak and inefficient to support public services. Doctors and teachers went months without receiving their salaries, leading many of them to look back nostalgically on the Soviet era. In her book *Sale of the Century*, Chrystia Freeland describes the economic system that resulted from privatization as a "capitalist politburo" supporting a "narrow layer of the super-rich."[4]

The bubble truly burst in 1998, when Yeltsin devalued the Russian ruble and froze bank accounts, which devastated the economic fortunes of the average Russian citizen. This decision, combined with his disastrous military intervention in 1994 into the Chechnya Republic to try to crush its bid for independence — which led to the deaths of thousands of civilians — sealed the president's reputation as the man who oversaw Russia's decline.

A CHILL IN THE AIR

In his 2005 State of the Nation address to the Russian people, Vladimir Putin lamented the demise of the Soviet Union as the "greatest political catastrophe" of the twentieth century. Its collapse had led to not only years of political and economic instability, he suggested, but also the loss of standing in the world for the Russian people, who had a proud and storied national history.

Commentators have since mused about whether Putin's speech, along with developments in Russian foreign and domestic policy, mark a return to those nerve-wracking Cold War days. With the annexation of Crimea, the volume of debate increased, with analysts and journalists referring to the "New Cold War" or "Cold War 2.0." In 2014, *Foreign Policy* magazine declared that events in Ukraine had "effectively put an end to the interregnum of partnership and cooperation between the West and Russia" and that the two decades after the fall of the Berlin Wall—often referred to as the "post–Cold War" period—would "be seen, in retrospect, as the inter–Cold War period."[5] The British newspaper the *Guardian* put it even more starkly: "Tanks and troops invading a satellite state, tit-for-tat spy expulsions, high-risk military games of chicken involving nuclear bombers and interceptor jets, gas supply cut-offs, and angry diplomatic exchanges — if it sounds familiar, then it should. Newspaper headlines from Moscow to Washington and Sydney to Kiev all agree: the Cold War is back."[6]

It is not only commentators in the media who have drawn parallels between today's situation and that of the Cold War. Russian Prime Minister Dmitry Medvedev has also suggested that strain between Russia and the West has reached Cold War intensity. "On an almost daily basis," he lamented in 2015 at the Munich Security Conference, "we are being described as the worst threat — be it to NATO as a whole, or to Europe, America or other countries. Sometimes I wonder if this is 2016 or 1962." Similarly, former U.S. Secretary of Defense Ashton Carter evoked the Cold War era by declaring that from "the Kamchatka peninsula through south Asia, into the Caucasus and around to the Baltics, Russia has continued to wrap itself in a shroud of isolation." With these words, he was echoing Winston Churchill's famous Iron Curtain speech of the mid-1940s, in which the British leader proclaimed: "From Stettin in the Baltic to Trieste in the Adriatic, an iron curtain has descended across the Continent."

While political players on both sides seem to agree that Cold War conditions have returned, they fundamentally disagree on who is to blame. From the Russian perspective, a continuing and aggressive eastward expansion of Western security and political organizations like NATO and the EU has forced Moscow to become more assertive in defending Russia's interests. Conversely, from the Western perspective, recent actions by Moscow are evidence of a Russian pivot toward authoritarianism and a more aggressive foreign policy, after its initial steps toward liberal democracy and free-market economics in the 1990s. Seen from this angle, developments in Russia point to a crumbling of the democratic peace that Fukuyama and others promised, as Putin's Russia pursues a deliberate strategy to position itself as a challenger to Europe and the United States.

The notion of challenger, rather than partner, was also at the heart of America's re-evaluation of the Soviet Union after the end of the Second World War, when the two countries emerged from that conflict as the two strongest states in the international system. In 1946, the veteran U.S. diplomat George Kennan (who was stationed in Moscow) penned his now famous "Long Telegram" to officials

in Washington, which detailed the essence of the
Soviet world outlook and foreign policy ambitions. According to Kennan, Moscow's greatest
fear was encirclement by the capitalist West, which
would not only pose a challenge to Soviet security but also potentially expose the weaknesses in
the Soviet Union's own domestic system. A hostile world was needed — in fact, was essential — to
justify the continuation of Joseph Stalin's oppressive rule, which married communism with authoritarianism. As a result, Kennan argued, the Soviet
Union sought to exploit differences between capitalist powers, openly challenge the West's economic and political values, and test Western resolve
with a series of moves to expand its influence in
Europe, and beyond. Of particular concern to the
U.S. was Moscow's apparent designs on Greece and
Turkey — through support to the communists in
the 1946 Greek Civil War and efforts to establish
military bases in the Turkish straits — and the failure of the Soviet Union to fulfil its agreement to
withdraw its troops from northern Iran after the
Second World War.

Kennan's key point, however, was that
Soviet expansionism stemmed from the traditional *Russian* sense of insecurity. As a country

with no natural borders, and a history of invasion from all directions — Sweden, France, and
Germany — Russia had sought to ensure friendly
and non-threatening states in its immediate neighbourhood and to extend its influence to ensure
access to key waterways and transit routes to
other parts of the world. In other words, Marxism-
Leninism was but a veneer for the older nationalism and imperialism of czarist Russia. The
best strategy, Kennan contended, was to contain the Soviet Union's efforts to expand in geographic areas of key strategic interest to the United
States — particularly in central Europe — and wait
for it to "mellow" and crumble from within.[7]

Today's Russia, under Putin, seems to many to
exhibit a similar combination of autocracy at home
and power projection abroad. It has also become
overtly hostile to Western values and interests, and
to the post–Cold War security order that was established in Europe in 1991 with the reunification of
Germany. Prior to 2005, President Putin's efforts to
turn back the clock and restore Russia's great power
status were focused primarily inward, through
steps to strengthen the Russian economy and stifle
political dissent that he viewed as fostering political instability. As former Clinton administration

official Strobe Talbott explains, the strategy was about "repudiating the transformational policies of his immediate predecessors and reinstating key attributes of the Soviet system *within* the borders of the Russian Federation." But there were also signs that Putin had grander designs, and "might extend his agenda, his rule, and what he hopes will be his legacy beyond those borders."[8] Unlike the first decade following the end of the Cold War, when Russia was finding its feet and was eager to "do business" (both literally and figuratively) with the West, Putin's Russia is pursuing an agenda that brings him into more frequent confrontation with the United States and its allies.

FLEXING ITS MUSCLES

The most obvious manifestation of Russia's more assertive posture abroad is the significant increase in its military budget (for example, an $11 billion increase from 2014 to 2015) and its greater willingness to use military power. In August 2008, it deployed its army, air force, and navy to Georgia to respond to that country's effort to counter separatist unrest in the Russian-speaking region of

South Ossetia. Russian and Ossetian forces fought together against the Georgians, eventually pushing back the Georgian army and temporarily occupying a number of Georgian cities until a ceasefire was reached. Many believe this episode was designed by Putin to test the waters with the West, to determine whether it would respond to Russian military action; the conclusion he drew was that Moscow could get away with it. The war was followed by Russia's de facto annexations of South Ossetia and Abkhazia, and the more recent intervention in Crimea.

At the more symbolic end of the spectrum, Russian assertiveness has taken the shape of military exercises on the borders of countries such as Ukraine, Poland, and the Baltic states, which are friendly to the West. In 2013, Russian and Belarusian military forces held joint exercises that simulated an incursion by foreign-backed "terrorist" groups originating from the Baltic states, involving tens of thousands of personnel and hundreds of vehicles and pieces of military equipment.[9] The mock response of the Russian and Belarus forces involved the kind of tactics and deployments that would be needed to invade and occupy the Baltic states, cutting off their land connection with Poland.

In addition, Putin announced publicly that he planned to add more nuclear missiles to the Russian arsenal and was building a new generation of non-nuclear arms that could strike U.S. soil. This decision seemed to defy the strategic arms reduction treaty signed by Barack Obama and then-President Medvedev in 2011, which had been designed to reduce the number of nuclear weapons and launchers deployed by the U.S. and Russia beyond the limits agreed to in 1991, when the Cold War was ending. It is also notable that Putin failed to attend the Nuclear Security Summit in April 2016 — a move that made Russia the only nuclear power apart from North Korea (which was not invited) that did not send senior officials to the summit.

Somewhere in between the symbolic and the real are a number of military "encounters" between Russian and Western militaries, in the air and on land. In the mid-2000s, Russia reignited the old Cold War practice of "skirting" Western countries' airspace; but a 2014 report by the European Leadership Network indicated that this practice had intensified and that close military encounters involving Russian and Western militaries were back up to levels not seen since the 1960s and '70s.

These events include violations of national airspace, narrowly avoided mid-air collisions between civilian airliners and Russian surveillance planes, close encounters at sea, close overflights of Western warships, and the shadowing of Western submarines.[10]

But it is in eastern Ukraine and Syria where the most serious standoffs between the West and Russia have taken place since the end of the Cold War, along with the most intensive shows of military force. In the wake of the annexation of Crimea, pro-Russian and anti-government demonstrations began in the Donetsk and Luhansk oblasts of Ukraine, together commonly called "Donbass." These protests soon escalated into open armed conflict between the separatist forces of the self-declared Donetsk and Luhansk People's Republics and the Ukrainian government. Many view these clashes as the direct result of covert Russian military intervention, a judgement substantiated by international monitors from the Organization for Security and Cooperation in Europe (the OSCE) and by the international press, both of which reported unmarked Russian military convoys crossing the border into rebel-controlled areas of eastern Ukraine, as well as vehicles transporting ammunition and soldiers' dead bodies across the Russian-Ukrainian border under the guise of humanitarian aid convoys. The July 2014 crash of Malaysia Airlines flight MH17 from Amsterdam to Kuala Lumpur in rebel-held Donetsk, in which all 283 passengers and 15 crew members died, is widely believed to have been the result of pro-Russia rebels mistakenly shooting the plane down with a Russian-made missile. Moscow denied involvement in the crash, opposed efforts to mount an international inquiry into the incident, and flooded its media with charges of blame on the Ukrainians.

According to the United Nations Human Rights Monitoring Mission, between April 2014 (when armed hostilities began) and February 2016 roughly 9,000 deaths and 21,000 injuries occurred as a result of the fighting in Ukraine.[11] And despite a second ceasefire agreement signed by Ukraine and Russia in February 2015, and backed by France and Germany, combatant and civilian deaths continued to mount — as did the presence of heavy weapons and artillery (in defiance of the agreement) and the daily crossing of men and women in military-style clothing over the Donetsk and Russian Federation border. Putin's interest in supporting the cause of Russian speakers in Ukraine, and in preventing closer relations between Kiev and Europe, continued unabated, despite the high costs of the ongoing war.

The intensity and impact of the armed conflict in Ukraine, so close to Europe's heartland, rattled not only member states of the European Union but also the United States. The February 2016 announcement by former President Obama to substantially increase the U.S. deployment of heavy weapons, armoured vehicles, and other equipment to NATO countries in Central and Eastern Europe — representing a four-fold increase in U.S. military spending for Europe — was aimed at deterring Russia from any further moves in its neighbourhood. The official name of the program — the European Reassurance Initiative — spoke volumes about the degree to which the security environment in Europe had deteriorated, particularly for states such as Romania, Poland, Latvia, Estonia, and Lithuania, who dared to believe in the 1990s that history, at least in the form of Russian aggression, might have come to an end. Today, the three Baltic states are actively reinvigorating their militaries to prepare for armed conflict and — in the case of Lithuania — reintroducing conscription.

Further afield, but still within what it considered an area of vital strategic interest, Russia has also continued to flex its muscles in the ongoing Syrian civil war. From the earliest days of the conflict in 2011, Russia steadfastly supported its ally in the region, the government of Bashar al-Assad, both politically and militarily. It also blocked three successive resolutions in the United Nations Security Council, tabled between the autumn of 2011 and the summer of 2012, as the violence intensified: the first resolution would have condemned the Syrian government's human rights violations and crackdown on protests; the second would have censured Assad's continued violence against opposition to his government and backed an Arab peace plan designed to bring about a political transition; and the third would have threatened economic sanctions against Syria's government for failing to implement the terms of a peace plan endorsed by the international community. With each Russian (and Chinese) veto, the critique of the Security Council's inability to fulfil its responsibilities under the UN Charter, and to mount a collective response, grew louder. The world was returning, it seemed, to the heights of the Cold War, when the Security Council was paralyzed by disagreement between the Soviet Union and the West. Like the Iran-Iraq War, which raged from 1980 to 1988 without resolution, the divisions between permanent members of the Security Council were preventing a concerted approach to ending the bloodshed in Syria.

The public rationale for the Russian position was straightforward: President Assad led the internationally recognized government of the Syrian Arab Republic and was countering a violent domestic opposition. In Moscow's view, it was morally and legally wrong, and politically unwise, for outside powers to attempt to bring about a regime change — particularly through forceful means. Such an approach, Russian officials insisted, was contrary to the UN Charter and subsequent General Assembly resolutions supporting the principle of non-intervention in the internal affairs of sovereign states. Moreover, they insisted, the West's strategy of regime change had a bad track record. Speaking to Western media in defence of Moscow's position, Russian Foreign Minister Sergey Lavrov asked rhetorically: "Saddam Hussein — hanged. Is Iraq a better place, a safer place? . . . Qaddafi murdered — you know in front of viewers. Is Libya a better place? Now we are demonizing Assad. Can we try to draw lessons?"[12]

By contrast, Lavrov and others contend, the outside world's approach must be balanced, rather

than seeking to "punish" only one side of the conflict or bring about a particular political solution.
Speaking after the Security Council debate over the
vetoed resolution in February 2012, Russian diplomat Vitaly Churkin claimed that the Western-
sponsored draft text sent an "unbalanced signal"
to the conflicting parties by calling on the Syrian
government to withdraw its forces from urban loca-
tions but not making the same demands of the
opposition forces.[13] Of course, Russia's own actions
called into question its professed neutrality. Just
as it accused the West of supporting rebel forces
in Syria, it had consistently been one of the major
suppliers of weapons to the Assad government. The
Russian position had been bolstered, however, by
the evolution of the Syrian conflict to involve violent extremists such as ISIS. In supporting the government in Damascus, Russian officials claimed
they were also promoting a broader international
counter-terrorism effort, which the West should
applaud rather than condemn.

In the autumn of 2015, with the Syrian conflict
spiralling out of control, Moscow took an even more
audacious step that caught Western powers by surprise. After an official request by the Syrian government for military help against jihadist groups,

including ISIS and the al-Nusra Front (al-Qaeda in the Levant), Russia launched a series of airstrikes in northwestern Syria — ostensibly designed to help the Syrian government retake territory. Rather than joining the broader U.S.-led coalition in its air war against ISIS (which had spread from Iraq to Syria), Moscow was attempting to build its own counter-alliance by deploying up to fifty combat aircraft and — in contrast to the West's aversion to "boots on the ground" — a contingent of 4,000 Russian troops. The seven-month-long campaign marked the first time Russia had intervened militarily in a country outside the former Soviet Union since the 1979 invasion of Afghanistan, thus signalling to the world both its capacity and its determination. But it also had significant implications for the military effort waged by the U.S. and its allies, and even created the possibility of clashes between Russia and Western forces.

As it turned out, Moscow's weapons systems were deployed to fight not just jihadi forces, but all opposition to the Syrian government — including rebel groups backed by the West. The location and nature of the deployment, which included anti-aircraft systems, also gave Russia a certain degree of leverage over the West's anti-ISIS campaign, forcing Western governments to collaborate with Moscow if they wanted to avoid direct contact. In one particularly tense moment during the Russian airstrikes, one of its jets was downed by the Turkish Air Force — an incident believed to be the first time a NATO country shot down a Russian plane in half a century.

In March 2016 President Putin ordered the withdrawal of the majority of Russian forces from Syria — again, without signalling his intentions to the West — declaring that the intervention had largely achieved its aim of assisting the Syrian government to strengthen its position against its terrorist opponents and retake ground. (According to the Syrian Observatory for Human Rights, meeting this objective had come at the cost of more than 5,000 deaths — 40 percent of which were civilians.[14]) Although Russia had not, and could not have, defeated ISIS, it had succeeded in achieving its larger purposes: defying the West's hope for regime change in Syria and demonstrating its military prowess. Through its intervention, Moscow had positioned itself as a central player in containing the violence in Syria and reaching a political solution. And as long as it was integral to the negotiations, the West would not be able to dictate the terms of Assad's fate. Through his bold and risky intervention in Syria, Putin had fulfilled his goal of reinserting Russia into the centre of great power politics. As White House official Robert Gates observed, Putin was "determined that no problem will be solved without Russia being at the table."

PIPELINES AND CYBER ATTACKS

What made the original Cold War so distinctive was the vast array of tools wielded by the capitalist West and communist East to undermine the other's quest for global supremacy. The confrontation between the superpowers was not just about armies stationed across the border from one another, as in West and East Germany, or the feverish accumulation of nuclear weapons. The Cold War also encompassed economic agreements designed to bolster states that were vulnerable to the ideology of the other side. In fact, the economic rescue package for Europe after 1945, known as the Marshall Plan, was viewed by George Kennan as a mechanism of containing the Soviet Union by stabilizing West European economies and thus having the psychological effect of restoring confidence in these societies, thereby making them less susceptible to radical political parties and "indigenous communism."[15]

The Cold War was also waged through preferential trading agreements with "like-minded" countries, as was the case, for example, with Moscow's creation of COMECON (the Council for Mutual Economic Assistance among communist states) or through promises of trade or foreign aid to so-called Third World countries to "buy" their allegiance to one or the other side. In the mid-1950s, the United States and Britain offered Egyptian President Gamal Abdel Nasser financing to build the massive Aswan Dam across the Nile River, with the hope that the aid would secure Nasser's allegiance and cooperation in the larger battle to contain communism. After Nasser valiantly tried to court both sides and remain neutral between East and West, the U.S. withdrew its support and the Soviet Union ultimately financed the dam's construction.

Just as during the Cold War, Russia's more muscular foreign policy today is not confined to overt military action or direct confrontation. Putin's government is also using different tactics to increase its influence over those on its borders and to create divisions within the West.

The most effective form of leverage has been Russia's energy policy toward neighbouring countries, particularly those in Europe that rely on its supplies of oil and gas. Russia has the largest known natural gas reserves of any state on earth and is the world's biggest producer of natural gas (one-fifth of the global total). It is also the world's second-largest oil producer after Saudi Arabia and has the world's second-largest reserves of coal. In addition to being a massive energy producer and exporter, Russia has inherited the oil and gas pipelines of the old Soviet Union; these assets enable Moscow to put political pressure on former satellite states that have no other independent sources of energy supply. Russia has exerted its energy power either by vastly increasing energy prices in a short period of time (as it did with Ukraine in the wake of the Orange Revolution in 2006) or by cutting off supply completely (as it did with Estonia in 2007). Russian officials frequently deny the cut-offs are the result of their direct action, but instead point to sabotage or natural disasters.

In order to enhance its position as an energy supplier, Moscow has pressed ahead with what is known as the Nord Stream submarine pipeline project, which would bring natural gas directly from Russia, under the Baltic Sea, to Germany, France, and the Netherlands. This move would connect Russia closely to Western Europe — bypassing Belarus, Poland, Ukraine, Slovakia, and the Czech Republic — and would thus enable Moscow to cut off energy supplies to Eastern European neighbours with whom it might be in conflict without risking more important customers further West. The Nord Stream project also contains a military dimension: Moscow has given the lead company, Gazprom, the unusual right to recruit and operate its own military forces to protect its overseas pipelines, and Russia is beefing up its Baltic fleet to help prospect the seabed and protect the pipeline once built.[16]

All of these initiatives in the energy sphere can be seen as part of a larger economic philosophy — one that is based more on national security interests than on liberal ideas of modernization or free trade. Analysts at the Finnish Institute of International Affairs have referred to Russia's strategic use of its energy resources as "energy geo-economics": what matters most is not the profitability of energy projects but rather their usefulness in achieving geo-strategic goals and securing the power and interests of the Putin government. With the Nord Stream gas pipeline project, for example, Russia could drive

a wedge through the European Union, exposing
the different interests that European states have
with respect to energy policy, depending on their
relative reliance on Russian supplies. In particular, the project could undermine the EU's official
efforts to maintain Ukraine's important strategic
status as a "transit state" for energy supplies, from
East to West.[17]

Beyond these traditional economic tools, Russia
is also destabilizing its opponents through twenty-
first-century means of cyber attack. This non-
military form of warfare includes denial of service attacks, hacker attacks, and the dissemina-
tion of disinformation over the Internet. In 2007, a
series of cyber attacks swamped the websites of key
Estonian organizations, including the Estonian parliament, banks, ministries, newspapers, and broadcasters. The attacks followed the Kremlin's strong
reaction to the decision of the Estonian government
to relocate the so-called Bronze Soldier of Tallinn,
a Soviet-era memorial statue designed to mark the
arrival of Soviet troops in the Estonian capital in
1944. For decades the monument had been located
in central Tallin, above a small burial site of Soviet
soldiers. Its relocation, along with the remains of
the soldiers, to a military cemetery outside the city

centre brought to the surface political differences between Russians and Estonians over the events of the Second World War — particularly the claim that Estonians had been liberated by the Red Army.

The effect of the cyber attacks was far-reaching, severely disrupting Estonia's links with the outside world. While the exact sources behind the attacks are difficult to determine, evidence points to Russia.[18] During the 2008 Russo-Georgian War, similar cyber attacks swamped and disabled numerous South Ossetian, Georgian, and Azerbaijani websites, though the Russian government has again denied being behind the disruption.

SPY GAMES

Aside from the nuclear arms race, espionage was the practice that most clearly defined the original Cold War. The vast networks of agents deployed by both the Soviet Union and the West to understand the strengths and weaknesses of the other side, and to anticipate moves on the international chessboard, have been immortalized in books, Hollywood movies, and television programs. These range from John le Carré's classic novel *Tinker Tailor Soldier*

Spy, about the uncovering of a mole in the British Intelligence Service, to the current hit TV series on Cable FX, *The Americans*, about two Soviet KGB officers posing as an ordinary American couple living in the suburbs of Washington in the early 1980s, running a travel agency by day, awaiting their orders from the homeland for the next mission. *The Americans* is based on the real story of Soviet agents operating undercover in the United States, who trained for years to assume their fake identities. Unlike their "legal" counterparts in Soviet embassies and consulates, who had immunity from prosecution as diplomats, the "illegals" (as they were known by the U.S. Department of Justice) operated without such protection and thus went to great lengths to maintain their cover.

While we might think these forms of espionage are confined to history books, Russian spying has reached unprecedented levels in recent years and the Illegals Program has returned in a new form. In 2006, Canadian officials deported a Russian citizen living in Montreal who was suspected of spying under a false Canadian identity. This arrest was the prelude to a larger investigation conducted by the FBI in 2010, which uncovered ten agents planted by the Russian Foreign Intelligence Service

(SVR) in the United States. The sleeper agents had been building contacts with academics, industrialists, and policy-makers in order to gain access to intelligence. They were subsequently charged with "carrying out long-term, 'deep-cover' assignments in the United States on behalf of the Russian Federation" and flown to Vienna after pleading guilty to charges of failing to register as a representative of a foreign government. (The Moscow legal court documents made public in 2011 revealed that another two Russian agents managed to flee the U.S. without being arrested.) The same day, the ten agents were exchanged for four Russian nationals, three of whom were convicted and imprisoned by Russia on espionage (high treason) charges.[19] During the Cold War freed Soviet spies typically kept a low profile after their return to Moscow; but the most famous member of the recent spy ring, Anna Chapman, became a lingerie model, corporate spokeswoman, and television personality.

GEOPOLITICS REDUX

Military confrontation. Economic blackmail. Espionage. Diplomatic standoffs. It is tempting to reach the conclusion that history has returned. But despite all of the signs of Russia's increasing assertiveness and competition with the West, the label "Cold War 2.0" is difficult to apply to our contemporary period. The four decades of superpower confrontation that marked the original Cold War differ in significant ways from the current tensions between Russia and the West.

First, and most important, was the Cold War's intense ideological character. Great power rivalry had been a common feature of international history for centuries, but it was the degree to which the Soviet Union and the United States saw their entire *systems* to be at war that made the original Cold War so distinctive. Our twenty-first-century vantage point magnifies the inevitability of liberal democracy. But as I suggested in Chapter One, this obscures the reality of competing political ideas and programs for much of the twentieth century, and particularly in the period following 1918 — the end of the cataclysmic First World War. The Great Depression called into question the capitalist economic model, and the carnage of the Second World War demonstrated the depths to which Western states, propelled by nationalist agendas, could descend. Moreover, the attack on the legitimacy of colonial empires, which had begun during the First World War and continued through the inter-war period, came to a climax in the 1940s with the launch of a series of independence struggles — some violent and some non-violent. The Marxist-Leninist world vision that underpinned the Soviet system drew its legitimacy from the promise of a revolution that would overthrow oppressive colonial rule and capitalist economic injustice, and the initiation of a system of greater equality for *all* classes and races. Under Stalin's leadership, the original Marxist idea that revolution would be spontaneous, and automatic, was replaced by a Soviet-centric ideology: the USSR was the centre from which socialism would spread and defeat capitalism. But the expansionist implications of this idea were equally powerful.

When the alliance of convenience against the common enemy of Hitler's Germany ended in 1945, the Soviet Union and the United States were faced with a new reality: a power vacuum in Europe and the prospect of a raft of newly independent states in the developing world. Much ink has been spilt by historians about why the practice of wartime cooperation between the two states did not endure into the post–World War II era. Much of it has to do with the profoundly different conceptions of security that each side had after 1945, based on their own experience of the war. The Soviet Union's experience of invasion, for example, led it to be dominated by a territorial conception of security, whereby a set of "buffer states" on its borders was the key objective. The United States, by contrast, was attempting to create a post-colonial world of self-determining states engaged in cooperation and free trade, and a collective security system in which the great powers would work in tandem to address shared challenges to peace and security.

A certain degree of friction was bound to mark relations between the two great powers that were left "still standing" after 1945 — even if both had been liberal democracies. But the level and nature of the confrontation was profoundly affected by their opposing ideologies, and more importantly, by their efforts to export and defend those ideologies globally. It was therefore not enough that Stalin's desired buffer states were militarily friendly; they also had to be ideologically aligned so as to pose no threat to the Soviet Union's own regime. Indeed, Stalin hoped their eventual success as socialist countries would bolster the legitimacy of the Soviet state as well. And similarly, while Washington's initial vision of the post-war economic order was a set of initiatives and institutions (such as the Marshall Plan and the World Bank) that would include the Soviet Union, this order soon morphed into a club of liberal capitalist states that, from Moscow's perspective, sought to spread the West's model through economic weapons.

During the Cold War, the two sides exploited every opportunity to demonstrate the superiority of their respective systems. Every defection of a Soviet artist to the West, or a Western spy to Moscow, was heralded as a sign of the triumph of capitalism or communism. Every Olympic medal for East Germany, or victory in ice hockey for a Western team, was proof of the excellence that each system could foster. Every foray into space, whether Moscow's launching of the satellite Sputnik in 1957 or NASA's successful man on the moon mission in 1969, was evidence of the scientific prowess of either side. And every civil conflict, whether in Asia or Africa, was a test, by proxy, of the power of capitalism and communism.

Today's relationship between Russia and the West is not characterized by the same kind of ideological fervour. Nor is it a struggle between "isms" or monolithic rival systems. In fact, today's Russia has embraced many aspects of capitalism, and its economic system is a long distance away from the managed and centrally planned economy of the Cold War. It is also integrated into the European economy, and with its vast natural resources is one of Europe's largest suppliers of natural gas, oil, and coal. Instead, the contemporary era is marked more by a clash of values — between the West's championing of open elections, freedom of expression and movement, and the rule of law, and Russia's hybrid version of democracy, with an oligarchic governance structure and limits on individual freedoms, in exchange for economic growth. The Russian model, with its emphasis on national identity and religion, also looks very conservative in its orientation, in contrast to the radicalism that underpinned Marxism-Leninism.

The rhetoric of state leaders also differs significantly from the dramatic and hostile language of the original Cold War, during which the Soviet Union and United States were "sworn enemies." Although the partnership established in the early 1990s has eroded, it does not mean there are no common interests or objectives between Russia and the West. In a July 2014 congratulatory message to then President Obama marking U.S. Independence Day, Vladimir Putin noted that, despite the differences between the two countries, Russian-American relations remain the most important factor of international stability and security. He also expressed confidence that Russia and the United States could find solutions to the most complicated international issues and meet global threats and challenges together "if they based their relationship on the principles of equality and respect for each other's interests."[20] This perspective has been reflected in the regular high-level talks that continue to take place between the U.S. secretary of state and the Russian foreign minister—a level of diplomacy that was absent during the Cold War—even if the encounters are frequently frosty. In addition, since the 9/11 terrorist attacks, Putin, Medvedev, and other Russian politicians have consistently tried to rally Russia and the West around the common enemy of Islamic terrorism and, more recently, ISIS.

A second difference between the original Cold War and the contemporary breakdown in relations between the U.S. and Russia is one of scope. It is crucial to remember that the original Cold War was a truly global competition. The United States and its allies confronted the Soviet Union and its allies. Sometimes that clash took place in the middle of Europe, as it did so symbolically with the division of Germany into East and West. But more often it took place in the so-called Third World — in Vietnam, Indonesia, Yemen, Angola, or Mozambique — or on the frontier of the superpowers' spheres of influence — whether that be in Central Europe for the Soviet Union or Latin America and the Caribbean for the United States. It is emblematic of the reach of Cold War rivalry that one of its hottest moments — the Cuban Missile Crisis of 1962, which brought the United States and Soviet Union to the brink of a nuclear war — occurred precisely on that frontier.

Although from a practical point of view it was probably unfeasible for Moscow to create a Caribbean outpost for communism in Cuba, from the *ideological* perspective that dominated the Cold War it made perfect sense. Each side sought an ideological foothold on every continent. As historians have discovered through the opening up of the Soviet archives in the early 1990s, Cuba was of paramount priority for the Kremlin because it promised to provide the spark that would ignite Marxist revolutions all over Latin America. The tantalizing prospect of communism spreading to that region, in the words of historian John Lewis Gaddis, "had an intense *emotional* hold in Moscow."[21]

The same could be said of the United States' long and ultimately futile attempt to hold back the communist onslaught in Southeast Asia, as was exemplified during the Vietnam War. Policy-makers in Washington, as well as in London and Paris, feared that the appeal of the Soviet Union as a *revolutionary* state would take hold in those countries in Africa, Asia, and Latin America that were emerging from colonial rule and claiming their independence. Their concern, as Gaddis points out, was that the "Cold War could yet be lost, so to speak, by the back door."[22] Looking back, it seems difficult to fathom how ensuring the continuation of a particular (and unpopular) non-communist government in Saigon was seen as the key to maintaining the credibility of the United States in the world. The assumption — so ill-conceived in retrospect — was that Vietnam's fate would dominate that of the entire region and that a set of countries with highly diverse populations and cultures would adopt a single ideology. But that was the mentality of the Cold War. Events anywhere had a bearing on the status of each superpower.

What we are witnessing today, then, is less the return of an ideological Cold War, and more the revival of old-fashioned geopolitics. The competition between Russia and the West is regionally focused, centring on Europe's eastern flank (including Ukraine and the Baltic states), southern parts of the post-Soviet region (for example, Georgia, Moldova, Azerbaijan, and Armenia), and on the age-old, pre–Cold War struggle for influence in the Middle East. Many commentators use the term "geopolitics" as shorthand for global rivalries in world politics. But in fact, it has a more precise meaning, which relates to the dynamic interaction of political power with geographic space. And for the British geographer Halford Mackinder, who first used the concept in 1904, geopolitics was about expansion into and competition over one specific territorial space: Eurasia and the "heartland" of Eastern Europe. Whoever controls this heartland, he famously quipped, also "controls the world."[23]

Following the end of the Cold War in the 1990s, Russia, the United States, and West European states converged on what American political commentator Walter Russell Mead has described as a set of shared "geopolitical foundations": a unified Germany, the dissolution of the USSR, and the integration of the former Warsaw Pact countries of Central and Eastern Europe into NATO and the European Union. In the Middle East, there was also a rough consensus on the dominance of Sunni powers allied to the United States (namely Saudi Arabia, Qatar, United Arab Emirates, Egypt, and Turkey) and the containment of Iran. But today, the early post–Cold War consensus has broken down and geopolitical rivalry has resumed. In the Middle East, it has taken the form of an internationalized sectarian conflict — with Iran, for example, pitted against Saudi Arabia in both Syria and Yemen. And with respect to the "heartland," President Putin has pursued the creation of a Eurasian Economic Union (which by 2015 included Russia, Belarus, Kazakhstan, Armenia, and Kyrgyzstan), opposed any further NATO expansion, and altered the territorial status of both Georgia and Ukraine.[24]

Despite the resumption of power political rivalry, including the willingness in some cases to deploy military force, today's competition between the great powers is regional rather than global. This is a function of both capacity and will: Russia cannot exert its influence beyond Eurasia — and even then, its gains are limited — and the United States has drastically curtailed its global ambitions and its willingness to deploy its forces abroad.

A third way that 2016 differs from 1946 relates to the status of the United States and Russia. During

the original Cold War these two countries were
unrivalled superpowers. The world was structured
on "bipolar" lines. The Russians and the Anglo-
Americans, as Alexis de Tocqueville had once proclaimed, were the two "great nations in the world"
that each seemed to "hold in its hands the desti-
nies of half the world."[25] But our contemporary
international system is much more "multipolar":
states such as China, India, Brazil, and South
Africa are on the rise and no longer in the pocket
of a superpower. They frequently and openly challenge the foreign policies of both the United States
and Russia, and are no longer reliant on them for
political and military support. States in the Soviet
Union's former sphere of influence in central and
eastern Europe have gone their own way, and
few would count themselves as staunch allies of
Russia. In fact, Russia has fewer allies today than
at perhaps any time in its history.[26] Furthermore,
there have been serious divisions even among
Western states that Washington cannot always
dampen in the name of alliance unity. These fis-
sures were perhaps most evident during the 2003
Iraq War, when states such as France and Canada
broke ranks with the United States over military intervention. But they have also been visible

during debates between the European Union and the U.S. over the most appropriate response to Russia's actions in Ukraine.

Fourth, the structure and dynamics of the original Cold War were heavily determined by the nuclear arms race. At its height, each side had tens of thousands of warheads that could annihilate the other many times over. The strategic doctrine that governed U.S.-Soviet relations was one of "mutually assured destruction" — or MAD, as it was ironically known. While the United States still has a nuclear arsenal, and Russia under President Putin has increased military spending, the two countries' missiles and warheads are nowhere near Cold War levels, thanks to a series of arms control agreements over the past two decades. Nor are the military doctrines of each side wholly defined by the objective of eliminating the other. As the American international affairs analyst James Stavridis reminds us, the original Cold War "featured millions of troops on the Fulda Gap in Europe, ready to attack each other; two huge battle fleets all around the world chasing each other in a massive *Hunt for Red October* world; and a couple of enormous nuclear arsenals on a hair-trigger alert poised to destroy the world."[27]

This leads to a final point. Despite bold claims of a return to greatness, Russia today is by many measures much weaker than the old Soviet Union — resulting in a striking power gap vis-à-vis the United States. The U.S. economy is eight times as large as Russia's and its military budget at least seven times higher.[28] Since the conflict in Ukraine began, Russia's economic position has become even weaker — partly as a result of Western sanctions and partly as a consequence of the sharp drop in the price of oil. In 2015, the value of the Russian ruble declined by 50 percent and the country suffered a severe recession, which resulted in a 5-percent economic *contraction*.[29] During his time in office, Putin's popularity has been linked to his capacity to deliver economic prosperity. Now, as growth declines and as the president rapidly burns through Russia's currency reserves, Putin has shifted to a sharper rhetoric in defence of traditional Russian (as opposed to Western) values and an assertive foreign policy. In fact, some analysts believe that the biggest concern for the West today is less a strong Russia than a relatively weak one, since it might resort to increasingly draconian tactics at home, and adventurism abroad, to maintain political control.[30] Putin's response to this decline has

been to initiate more isolationist economic policies by restricting foreign ownership and investment to make the country less dependent on the
West. But as former U.S. Ambassador to Moscow
Michael McFaul argues, history shows us that this
may not be a recipe for prosperity, but for further
economic crisis and instability.[31]

RUSSIA'S ILLIBERAL DEMOCRACY

Even if relations between Russia and the West do
not amount to a new Cold War, Russia's political
trajectory is not following the liberal democratic
path prescribed by triumphalist Western commentators and policy-makers following the fall of the
Berlin Wall. For many in the West, Russia's apparent slide toward authoritarianism under Putin is not
only devastating for supporters of liberal democracy within Russia, but potentially destabilizing
for broader international efforts to expand the zone
of peace among liberal democracies. As Russian
political scientist Sergey Karaganov has noted: "It is
obvious that Russia is firmly determined to change
the rules of the game that have been dictated to it
for the past 25 years. Unable and reluctant to toe

the line, Russia has given up attempts to become part of the West."[32]

Compared to Boris Yeltsin's leadership in the early 1990s, when corruption was rampant but the political system and the press mostly free, Putin has overseen a progressively elaborate repression of opposition parties, the media, and outspoken critics of the regime. He has also built up a sophisticated propaganda machine, and inflamed extreme nationalist and xenophobic sentiments among parts of the Russian population. Throughout this process, Putin has managed to consistently secure the approval of a strong majority of Russian citizens, raising questions about whether an authoritarian regime such as his can nevertheless continue to be regarded as having democratic legitimacy.

Opposition movements and parties have been increasingly marginalized under Putin's leadership. Even though there is no formal censorship or outright prohibition on oppositional political activity, legal mechanisms have been stretched to enable selective crackdowns against both prominent dissidents — for example, through trumped-up economic or financial charges — and rank-and-file activists. Under recently introduced legislation that bans calls for separatism, Tatar activist Rafis

Kashapov was jailed for three years for publishing articles that denounced Russia's annexation of Crimea on the VKontakte social network. Under the same legislation, a single mother was sentenced to one year of community work for reposting a pro-Ukrainian article. As noted by the European Council on Foreign Relations, when these selective prosecutions are publicized by Russia's mass media, they serve to frighten others and create an environment of pervasive "self-censorship."[33]

Russian elections under President Putin have also come under increasing international criticism. With respect to the 2007 parliamentary election, in which Putin's United Russia party won 64 percent of the vote, both the OSCE and Council of Europe concluded that the vote failed to meet their standards for fair democratic elections, criticizing the "abuse of administrative resources" and "media coverage strongly in favour of the ruling party." The two organizations also claimed that the polls "took place in an atmosphere which seriously limited political competition" and thus did not create a "level political playing field."[34] Amnesty International decried the Russian authorities' systematic disregard for human rights in the run-up to the elections through their efforts to prevent freedom of assembly and expression, including the beatings of journalists and human rights defenders and detention of demonstrators. One prominent case was the arrest and five-day administrative detention of opposition leader and former chess champion Garry Kasparov for allegedly leading an unsanctioned demonstration and resisting arrest.[35]

Similarly, Putin's landslide 2012 victory that returned him to the presidency was marred by allegations of fraud, backed by video evidence of ballot-stuffing and "carousel voting" — a practice where citizens are employed to cast their vote several times at various polling stations.[36] The OSCE declared in its statement: "There were serious problems from the very start of this election. The point of elections is that the outcome should be uncertain. This was not the case in Russia. There was no real competition and abuse of government resources ensured that the ultimate winner of the election was never in doubt."[37]

In 2011, tens of thousands of protesters called for a "Russia without Putin" and decried the alleged election fraud of previous contests. The government responded by adopting strong measures to prevent large-scale demonstrations, including an anti-protest law — described by authorities as a measure to fight terrorism — that enables Federal Security Service agents to open fire on crowds and grants them the "right to withhold any warnings of their intention to use weapons, special means or physical force." Steps have also been undertaken to ensure that the election outcomes maintain the parliamentary status quo — i.e., the dominance of Putin's Party of United Russia supported by a communist opposition — including by barring opposition figures from entering the Russian Duma. Finally, the Kremlin has taken pains to limit the influence of "undesirable" non-governmental organizations that are frequently branded as "foreign agents." This move has effectively deprived opposition politicians of grassroots assistance that might have helped them to counter the multiple advantages of regime-supported candidates.[38]

The Russian government has also employed more extreme measures to silence its domestic critics. The British journalist Edward Lucas uncovered the story of Sergei Magnitsky, an auditor at a Moscow law firm who exposed a multi-million-dollar fraud perpetrated by Russian officials against their own taxpayers and who was subsequently arrested on trumped-up charges. He died a year later in pre-trial detention, where he had been held in dreadful conditions, receiving a severe beating on the day of his death. In response, the Russian authorities blamed Magnitsky himself for the fraud he uncovered and put him on trial posthumously.[39] In October 2006, Russian journalist Anna Politkovskaya, critic of the Kremlin's military strategy in Chechnya, was gunned down in front of her house after turning up on a blacklist of "enemies of the nation." But perhaps the most infamous case is that of Alexander Litvinenko, a former officer of Russia's internal security forces (FSB) who had fallen out with the authorities and fled to London. A few weeks after Politkovskaya's death, Litvinenko's cup of tea was poisoned with a rare radioactive isotope (polonium-210) in a hotel in Mayfair and he subsequently perished. A public inquiry held in the U.K., presided over by a retired judge, concluded in early 2016 that there was "strong circumstantial evidence of Russian state responsibility" and that the acts of the Russian security agents who administered the poison likely had approval from the highest levels of government.[40]

President Putin and the United Russia Party have also gradually asserted their dominance over the country's media by acquiring independent media outlets and exerting control over what is broadcast. This is particularly true with respect to television (watched by at least 90 percent of the Russian population[41]) but also affects the content in newspapers, on radio stations, and increasingly on the Internet. Many analysts of democracy believe the state media under Putin has simply become an instrument of propaganda, as opposed to a robust institution of civil society. At his 2013 annual news conference Putin told reporters: "There should be patriotically minded people at the head of state information resources, people who uphold the interests of the Russian Federation...These are state resources; this is the way it is going to be." But privately owned broadcasters have also largely succumbed to Kremlin influence, and outlets that have resisted such control are subject to marginal-ization and frequent harassment, often under the header of antiterrorist action or tax inspections.[42]

This media dominance has allowed the govern-ment to create an ever-growing cult of personal-ity around their leader, a phenomenon that Edward Lucas describes as *the* key feature of Russian poli-tics. The "modest, taciturn man who took power in 1999," he writes, "is barely a memory...Mr. Putin has piloted a microlight to guide migrating cranes, stunned a Siberian tiger which was supposedly menacing a female journalist, flown a fighter plane, and dived down to the Black Sea seabed to 'find' two antique amphorae (which turned out to have been borrowed for the occasion from a museum)."[43]

As a final element of the strategy, Putin's government has cultivated nominally independent but Kremlin-friendly civil society organizations and movements. The most prominent of these is the patriotic youth league called Nashi ("Ours"), established with the government's support in 2005 — seemingly in direct response to the success of anti-regime demonstrators in Ukraine's 2004 Orange Revolution. By late 2007, the organization had grown to at least 120,000 members and was able to deploy thousands of uniformed young people to counter political opposition at a moment's notice. Illustrating this strength were the counter-demonstrations it organized in response to the anti-government protests in Russia in late 2011.[44] Western commentators have thus dubbed the organization as "Putinjugend," or "Putinyouth" – a nod to the Nazi-era Hitlerjugend – and compared it to the Soviet-era Young Communist Leagues.

To many in the West, all of these developments are evidence of Russia's incapacity and unwillingness to evolve into a liberal democracy, along the lines of most post-communist states in Eastern Europe. While Yeltsin's Russia initially appeared committed to the liberal model of political economy and closer integration with the West, Putin's Russia is taking a page from the Chinese playbook and rejecting political and social liberalization. The veteran analyst of international affairs Robert Kagan argues that Russia is pursuing "divergence" rather than the promised "convergence" with the West. Elections are simply an opportunity to ratify decisions made by Putin; the legal system is a tool to be used against political opponents; and the media is in the hands of the government. In Kagan's view, this "Czarist" political system in contemporary Russia places the country firmly in the autocracy camp, and thus revives a much older battle between liberalism and autocracy that began in the late eighteenth century and carried through the First and Second World Wars.[45]

What we are seeing in Russia, however, is not necessarily the return of nineteenth-century autocracy or of Soviet-style dictatorship. Instead, it appears to be a modern political hybrid. As worrying as the erosion of liberties may be, twenty-first century Russia is a significant distance away from the closed society of the Soviet era, when the Communist Party and KGB controlled much of daily life and when foreign travel was not a right but a rare privilege. Religious and private enterprise, which were outlawed in the former USSR, are an integral part of Russian society. Above all, opposition parties actually exist — even if they are kept on the fringes of the political system, cannot demonstrate freely or easily, and have no significant access to the media.[46]

Thus, while today's Russia is clearly illiberal, it is harder to argue that it is deeply undemocratic. Putin's government does seem to correspond to preferences of many Russians for authoritarianism and populism over liberalism.[47] The president's personal approval ratings within Russia have consistently been high compared to those of Western leaders, reaching an all-time peak of 87 percent in June 2015.[48] These figures suggest that Putin's Russia may not be so much abandoning democracy as offering an alternative model to the West's version of *liberal* democracy. And it is doing so at a time when liberal democracies themselves are facing economic and political turmoil. As Russian Foreign Minister Lavrov claims: "For the first time in many years, a real competitive environment has emerged on the market of ideas."[49]

SOVEREIGN DEMOCRACY AS
THE NEW RUSSIAN DOCTRINE

Lavrov's suggestion challenges Fukuyama's prediction that with the death of the Soviet Union the progression of human history would no longer be driven by a struggle between political ideas. While adopting the institution of competitive elections, post-Soviet Russia has moved in a distinctly illiberal direction when it comes to free speech, an accessible and critical media, and freedom of association. In *The Future of Freedom,* Fareed Zakaria — who coined the term "illiberal democracy"— explains that individual liberty and democracy may go together in the West, but that they are not necessarily connected everywhere. In many countries, the curtailment of liberties may even have the support of a majority of voters.[50]

It is less clear, however, whether this illiberal democratic system constitutes or is backed by an emerging ideology. Many critics of Putin assume that the values he espouses are merely a cynical mechanism for retaining power and authoritarian control. But as Kagan suggests, it is the West's folly to think that those who do not embrace liberal democracy are simply interested in enhancing their

own position or "lining their pockets." Personal economic motives are no doubt present, but so too is
the belief that their model is serving a higher cause..
In Putin's case, these causes include political order,
domestic economic success, international influence, and great-power status. Russia's leaders, like
those of China, worry about holding their vast polity — with multiple time zones, nationalities, and
religions — together. The liberal democratic system of the West, with its frequent shifts in power
and changing political agenda, seems ill-suited to
the task of creating stability.

To legitimize their alternative model, Putin
and his closest circle have endeavoured to give the
Russian polity its own normative underpinning by
branding their form of governance as a "sovereign
democracy." This doctrine is less a coherent political
philosophy or ideological call for world revolution,
as with Marxism-Leninism, than an effort at self-
justification: its chief role, argues Edward Lucas, is
"to explain why the Kremlin's overweening political and economic power is part of the natural order,
not an aberration from the European mainstream."[51]
It is also a different kind of challenge to Western
ideas — one that emerges from *within* the broad tent
of democracy rather than from without.

The idea of sovereign democracy, which draws on two key concepts in the preamble to the Russian constitution, was forwarded by Vladislav Surkov, deputy chief of the Russian presidential administration and widely seen as a key political strategist in the Kremlin. In a speech to the United Russia party in February 2006, he described sovereign democracy as a system in which the powers and decisions of political authorities "are decided and controlled by a diverse Russian nation for the purpose of reaching material welfare, freedom and fairness by all citizens, social groups and nationalities, by the people that formed it."[52] The term has since been repeated by leading Kremlin figures and, most notably, by Putin himself, as a means of distinguishing today's Russian democracy from that of former President Yeltsin's, which is depicted as weak and susceptible to foreign domination.

The notion of sovereign democracy has two dimensions. The first is inward-looking, designed to legitimize the rule and agenda of the current party in power (United Russia) and insulate it from the kind of popular and destabilizing pressures that led to "revolutions" in other post-Soviet countries such as Georgia and Ukraine. It promotes a conception of democracy that is both anti-pluralist and anti-populist. Elections are designed not so much to express differences and conflicting interests, but rather to clearly delineate the contours of power: who are the governors and who are the governed. Or, as analyst Ivan Krastev puts it, elections are seen not as tools to represent people but rather to represent power "in front of the people."[53]

Religion also plays an important role in this Russian model: unlike communism, sovereign democracy takes an important part of its moral and spiritual legitimacy from the leadership of the Russian Orthodox Church — a key part of the country's history and what contributed to its past stature and influence. Putin himself regularly attends church services and frequently shows his interlocutors a crucifix that he rescued from a fire at his family home. After the presidency, the Church is the second-most trusted institution in Russia. In exchange for state protection and general tax and legal privileges, the Church bolsters the Kremlin's efforts to differentiate Russian and Western civilization. It depicts the concept of individual human rights as codified in the UN Declaration as a Western-sponsored construct, and as an alternative has adopted a Declaration of Human Dignity and Rights which stresses "faith, ethics, [national]

sacraments, Fatherland" as values "no less important than human rights."[54] The Church also defines
itself against so-called foreign religions, most notably the Roman Catholic Church, in a way that mir-
rors the Kremlin's strategy of setting itself against
the EU and NATO.

The second dimension of sovereign democracy
is more outward-looking and aimed at insulating
Russia from external pressures, such as globalization, terrorism, and mass migration, that have
marked the early twenty-first century. It entails
a strong conception of sovereignty based on freedom from foreign interference and domestic self-
determination, and implies a critique of Western
meddling in countries undergoing political transition. In the words of one media outlet sponsored
by the Kremlin: "[Sovereign democracy] is an efficient answer to Russia's search for a term that could
organically blend its foreign and domestic priorities, its national interests in dealing with the world
and an effective social arrangement, which would
enable Russia to react to outside changes and ensure
a comfortable life for its citizens. This is no small
task and is by no means limited to the right choice
of words. The crux of the problem is that the ability
of a country to consistently uphold and implement

its national interests in the world arena cannot be taken for granted. On paper there are about 200 sovereign states in the world, but very few are genuinely sovereign."[55] To be truly independent, Putin and his political supporters believe, countries must be able to resist the pressure exerted by "foreign centers of power" — particularly the United States and its ongoing efforts to democratize the world.

DIFFUSING THE RUSSIAN MODEL

The doctrine of sovereign democracy, as Kagan suggests, evokes the idea of Russia's "return to greatness."[56] It is also designed to assert the country's democratic credentials and to present itself as an alternative model for other states — particularly those that wish to insulate themselves from the economic pressures of globalization and the political pressures of Western-led democratization. This inspirational potential is already evident in the admiration expressed for Putin in several anti-establishment parties in the West, on both the right and the left end of the political spectrum.

Marine Le Pen of France's Front National has made no secret of her admiration for Putin. Her party has links to senior Kremlin figures, including Russia's Deputy Prime Minister Dmitry Rogozin, who in 2005 ran an anti-immigrant campaign under the slogan "Clean Up Moscow's Trash." But the connections are also material: the Front National has confirmed that it has received the first tranche of a loan (which will total forty million euros) from Russian supporters and the party's founder, Jean-Marie Le Pen, was separately revealed to have borrowed another two million euros from a mysterious company based in Cyprus with suspected Kremlin links.[57]

From as early as 2009, Russia has also been actively cultivating links with far-right organizations in eastern Europe, establishing ties with Slovakia's People's Party, Bulgaria's nationalist anti-EU Attack Movement, and Hungary's far-right party Jobbik. The latter, which won 20 percent of the vote in the April 2015 parliamentary elections, is avowedly pro-Russian. In 2013, its leader described Russia as the guardian of Europe's heritage, contrasting it with the "treacherous" EU. Its most controversial figure, Béla Kovács, who is a member of the European Parliament, has lobbied on behalf of Russian interests and supported the invasion of Crimea. More surprisingly, Hungary's ruling party, Fidesz, which was once fiercely anti-communist, has also been cultivating closer Russian ties. In a July 2014 speech, Prime Minister Viktor Orbán hailed Russia as a successful example of the "illiberal democracies" he wishes to emulate. He echoed the Kremlin's defence of its approach: "[T]he Hungarian nation is not simply a group of individuals but a community that must be organized, reinforced and in fact constructed. And so in this sense the new state that we are constructing in Hungary is an illiberal state, a non-liberal state."[58]

Support for Putin and his vision of democracy is also evident on the left. At the height of the Greek Euro crisis in 2015, when the country's negotiations with its Brussels creditors had collapsed, Alexis Tsipras — prime minister of Greece and head of the populist and leftist Syriza Party — shared a platform with President Putin at the St. Petersburg Economic Forum. Tsipras described Russia as one of "Greece's most important partners," and hinted that Greece could one day make an alliance with Russia if his country exited the Eurozone. In suggesting that the world was becoming more multipolar, Tsipras was sending a clear message to those in the West: his country had other options — financial and political — outside of Europe.[59]

A significant driver of the increasingly cosy relationship between Putin's Russia and populist political forces in the West is the Kremlin's conscious strategy of fostering links by way of financial support. But there is also an ideological dimension to these growing ties, particularly in Central and Eastern Europe. Here, populist parties and Putin's United Russia Party have converged on a kind of post-communist neo-conservatism, united by their suspicion of and resistance to the modernizing agenda of the European Union. The *New York Times* journalist Jochen Bittner calls it a shared "nostalgia over lost worlds": a preference for simple social and moral orders rooted in national communities over the EU's complex vision of open borders, shared sovereignty, and multiple identities. A quarter of a century after the end of the Cold War, many Russians blame democratization and liberalism for the breakdown in social order, corruption, and a general loss of certainty about the future. In parts of Europe, too, globalization is resisted for its alleged destruction of local industries, attack on community cohesion, and loss of political accountability.[60]

A WORLD OF OUR OWN MAKING

Populist figures in the West do not stop at voicing their respect for Putin; they also openly criticize Western policies designed to pressure or punish his government — especially those enacted in the wake of the annexation of Crimea. Some go even further, arguing that the West's efforts to incorporate countries from the former Soviet sphere of influence into its own security and economic institutions are to blame for the current tensions with Russia. In this view, an overconfident West paid insufficient attention to Russia's legitimate national interests and concerns after the end of the Cold War, and pursued a policy agenda destined to be perceived as threatening by Moscow.

This line of argument strips too much agency from Russia, depicting it as the hapless victim of a series of Western policies. The evolution of Russian society since the end of the Cold War has been profoundly affected by the choices of its political leaders — most notably Putin — and the willingness of elites and the broader public to support such choices. Nevertheless, there is an important lesson to be drawn from the original Cold War, especially its early years. Then, as now, it was not the action of only one side, but the *interaction* between the two sides, that created the spiral in tension. And so in asking the question "What to do about Russia" today, policy-makers in the West need to re-examine their own foreign policies and revisit their own decisions in the aftermath of the fall of the Berlin Wall.

The West's strategy of enlargement after 1991 — which resulted in the reunification of Germany, the extension eastward of institutions such as NATO and the EU, and the democratization of countries from the Soviet bloc — was in many respects the embodiment of Fukuyama's "end of history" thesis. It was also the fulfilment of a dream for many liberal democrats in Central and Eastern Europe and the Baltic states. The weak spot in the strategy, however, was that this Euro-Atlantic institutional order did not evolve to accommodate Russia. Indeed, institutions such as NATO and the EU had such leverage over aspiring members that they did not believe they *needed* to change. Instead, the burden of transformation was shifted onto others: reform your political and economic systems to conform to the tenets of liberal democracy or stay outside the club.

The big problem, of course, was Russia. As

many analysts agree, even if Russia *had* under-
gone a successful transformation and sought membership in Western-led institutions, neither NATO
nor the EU would have been able to absorb such
a large country — with its associated economic,
social, and security-related issues — without some
significant institutional change. And so Russia
was offered what former U.S. State Department
officials Samuel Charap and Jeremy Shapiro call
"partnership without membership." But the lack of
institutional change, and the continued march of
enlargement, created an impression in Moscow that
NATO and the EU were simply "continuing their
original purpose of containing Soviet/Russian
influence through new, more modern means."[61]

Of course, it is always difficult to answer the
counter-factual question "What if?" What if the
West had tried harder to accommodate Russia?
Would our current reality look different? How
should the historians judge the Western strategy of
enlargement — as an act of encroachment that provoked Putin's actions in Ukraine[62] or as a far-sighted
policy of protection that consolidated democratic
gains in post-communist Europe and protected vulnerable states from Russian aggression? And how
could Ukrainians have better resolved the issues

their country inherited when it became independent — namely, proximity to both East and West and the presence of a significant Russian-speaking minority?

Instead of concluding that the last twenty-five years have shown that Russia is innately hostile to the West and its values, a more promising and more humble approach would subject some of the West's own assumptions to greater scrutiny and endeavour to see the world through Russian eyes. In so doing, Putin's moves in Crimea, while certainly not to be exonerated or accepted, could at least be (partly) explicable. We would realize that the "colour revolutions" that shook countries like Ukraine — which the West supported with money and organizational assistance and later celebrated as evidence of democracy's continued triumph — were viewed in Moscow not only as a threat to Russia's regional influence but also as something that could be repeated in Russia itself.[63] We would also come to see that unilateral enlargement, to create Western strongholds on Russia's frontier, is a step too far. Perhaps Western hubris, as well as Russian hubris, is at the heart of today's icy relationship. With this recognition could come a wiser and more effective response to the next crisis — one that would consistently sanction Russia both when it transgresses important international norms and agreements and when it lapses into authoritarianism, but which keeps the door open for a better relationship. This isn't Cold War 2.0, but rather the prudent management of geopolitics in the twenty-first century.

Another way in which the West could re-examine its recent history and temper its triumphalism would be to look inward and reassess the health of its own political and economic model in this renewed era of competition with Russia. After all, George Kennan's Long Telegram reached the conclusion that the best way to counter Soviet expansion was not through military confrontation, which carried excessive risk, but rather through the preservation of a strong and cohesive society *at home*. The strength of the Soviet threat to the West, he argued, was rooted not in its military potential, but "in the terrible truths which the Russians have discovered about the vulnerability of liberal democratic society." The priority for the United States and its allies was thus to "measure up to its own best traditions."[64]

The aftermath of the Cold War has not brought about unrivalled superpower status for the United

States — in spite of the so-called "unipolar" moment in the 1990s. The U.S. has also been weakened, both by its adventurist foreign policy and by worrying economic and political developments within its own borders. More broadly, in this second decade of the twenty-first century, the West's geopolitical influence, as well as its political and economic model, is being challenged by traditional great powers such as Russia — as well as China. The West must again defend itself, not primarily through military prowess, but by re-cultivating its liberal democratic ideal.

FIVE

THE RETURN OF INEQUALITY

OUR RECOLLECTIONS ABOUT THE Cold War are mostly about external relations, or foreign policy — about the great global contest between liberal capitalism and communism. But it is also worth remembering that George Kennan, the key architect of the West's strategy for containing the old Soviet Union, was equally concerned about *domestic* policy and the condition of American democracy. The "greatest danger that can befall us in coping with this problem of Soviet communism," he wrote, "is that we shall allow ourselves to become like those with whom we are coping."[1]

His worst fear — that the United States might embrace its own form of totalitarianism — did not come to pass. Liberal democracy endured and eventually triumphed over communism, much as Kennan had hoped. But seventy years on from the drafting of his Long Telegram, there are reasons to believe that he would be alarmed at the current state of the American polity, and with the condition of democracy in the West more generally. In his own United States, the wrangling between the executive and legislative branches has reached unprecedented levels of dysfunction, making it almost impossible for the federal government to pass legislation. Populist politics are at a fever pitch, as demonstrated by rhetoric in the 2016 primaries and presidential election. And most worryingly, historically high levels of economic inequality have all but killed the American dream for millions of U.S. citizens and are depriving many in the younger generation of the ability to fulfil their true potential. Indeed, one out of four American children is now growing up in poverty.[2]

In this final chapter, I therefore want to turn our gaze inward — away from the big and sometimes seemingly intractable problems of war, migration, and geopolitics, to what is happening in our own countries, cities, and local communities. Here, too, I will argue, history is returning — most notably in the form of extreme inequality. The weakness of the "end of history" thesis is thus apparent not only outside our borders, but also within them. Liberal democracy itself is less stable, and less admirable, than it was at the end of the Cold War. It should also be less confident about its longevity.

In addition to showing how inequality has returned, I want to emphasize its corrosive effects. As prominent economists such as Joseph Stiglitz and Thomas Piketty have argued, inequality is not only bad for the economy — a message that many supporters of neo-liberalism have not wanted to admit — but also for social cohesion.[3] I will also call upon some provocative research by social psychologists to suggest that inequality can profoundly, and negatively, affect individual behaviour and thereby contribute to decreased levels of empathy and social cooperation.

Ultimately, I will contend that it's time to emphatically challenge the myths that continue to circulate — about how inequality helps our economies grow or about how high wealth and income are the justified results of "hard work" — and to take much more seriously the threat that inequality poses to our twenty-first-century liberal democracies. This entails tackling political taboos, such as talk of redistribution or additional taxation, and a willingness to challenge the austerity policies we have been told are unavoidable. It also implies that each of us, as individuals, must become much more active in fighting to maintain our liberal democratic model and its foundational ideas, particularly the value of fairness. As I suggested in the first chapter, grand narratives like the "end of history" can make us fatalistic about the direction in which the world is headed and over-optimistic about the inevitable triumph of our way of life. They can also sideline the important impact of courageous individuals, including — potentially — ourselves.

Much of this book has operated at the macro-level — the changing patterns of migration across borders, international terrorism, deteriorating relations between great powers. In short, about what is happening, and what needs to be done, "out there." But as we witness the return of history right here, with the growing gap between the rich and the poor in Western countries, the story has to come full circle to what Kennan rightly pointed to — the "health and vigor of our own society."[4]

THE CONTOURS OF ECONOMIC INEQUALITY

One of the most oft-cited benefits of globalization is its fostering of economic growth and, by extension, its contribution to reducing poverty levels worldwide. Branko Milanović, who for more than a decade was the lead economist at the World Bank, has demonstrated how the mean incomes of countries across the globe have begun to converge since the end of the Cold War. According to his data, the period between 1988 and 2008 marked the first decline in economic inequality among world citizens since the dawn of the Industrial Revolution. This trend has been accompanied by a significant expansion of the global middle class — thanks mainly to the growth of this class in China — and a marked decrease in the share of world's population living on $1.25 per day (the World Bank's definition of "absolute poverty").[5]

These figures undoubtedly signify progress. But as Milanović notes, globalization has both its winners and losers. Those at the top of the economic pyramid — the so-called global 1 percent — have done spectacularly well, increasing their real incomes by 60 percent during this twenty-year period. Thomas Piketty's bestselling book, *Capital in the Twenty-First Century,* tells the grand history of capitalism's circular path, from the high levels of economic inequality at the start of the Industrial Revolution, to more equitable levels in the twentieth century with increases in taxation and the rise of welfare states, and back to the nineteenth-century disparities in the second decade of the new millennium. To appreciate this cycle, we need to understand better the distinction between wealth and income.

Piketty reminds us that national wealth (or what he calls national capital) is a stock: it refers to the total market value of everything owned by the residents and government of a given country at a given point in time (including wealth appropriated or accumulated in previous years). National income, on the other hand, is a flow: it is the quantity of goods produced and distributed in a given period, usually a year. The capital/income ratio divides a country's stock by its annual flow of income. So, for example, a ratio of 6 means that a country's capital stock is the equivalent of six years of national income.[6] The evolution of that ratio, in any given country, allows us to understand the importance of accumulated wealth — as opposed to income from labour — in different historical periods.

The period just prior to the First World War saw a heavy concentration of wealth in the top 1 percent of the population, particularly in Great Britain and the United States (the world's leading democracies). At the time, owners of capital could expect to earn 4 to 5 percent on their investments, with very little or no taxation. They also tended to reinvest most of their income — after skimming some off the top to live in luxury — which ensured that their own private wealth was growing faster than that of the national economy. In short, the capital income ratio was relatively high.

This system persisted well into the twentieth century, despite the development of organized labour and increased wages for workers. More fundamental change came only after the Great Depression and the Second World War, when a combination of investment in public infrastructure (part of the post-war reconstruction) and favourable demographics — a high birth rate and a relatively young population — facilitated more ambitious schemes for income redistribution and flattened out the capital/income ratio.[7] But by the early 1980s, with the free market and low-taxation programs led by U.S. President Ronald Reagan and British Prime Minister Margaret Thatcher, the ratio of capital to income began to creep up again — and with it, the widening of the gap between the top 1 percent and the rest.

Since the 1980s, this trend has been particularly pronounced in developed Western nations, including the United States. And this shift in economic inequality *within* these nations has had profound implications for the health of liberal democracy.

AMERICAN EXCEPTIONALISM?

When he penned his "end of history" thesis at the end of the 1980s, Fukuyama praised America's egalitarianism, describing it as the "essential achievement of the classless society." While some gaps between rich and poor might exist, he conceded, they were not due to any fundamental legal or social arrangements. The United States was the place where "existential inequality"[8] — the phrase coined by Swedish sociologist Göran Therborn to refer to inequality among certain categories of persons, based on race or gender — had been erased, through progressive laws and social mores that gave every citizen an equal chance to realize her dream.

Today, however, the leader of the world's liberal democratic club also has the dubious honour of having the highest level of income inequality. In 2011, New York's financial district became the target of the Occupy Wall Street demonstrations, which rallied around the famous ratio, 1:99. The OWS slogan, "We are the 99 percent," referred to the inequitable distribution of income between the top 1 percent — which brought home more than 20 percent of all income earned in the United States — and the rest of the population. The gap is even greater when we consider wealth (which is based on ownership of assets) rather than income. In 2016, the wealthiest 1 percent of Americans held 35 percent of the country's wealth — and that concentration increased even further when housing assets were taken out of the mix.

The gains from economic recovery were also skewed toward the rich. After the 2008 financial crisis, just over 90 percent of all income growth between 2009 and 2012 was enjoyed by the wealthiest 1 percent of Americans.[9] This figure suggests that those who played a large role in the origins of the Great Recession (namely, professionals in the financial sector) did not really suffer the consequences. While stock prices did drop, and rich

THE RETURN OF HISTORY

Americans saw their wealth temporarily decline, their fortunes soon rebounded. Meanwhile, many ordinary Americans suffered the loss of their entire savings with the collapse of the housing market.

Some may consider these figures and wonder what is new. Haven't the poor — and the extremely wealthy — always been with us? The answer is, not quite. Inequality in liberal democracies such as the United States is back at the levels it was around the time of the First World War, and in some cases is getting worse.

In order to appreciate the increasing levels of inequality in the twenty-first century, we need to understand what the American Nobel Prize–winning economist Joseph Stiglitz has identified as the "increasing disparity between the mean and the median" — between what is happening on average and what is happening to the typical individual or household. The median household income in the United States, adjusted for inflation, is lower today than what it was in 1989. By contrast, the wealthiest 1 percent of households have 225 times the wealth of the typical American household — a figure that is double the ratio of what it was thirty years ago, just before the Cold War ended.

Even within the 1 percent of top earners and

wealth holders, there is great variation. The top 0.1 percent of the U.S. population, the so-called super-rich, takes home just over 11 percent of the nation's total income — three to four times what it was three decades ago.[10] Increasingly, this upper echelon in America's economic hierarchy has more in common with the super-rich in other countries than it does with its fellow citizens. Canada's foreign affairs minister and former journalist Chrystia Freeland uses the term "plutocrats" to refer to the transglobal community of economic peers, whose jet-setting lifestyle has made them "a nation unto themselves." Most members of this ultra-elite are hardworking and highly educated meritocrats who feel they are the deserving winners of a tough, worldwide economic competition. As a result, Freeland argues, they have an ambivalent attitude toward those who haven't succeeded quite so spectacularly and are decidedly lukewarm about new forms of economic redistribution.[11]

The increasing gradations of wealth within the top 1 percent, while interesting for those retail and financial institutions that hope to capitalize on the rising fortunes of the plutocrats, are occurring against the backdrop of significant underemployment and declining living standards among the working class. Since the victory of liberal democracy over communism in the late 1980s, ordinary Americans have seen their incomes stagnate or decline — often referred to as the "hollowing out" of the middle class — while the rich and ultra-rich have flourished. This trend also deals a mortal blow to proponents of trickle-down economics, made popular during the Reagan era, which theorizes that when the rich do well the rest of the population will also benefit. In today's United States, this process doesn't necessarily unfold: those in the top 1 percent can see income gains, while those in the 99 percent can actually see income losses.

This pattern of increasing inequality repeats itself to differing degrees around the world. The main indicator for inequality within countries is known as the Gini coefficient, which measures the extent to which the distribution of income among individuals (or households) within an economy deviates from a perfectly equal distribution. Thus, if perfect equality is 0, maximum inequality is 1. All but five out of the twenty-one OECD member states have seen a rise in inequality.[12] Moreover, there are troubling signs within developing countries whose economies are in transition: China's Gini coefficient, which in the 1980s hovered around

0.30, is now at 0.49 — higher than that of the United States. The World Bank considers a coefficient above 0.40 to represent severe income inequality.

The trends in Canada may not be quite as pronounced as those in the U.S. or China, but they are similarly worrying. Whereas in the 1980s and early 1990s government policies of redistribution significantly reduced income gaps, from the mid-1990s onward inequality has been on the rise. Canadian public policy scholars Keith Banting and John Myles refer to this trend as a "redistributive fade"[13] and Canada's was among the most dramatic among OECD countries. Over the past three decades, the top 1 percent of Canada's income earners captured 37 percent of total income growth in this country. Their share of total income has thus also increased, from roughly 7 percent in the 1980s to 12 percent just before the 2008 financial crisis (since the Great Recession this figure has decreased somewhat to 10 percent). Finally, the rise in top incomes has been much greater in certain sectors, such as finance, and among senior executives. This increase is not wholly reflective of a competitive market for skills, and thus confirms the argument of some economists that the high incomes of the top 1 percent are a function of "rent extraction."[14]

The inequality story also has a local dimension. The city of Toronto has become Canada's inequality capital, with the gap between rich and poor households widening at double the national pace — a 31 percent increase between 1980 and 2005. The city has also seen a growing concentration of working poor toiling in the service of high-paid professionals from the knowledge sector in a kind of modern-day *Downton Abbey.*[15] David Hulchanski, professor of housing and social work at the University of Toronto and author of the study *The Three Cities Within Toronto,*[16] tracks the disappearance of middle-income communities and the gradual creation of an island of wealth surrounded by a sea of poor suburbs. "Instead of living together harmoniously, with mutual respect," Hulchanski claims, "we are setting up two extreme lifestyles — one where people struggle just to get by and another where every option in the world is open to them. No country is ever perfect in terms of equality, but we're going in the opposite direction."

The upward creep in Canada's Gini coefficient has a variety of causes: some point to long-term processes of de-industralization via free trade; others to tax cuts and public policies designed particularly for society's top earners; others to low wages in a labour market that is becoming more deregulated and contract-oriented; and others to cuts in social spending and social program transfers and the "offshoring" of corporation profits to avoid Canadian taxes. But whatever the driving factors, the result is the same: Canada is no exception to the return of inequality.

THE GILDED AGE: A TALE OF TODAY?

Even more alarming is the source and nature of today's inequality, in particular how it is undermining the meritocratic values upon which liberal democracies are based. Piketty posits that a high capital/income ratio tends to make accumulated and inherited wealth disproportionately influential in determining an individual's well-being. This is partly why so many nineteenth-century novels, such as Charlotte Brontë's *Jane Eyre*, are about marrying into wealth, or of the struggle of the poor to reach affluence, such as Mark Twain and Charlie Dudley Warner's *The Gilded Age*, which chronicles the futile efforts of a Tennessee family — led by patriarch Si Hawkins — to sell 75,000 acres of land in an attempt to join the affluent club.

The title of this satirical tale about the lust for wealth is drawn from a scene in Shakespeare's play *King John*, in which the Earl of Salisbury derides the practice of gilding — putting gold on top of gold — as wasteful and excessive. *The Gilded Age* thus became a metaphor for an entire historical period, from the mid-nineteenth to the early twentieth century, when the United States, as well as Great Britain, France, and Russia, saw a combination of materialistic excess and extreme poverty. On the one hand, this period gave rise to exotic fashion and haute couture, great restaurants like Maxim's, and grand Victorian architecture; on the other hand, it also witnessed grotty urban slums and the passage of "Poor Laws" designed to limit who could claim economic relief. In Benjamin Disraeli's 1845 novel *Sybil*, the character Walter Gerard — a working-class radical — laments that the rich and poor in England inhabit "two nations...between whom there is no intercourse and no sympathy; who are as ignorant of each other's habits, thoughts, and feelings, as if they were dwellers in different zones, or inhabitants of different planets."[17]

In shifting our gaze back to this era, today's economists of inequality also remind us of its dark underbelly. Piketty argues that contemporary economic disparity is driven primarily by unequal ownership of assets — much the same way as in the period leading up to the First World War, when wealth was concentrated in the hands of a few rich families. His central finding is that in an economy where the rate of return on capital (assets) is greater than the rate of growth of output and income — which was the case in the late nineteenth century and is also the case today — inherited wealth rises in importance and capitalism "automatically generates arbitrary and unsustainable inequalities."[18]

What is especially striking about the current period in the United States is that more and more people within the top 1 percent are rich *both* in terms of their ownership of capital and through their earnings from high-salaried jobs. Consider it another version of American exceptionalism. Nevertheless, the overall implication remains the same: individuals generally become rich not through a lifetime of hard work — as suggested by the American dream — but through how much capital they inherit. As the American economist and *New York Times* columnist Paul Krugman has concluded: "It's generally more valuable to have the right parents (or to marry into having the right in-laws) than to have the right job."[19]

By presenting these cold hard facts, contemporary economists have broken a taboo by contributing to a greater willingness to talk openly about inequality. They have also laid bare many planks of the received wisdom of how modern Western liberal economies would evolve in the twentieth century. One such example is the so-called Kuznets curve, named after the famous post-war American economist Simon Kuznets, who in the 1950s argued that as societies underwent industrialization they would initially become less economically equal — particularly as labour moved from agriculture to industry — but would then move into a period of declining inequality as economic growth took effect. In short, inequality would follow a bell-shaped curve. Through an increasingly educated and skilled labour force, and broader social transfers, richer countries would become more egalitarian.

Piketty, by contrast, suggests that the decades after 1945 were not a story of progress, which might be repeated elsewhere, but a blip in history. Specific historical conditions, facilitated by disasters such as war, drought, and economic recession, brought about the levelling of inequality in the twentieth century. But now the trend has reversed. The future

Piketty depicts for economically advanced Western societies is one of low-growth capitalism, combined with high levels of inequality and low levels of social mobility. This scenario could also unfold, eventually, for developing countries, once their process of industrialization slows in pace.

Other economists are slightly less deterministic. Branko Milanović, for example, adopts a longer historical frame of reference — going as far back as the Byzantine era — and takes into consideration the ebbs and flows in inequality over the centuries. He speaks in terms of "Kuznets waves" — with cycles of increasing and decreasing inequality within countries — rather than a definitive reversal of the Kuznets bell curve.[20] Still, his prognosis for Western governments is no less stark: the entrenchment of deep inequality is creating a global super-elite, which will force us to revise our collective conceptions of what is fair and just.

INEQUALITY'S CHALLENGE TO LIBERAL DEMOCRACY

After the end of the Cold War, economic growth appeared to be the inevitable product of the spread of globalization. Within Western societies, the focus of social democratic parties, such as New Labour in the United Kingdom or the New Democratic Party in Canada, was therefore on poverty alleviation, rather than addressing broader and deeper forms of economic inequality. As the former British Labour politician Peter Mandelson famously quipped in 1998, his party was "intensely relaxed about people getting filthy rich as long as they pay their taxes."[21] Those taxes were designed to bring individuals living below the poverty line up to a more respectable level and to improve and expand social services. What happened above that basic level was deemed acceptable in the name of continued economic expansion.

There are a number of reasons, however, why a focus on people's *relative* economic position, and not just their absolute levels of economic well-being, is important for maintaining the health of liberal democracy. In short, economic inequality — especially at today's historic levels — cannot simply be accepted as part and parcel of capitalism.

The first and most basic reason is that inequality has proven to be detrimental for the economy. In his book *The Great Divide*, Stiglitz debunks the idea that increased inequality is the corollary of economic success. If the top 1 percent is reaping almost all of the growth in income, then the middle class is too weak to create the kind of consumer spending that has historically driven economic growth. As a consequence, the vast majority ends up borrowing — usually beyond its means — thus making the economy even more volatile and susceptible to shocks.[22] Prior to the 2008 financial crisis — a time that some now nostalgically pine for — the economy was already creaking and rotting: the financial bubble and unsustainable levels of consumption, Stiglitz writes, were "simply acting as life support."[23]

The International Monetary Fund has also warned of the negative economic effects of inequality, particularly on efficiency and stability. The Fund's research has shown that countries with high levels of economic inequality tend to be marked by lower rates of growth and higher levels of instability[24] — thus challenging the oft-heard argument that efforts to create greater equality will harm economic performance. Findings like these have resulted in alternative proposals for how to conceive of economic growth and well-being, beyond measures like gross domestic product. The OECD, for example, has launched the Better Life Initiative, which seeks to employ a multi-dimensional measure of economic performance and social progress, including the diverse experience and living conditions of individuals and households. Its studies have found that while OECD countries with high GDP per capita predictably do (relatively) better in terms of measures like household income, there is a great diversity among them in terms of job security, housing affordability, and work-life balance.[25] Public health researchers Richard Wilkinson and Kate Pickett have also argued for the need to evaluate societal success with a broader array of measures, beyond just economic ones. Their bestselling book, *The Spirit Level*, observed that society's greatest ills — including mental illness, drug addiction, obesity, loss of community life, imprisonment, and poorer well-being for children — increase in prevalence as societies become more economically unequal. Thus the effects of inequality are not confined only to the poor but damage the entire social fabric.[26]

The second pernicious effect of economic inequality is that it can very quickly translate into inequality of opportunity. This result runs counter to the mantra in the United States that "anyone can succeed in America." Those in the top income echelons can buy privileges for their children, particularly in the realm of education, which provides more direct access to certain kinds of jobs and opportunities. They are also less likely to see the need for common public infrastructure — including public transportation — thus reducing the propensity for unequal societies to invest in the common good.

These effects chip away at Fukuyama's image of the classless society and raise questions about an exclusive focus on addressing "existential inequality" between races or between genders. Citizens of liberal democracies have used law to win important battles against existential inequality, and these victories should be celebrated; but on their own they are insufficient to reduce social injustice. As Milanović has argued, while legal equality puts everyone on the same starting line, it "[does] not care that some come to the starting line with Ferraris and others with bicycles."[27] In order to address the real barriers to social mobility and better social outcomes, we also need to pay attention to inequality of income and wealth.

This erosion of equality of opportunity is even more problematic if we accept Stiglitz's claim that the earnings of the top 1 percent are not necessarily "just desserts" for its contribution to society's prosperity. This is where his argument starts to hit a raw nerve: one of the greatest defences of inequality — its last bastion, perhaps — is the claim that wealth is earned. Those who have more have worked harder, possess special talents, or have taken extraordinary risks. But in today's world of economic inequality, that justification is harder to sustain.

With some notable exceptions — a prominent example being Microsoft founder Bill Gates — the individuals at the top are not usually those who have engineered great innovations for society's benefit. Nor are they necessarily the greatest job creators. Instead, the vast majority within the top 1 percent pursues what economists call "rent-seeking" — appropriating a greater share of existing wealth rather than creating new wealth. Many derive their wealth from connections — whether familial or political — and as Stiglitz notes, excel "in figuring out how to get a larger share of the nation's pie, rather than enhancing the size of that pie."[28] A disproportionate number of those in the top economic echelon work in the financial sector, and some were direct contributors to the Great Recession that began in 2008 through questionable lending practices and market manipulation.

An additional concern about inequality, which has long bothered political theorists, is its potential to turn economic advantage into political power. This dynamic eats away at liberal democracy's fundamental premise: that each citizen ought to have an equal say in the political process that sets law and public policy for his or her society.

It has long been suspected that wealth buys political influence, and American political scientist Martin Gilens has amassed the evidence to prove it. By examining the outcome of, and attitudes toward, thousands of proposed policy changes in the United States, he demonstrates that those public policies that are favoured by the rich — for example, certain forms of taxation policy — are much more likely to be acted upon by their political representatives (i.e., senators and congressmen) than those that are favoured by the lower or middle classes. Furthermore, the significant difference in levels of influence among classes is truer today than it was a few decades ago. As Stiglitz has memorably quipped, U.S. politics is no longer about "one person, one vote," but increasingly about "one dollar, one vote."

A feedback loop has thus been established whereby economic inequality translates into political inequality, and political inequality creates further economic and social stratification. This is why so many commentators have begun to describe the United States not as a democracy but rather as a "plutocracy": rule by the rich.[29] Even if those who hold public office are not all in the top echelons of wealth (though many of them are), the rich in America have disproportionate influence over who holds office and the actions that they take. Examples of legislation and policy initiatives that have benefitted big businesses and wealthy Americans include the weakening of the apparatus to regulate financial activities (which began during the Clinton administration in the 1990s), the reversal of judgements of the Environmental Protection Agency in the face of commercial pressure, tolerance for the concealment of offshore profits — as was so starkly revealed in the so-called Panama Papers — and "relaxed interpretations" of tax laws by the Internal Revenue Service to the advantage of high-income Americans.[30]

While a variety of factors contribute to the strong relationship between the preferences of affluent Americans and particular policy outcomes favourable to the rich — such as particular party structures, campaign financing laws, and the dominance of special economic interest groups — Gilens makes the broader point that it is the lack of genuine political competition and the convergence on a narrow set of ideas that is undermining representative democracy in the U.S., and potentially elsewhere.[31]

THE DEFICIT IN POLITICAL WILL

In *The Age of Acquiescence*, American labour historian Steve Fraser laments the incapacity of Americans to imagine a better or alternative system to predatory capitalism. The mid-nineteenth and early twentieth centuries were a time of outrage and protest against social and economic privilege in the United States, particularly the "robber barons" of big business who amassed their fortunes on the backs of workers. Examples include the 1874 "bread or blood" protest, when unemployed women and their children marched on New York's City Hall, and the 1877 railway strike that began in West Virginia in protest against reductions in wages but expanded to become the first nationwide strike in U.S. history. This kind of popular mobilization contributed to a series of progressive changes, including the passage of anti-trust legislation, the launch of the trade unionist movement, and the creation of the eight-hour workday.[32]

Today, by contrast, there is little to no popular challenge to similar levels of economic inequality. While the Occupy Wall Street movement stole headlines for the latter months of 2011, it ultimately fizzled given a lack of agreement among its members on a concrete agenda and its unwillingness to engage—even minimally—with existing political institutions. Twenty-first-century Americans—and the same might be said for citizens of other liberal democracies—have by and large submitted to a system whose permanence is assumed; they focus their energies on the private pleasures of consumerism rather than on cultivating the public good or the political or economic interests they share with others. Fukuyama's fear that the end of history would foster a consumerist culture, and expose an "emptiness at the core of liberalism," seems to have been fulfilled.

As a result, any political figure that dares to question the excesses of free-market capitalism is characterized, at best, as part of the fringe, or at worst, as an enemy to national security and prosperity. The reaction to the election of leftist politician Jeremy Corbyn as head of the British Labour Party is a clear example of this kind of narrative. In the autumn of 2015, Corbyn defied expectations to win a surprise first-ballot victory in Labour's leadership contest with the support of close to 60 percent of the party's members — an even stronger mandate than that given to former leader Tony Blair in 1994. Indeed, Corbyn was elected by 100,000 more voters than David Cameron when he was selected as leader of the U.K. Conservative Party in 2005. Yet, no sooner than the votes were counted, a barrage of criticism against Corbyn's political views was unleashed — most notably by many Labour MPs, several of whom declared that they could not serve under him as part of the shadow cabinet. Corbyn's strong critique of inequality and the ruling economic policy of austerity were deemed to have made him implausible and unelectable — an economic dinosaur that had stepped outside the boundaries of acceptable opinion. He also mused about nationalizing the railways, apologized for Britain's entry in the Iraq War, and called for a more progressive taxation regime in a country which has seen the overall wealth of the 1,000 richest citizens double over a six-year period (from 2009 to 2016), while food banks have

proliferated and the rate of evictions has acceler-
ated, due to ever-increasing rents.

Media watchdogs have shown that large sections
of the British press set out to systematically undermine Labour's new leader in the wake of his victory.[33] Journalists accused him of "not playing the
game" or not recognizing the need, in one columnist's words, to choose between "purity or power."[34]
Even the BBC, the bellwether of the British's media's
view on the electability of politicians, seemed completely perplexed by Corbyn's victory. Largely as
a result of years of New Labour, the fulcrum for
the BBC's prized impartiality had shifted to the
right, leading it to present a much narrower range
of political opinion. *London Review of Books* editor
Paul Myerscough sums it up nicely with a sports
analogy: "By defining himself against the establishment, Corbyn becomes an outsider, an insur-
gent, who can be discussed 'fairly' by the BBC only
in the way that, say, Radio 5 Live [the BBC's sports
channel] can 'fairly' cover England's opponents at
the World Cup."[35]

The response to the staying power of Bernie
Sanders in the 2016 Democratic primaries in the
U.S. is also emblematic of how the parameters of
mainstream political consensus have narrowed in

recent years. Sanders — a left-leaning senator from Vermont — portrayed himself as the quintessential outsider, running against the Democratic Party's establishment candidate Hillary Clinton, with the message that economic disparity had brought America to a breaking point. The proposed antidote to that disparity? Raising minimum wage to $15 an hour. Expanded social security benefits. A more progressive taxation scheme. A single-payer health care system. Free tuition at public universities. Once upon a time, these issues were regularly debated in mainstream American politics. But after Ronald Reagan put a stop to progressive taxes in the mid-1980s and froze the minimum wage — policy measures which neither the Clinton nor the Obama administrations have really challenged — Sanders's policy program appeared to the centrists in the Democratic Party as little more than the idealistic musings of a raving socialist.

Nevertheless, the party had to sit up and take notice. The Vermont senator's battle against inequality struck a chord with a significantly large constituency, particularly with young Americans, many of whom are experiencing an additional form of inequity between themselves and the relatively well-off Baby Boom generation. For these new voters, Sanders's willingness to challenge the economic framework inaugurated by Reagan was his strongest selling point.

This raises a broader political point: the economic inequality we see today is not something that has been thrust upon us, as the necessary product of economic forces. It is the result of conscious policy choices. This is the message that leading economists such as Piketty, Stiglitz, and Milanović most want us to take away from their painstaking work on inequality—that we have the power to reverse the negative spiral. If the laws of economics are so universal, Stiglitz asks, why is inequality not rising at the same alarming levels everywhere? Among developed economies, Norway and France seem to have avoided the extreme changes, and in Latin America, many countries have actually reduced economic inequality.[36] It is our particular economic, legal, and social frameworks that create and perpetuate inequality—whether in education, taxation, corporate governance, or anti-trust and bankruptcy law.

These decisions are undermining the foundations of contemporary liberal democracy and compromising the egalitarianism that inspired democracy's earliest champions. Thomas Rainsborough, who debated Oliver Cromwell during the famous Putney Debates of 1647 over the future shape of the English constitution, captured most eloquently the democratic value of equal political participation. While Cromwell believed that manhood suffrage would be tantamount to anarchy, and argued that the vote had to be restricted to property owners, Rainsborough attacked the idea of rule by the rich and defended the principle of one man, one vote: "I think that the poorest he that is in England has a life to live as the greatest he; and therefore truly, sir, I think it's clear that every man that is to live under a government ought first by his own consent to put himself under that government."[37]

In many of today's liberal democracies, the main alternative to a plutocratic system that continues to favour the rich seems to be an angry populism that reflects the increasing frustration of the middle class. If equal opportunity is undermined and merit no longer secures advancement, if political influence is skewed toward the wealthy, and if those who do well are not necessarily net contributors to society, then citizens become alienated from the political and economic system. Trump traded heavily on this disenchantment throughout the 2016 presidential campaign. His principal enemy was globalization and its alleged attack on middle-class jobs and livelihoods in the United States. In the Trump worldview, there is a zero-sum game between the poor in developing countries such as China, who have seen their fortunes rise, and the working class in America, whose interests are being sidelined by politicians. Trump's path to victory was fuelled by his capacity — seemingly ironic, given his own astronomical wealth — to empathize with those experiencing stagnating incomes and a loss of dreams. In response, he has promised to forge "better deals" with America's economic rivals, to turn back the globalization clock, and to re-impose tariffs and tougher immigration rules to protect jobs. What he offered his supporters are not really concrete economic solutions, but rather the negative promise to undo the policy decisions that he believes have resulted in national weakness.

But this agenda gives way to another, unproductive form of political polarization — this time between the world's poor and the middle class in developed countries.[38] It is also a convenient distraction for the top 1 percent in the U.S., whose capacity to accumulate and perpetuate their wealth is left largely untouched. Playing an unhappy domestic constituency against a remote and foreign one doesn't resolve the issue of aligning the policy priorities of the political elite with the interests of a broader set of stakeholders.

For years to come, political scientists and commentators will be dissecting the long-term and intermediate causes that bred Trump's political victories. However, one common feature of that analysis has already emerged: the success of his populism rests on his ability to leverage feelings of resentment and fear that have been building for decades and that regular politics proved incapable of understanding, let alone addressing. Millions of Americans were already suffering from what behavioural economists call "loss aversion": the tendency for individuals to fear losing a good of a certain value more than they celebrate a gain of the same size. The source of that aversion, economists argue, is the stronger psychological pain associated with loss.[39] Trump capitalized on this fear of (further) loss and channelled it into positions that sow discord — by pitting Muslims against non-Muslims, and regular citizens against "illegal" immigrants — and further erode social cohesion. But the raw material for his oppositional politics was already there, long before he strode into the political limelight.

HISTORY RETURNING? THIS TIME IT'S DIFFERENT.

A common response to these alarming circumstances is to say, "We've been here before." The twentieth century saw a series of crises that seemed, at the time, to spell the demise of liberal democracy. Some of these challenges were economic, such as the Great Depression of the 1930s or the oil shocks and high inflation of the 1970s. Others were political, either in the form of ideological rivals — as in the case of fascism and communism in the period between the two World Wars — or in the form of particular crises within democratic institutions — as in the Watergate scandal of the 1970s. At each of these junctures, commentators were fixated on the prospect of democracy's failure, concentrating on its weaknesses rather than its strengths. As the British novelist and historian H. G. Wells predicted in 1933, when it seemed that fascist dictatorships were in the ascendant, democracy would soon be discarded as "altogether too slow-witted for the urgent political and social riddles, with ruin and death at hand."[40]

The British political scientist David Runciman argues that this preoccupation with crisis and failure is a key feature of the evolution of liberal democracy. Its "onward march," he observes, has always "been accompanied by a constant drumbeat of intellectual anxiety."[41] In retrospect, this anxiety appears to be misplaced: liberal democracy has also proven remarkably good at recovering from crises — even very big ones, such as war and economic recession. "Success and failure," Runciman claims, "go hand in hand. This is the democratic condition." The very factors that make liberal democracy work over time — its flexibility and its responsiveness — are also what make it occasionally go wrong. But the good news is that it has the capacity to self-correct. Autocratic societies lack checks to prevent their rulers from leading them headlong into disaster. Democracies, by contrast, have political and constitutional safeguards that prevent them from "going over a cliff."[42]

While Runciman believes that democracy's hidden talents have helped to ensure its longevity, he also points to an associated danger: complacency and overconfidence. If every warning bell starts to sound the same, we screen them out. And so rather than learning from crisis and becoming more farsighted, liberal democracies keep making the same mistakes. "Democracy has triumphed," Runciman writes, "but it has not grown up." The only lesson liberal democracies seem to have learned from history is that no crisis is *really* as bad as it seems. Whenever democracies get too close to the edge, they eventually see sense and pull back. But this dynamic can also breed recklessness and turn democracy into a dangerous game of chicken: "When things get really bad, we will adapt. Until they get really bad, we need not adapt, because democracies are ultimately adaptable. Both sides play this game. Games of chicken are harmless, until they go wrong, at which point they become lethal."[43]

And so the question arises: Is it different *this* time? Are we really in trouble today, or is this just one more challenging period that liberal democracy will — eventually — overcome? Fukuyama is still an optimist. While he acknowledges the cracks in liberal democracy, and that it has been taken hostage by political elites for their own gains (particularly in the United States), he sees no rival political ideal. His eye remains fixed on the bigger, more positive trends — such as the fact that the number of democratic states is three times higher today than it was in 1970.

I am more of a Chicken Little about liberal democracy's future, and only history, as it unfolds, will prove me right or wrong. It may be true that liberal democracies have proven adept, in the past, at navigating crises. But as Runciman reminds us, they have not been particularly astute in recognizing or avoiding such calamities — despite ample warning signs. This is because all of the "surface noise" of democratic politics often makes it hard to see real turning or tipping points.[44]

Moreover, as we get further away historically from liberal democracy's origins, our attraction to it has become driven disproportionately by a negative argument: at least our political system lets us get rid of the bad guys (every four to five years). "Democracy is the worst form of government," Churchill was said to have lamented, "except for all those other forms that have been tried from time to time."[45]

But what has happened to the positive allure of liberal democracy? Where are the voices trumpeting its capacity to bring dignity, to empower, and to build collective consciousness? Growing inequality has fostered widespread amnesia about democracy's positive, foundational values — above all the value of fairness.

FAIRNESS AND LIBERAL DEMOCRACY

The breakdown in social solidarity that afflicts many of today's liberal democracies happens at an even more micro and private level. This is because economic inequality can change individual expectations and behaviour. For those on the lower end of the scale, we know that it can sap initiative or — worse — breed grievances that can become revolutionary or violent.

For the upper echelons in society inequality often morphs into a feeling of entitlement, which can then translate into actions that further undermine social trust and common purpose. Over the past decade, groundbreaking research by behavioural psychologists illustrates how inequality actually *shifts states of mind*. In other words, there is a certain psychology to wealth and privilege.

While we all struggle in our lives with competing motivations — for example, whether to take time to help others or to focus on pursuing our own goals — professor of psychology Paul Piff and his team at the University of California have shown that the wealthier people are, the more likely they are to pursue self-interest to the detriment of others. Through dozens of experimental studies with thousands of human participants, researchers consistently found that as levels of wealth increase, feelings of entitlement also rise and levels of empathy and obligation toward others decline. Although there are always notable exceptions to this trend — we can all point to billionaire philanthropists — Piff argues that, statistically speaking, the tendency to "look out for number one" increases as a person rises to the top of the income and status hierarchy.[46] In his experiments, this phenomenon translates into a greater propensity to engage in self-regarding and unethical behaviour — including cheating to increase one's chances of winning a prize, endorsing unethical behaviour at work, or breaking the law while driving.

Consider two experiments. In the first, drivers of different types of cars are observed at a pedestrian crosswalk. In 90 percent of cases, drivers stop when they see a pedestrian nearing the intersection — *except* for those driving luxury cars. Piff's study found that the latter are almost as likely to run the intersection as they are to wait for the person to cross the street (46 percent did not stop). In a second experiment, researchers create a rigged game of Monopoly — in which one player is given more money (resources) and more dice (opportunity) — and watch how his behaviour changes relative to the other player. In game after game, Piff and his team observe that the better-off player develops a strong sense of self — he becomes louder, ruder, and less sensitive toward the other player. He also feels more entitled than his opponent to take from a plate of pretzels that is placed next to the board.

Although greed affects all people, these studies indicate that it is not present equally across all social strata. The greater resources and independence available to those at the top of the economic hierarchy have a distinct effect on their behaviour. Those with greater wealth can deal more effectively with the "downstream costs" of acting unethically, while reduced dependency makes them less concerned with others' evaluation. This combination can give rise to the positive values of greed and self-focused behaviour. Indeed, this sense of autonomy can manifest itself even in ordinary human interactions: experiments have shown that those in the high economic echelons are more disengaged in social settings — frequently doodling or checking their cellphones — and are worse at identifying and responding to the emotions of others.[47]

Behavioural psychologists have therefore

concluded that high levels of inequality facilitate behaviour that undermines social cohesion and create what Piff calls a "vicious cycle of stratification."[48] Those at the top feel more deserving than those at the bottom; having more means that you can rely less on others, leading to a reduced feeling that you owe anyone anything. This might help to explain why the wealthy tend to be more economically conservative and often object to increased taxation or public spending. To repeat: it is not just that these measures appear to work to their economic advantage; there is also a psychological element at work — a sense of entitlement which increases as perceived wealth increases. These psychological factors can then compound inequality, since the economic hierarchy largely depends upon policies and institutions over which the very wealthy have disproportionate control. For their part, those with less begin to expect the worst from their governments and leaders. And society's sense of common purpose is gradually eroded.

But there is also an upside to this story. Our psychological states and accompanying behaviours are malleable. Lab experiments have shown that the process can work in reverse. Wealthy people who are made to feel poor relative to others experience a lower sense of entitlement. Moreover, if they are asked to list three benefits of cooperating or treating others as equals, their subsequent behaviour demonstrates reduced levels of entitlement akin to those of the lower classes.[49] These results suggest that psychological interventions — what scientists call "nudges" — can potentially slow the vicious cycle of stratification. They also show that, as the philosopher Elizabeth Anderson powerfully argued, equality is a social relationship and not merely a pattern of distribution.[50] But such interventions or nudges need to be matched by supporting public policies and a new political discourse that emphasizes fairness.

Deepening economic inequality is a moral issue — it erodes individuals' capacity to see one another as worthy of respect and weakens social cohesion. Economists have demonstrated its pernicious effects on economic growth. Sociologists and medical researchers have outlined its devastating effects on health outcomes and life expectancy. And political scientists have illustrated how it undercuts the value of fairness, which is a critical foundation of liberal democracy.

I've called fairness a basic human value, but it actually extends beyond, to all primates. In a famous experiment conducted by the Dutch primatologist Frans de Waal, two capuchin monkeys were asked to do a routine job — handing a lab worker a small rock — in return for a reward. At the beginning of the experiment the monkeys fulfill their task and each gets a cucumber. They are happy to repeat the exercise twenty-five times or more for this reward. Then, the parameters are changed: Monkey A is given a piece of cucumber after completing his job, but Monkey B receives a grape (a higher-value treat for monkeys). The first monkey is initially perplexed and quickly repeats the task to see if he will receive a grape. But as the sequence is repeated, and the differential treatment continues, Monkey A becomes increasingly incensed that he receives a cucumber each time while the other monkey receives a grape. He begins to throw the cucumber at the lab worker, pound the table, and then rattle his cage in anger. It is the unfairness of it all — a different reward for the same hard work — that provokes the Monkey A into despair and, ultimately, violence.

In liberal democracies, risk and reward are designed to be shared. We are all in it together through our equal right to participate in debate and decision-making. Fairness is part of democracy's very DNA. When we compromise that basic and common moral sentiment, we also start to destroy what courageous individuals — working together — built up brick by brick. Yet there is too little willingness to talk openly about fairness in contemporary liberal democracies and to take seriously the policies that would enhance it. Centrist and left-leaning political parties flout mild redistributive policies through changes to income tax and programs to enhance the skills of the workforce. These are good ideas, in and of themselves. But they dance around the edges. All that current policies can produce, writes the *Guardian's* Paul Mason, "is the oligarch's yacht co-existing with the food bank forever."[51] Unless we are prepared to address wealth inequality, we are not changing the entrenched patterns that are undermining fairness. The economists who chronicle inequality are therefore posing more fundamental redistributive solutions, including a progressive tax on private wealth, a reverse estate tax to address one-time gains from property sales, and enforced transparency for all bank transactions.

These bolder prescriptions seem out of reach to our contemporary political class. Ultimately, however, a shift in our ways of thinking about social ills like inequality requires a deeper transformation in politics. And in a liberal democracy, if we want that deeper transformation, we have to initiate it ourselves. That is what the history of the twentieth century revealed: individuals stepping up to draw attention to injustice, to demand greater equality of participation, and to stand up for fairness. And they did so knowing that their demands would likely involve some personal sacrifice. The crises facing today's liberal democracies suggest that we need to re-read our history, to learn more about how our societies coped with both global and domestic challenges, and about the particular battles fought in the name of creating the world's best political system. And then we need to take that history into the present and give it our own modern twist.

AFTERWORD

DURING THE AUTUMN OF 2016, while travelling across Canada to deliver the Massey Lectures, I frequently received one of two responses. The first was fascination: "How did you manage to predict the future? All the trends you talked about came to a head this year." The other was frustration: "Why do you see the glass as being so half empty? Isn't the world a healthier, safer and more prosperous place than it was a hundred years ago?"

Let's deal with the first reaction. I certainly didn't have a crystal ball, or any finely honed predictive powers, when I conceived *The Return of History* in the summer of 2015. What I did have before me was a panoply of evidence, and wise commentary, that pointed to a series of global challenges that were combining in particularly potent ways. The seeds of those challenges — whether we think of protracted civil wars, governance failures, deteriorating relations between the West and Russia, or rising economic inequality — had been planted long before. But it was the complacency and overconfidence of liberal democracies that had blinded many to their potential trajectory. Moreover, it has taken time for some analysts and policy-makers to acknowledge the *interdependence* between the phenomena at the heart of my lectures. The continuation of Syria's devastating war contributed to a wave of mass flight, which in turn catalyzed nativist and anti-immigrant opinion in Europe, which then helped to fuel the electoral success of populist parties. It is ironic that at the very moment when isolationist and nationalist sentiment — *America First!* — is at its most raucous, we are witnessing in vivid colour how peoples and forces are interconnected.

And so on to the charge of pessimism. Like many, I counted down the last days of 2016. The year that had seen Brexit, the terrorist attacks on French boulevards, the election of Donald J. Trump to the U.S. presidency, and the relentless siege of the Syrian city of Aleppo, couldn't end fast enough. But while 2016 was a kind of *annus horribilis*, it has to be placed in context. The macro picture, on many social, economic, and political indicators, remains *relatively* rosy for many populations around the globe. And so we should resist the cognitive tendency to fixate on crisis, and cherish the broadly peaceful and prosperous world we inhabit.

Of course, it all depends on who you are and where you live. For civilian populations in South Sudan and Yemen, who have been subjected to indiscriminate violence and *human-made* famine, 2016 does look like a return to the conflicts of earlier centuries. For democratic activists in Turkey and Hungary, who have witnessed first hand abrupt revisions to constitutions and the closing of space for political debate and free media, 2016 does look like the year in which claims about the magnetic pull of liberal democracy have been punctured. And for the non-governmental organizations mounting search and rescue operations on the Mediterranean, who have been accused of "colluding" with smuggling networks and providing a "free ticket to Europe" for migrants, 2016 does look like the year that Western politicians completely lost sight of their humanitarian responsibilities.

SIGNS OF DEMOCRATIC REGRESS

The central goal of *The Return of History* was not to paint a canvas with one solid colour — unmitigated disaster — but rather to question the progressivist assumptions that have dominated the three decades since the end of the Cold War. The gains that have been made in the political, economic, and security realms can be reversed, and trends from the past few years suggest that forms of regress are already underway.

I'll begin at the point where I ended the book, with the state of democracy itself. The NGO Freedom House's annual report shows that in 2016 the number of countries around the world suffering net declines in political rights and civil liberties is almost double the number that has registered improvements. More troubling, Freedom House analysis indicates that this decline in the quality of democracies is no longer concentrated among autocracies and dictatorships, but has also infected countries traditionally rated "free."[1] The picture is particularly bleak if we zoom in on the area of the world associated with the greatest optimism in 1989 — the twenty-nine former communist countries that comprised the former Soviet bloc.

Over the past year, eighteen of these states saw a fall in their democracy scores, producing a situation in which there are now more consolidated authoritarian regimes in Eurasia than consolidated democracies.[2] These trends indicate that the slow diffusion of democracy to all parts of the globe is by no means a foregone conclusion. Or, to put it in Fukuyaman terms, many populations still appear to be mired in "History."

But even for those of us who have allegedly crossed the Rubicon into a post-historical era, the events of 2016 and early 2017 have brought private musings about the fate of liberal democracy into the pubic realm. Harvard University's Yascha Mounk has raised the possibility — unthinkable to most political scientists a decade ago — of "democratic deconsolidation," a process whereby the citizens of prosperous and mature democracies become positively disposed to alternative political systems (including authoritarian ones) and the key institutional features of those democracies, such as competitive party systems, become dysfunctional.[3] Deconsolidation can also be driven by the erosion of key norms and rules of behaviour typically respected and followed by prominent political players — a trend that Mounk sees as even more undermining of Western democracies than any particular illiberal policy.

Key liberal democratic countries in the West have certainly laid to rest any pretense of "leading by example," in light of the speed with which political leaders have latched onto nationalist and anti-immigration rhetoric. Over the past year, the populist temptation to play on fears about immigration had a game-changing effect on democratic elections throughout Europe, catapulting former fringe parties to the centre and mobilizing unprecedented coalitions to keep populists from power. The electoral defeat of far-right parties in the Netherlands, Austria, and France is rightly hailed as evidence that when moderates band together, and come out to vote, they can stem the populist tide. But it's crucial to read the fine print to understand how mainstream parties managed to win: it was often by co-opting elements of the nationalist trope, rather than challenging it. The post-election Dutch parliament, for example, lacks a pro-immigration majority and is likely to move away from the multiculturalist agenda of the recent past.

All of these elections laid bare what Fukuyama himself points to as a key sign of democratic decay: polarization. Democratic politics, which ensures peaceful transitions of power, both requires and is designed to foster moderation and compromise. Yet political opinion in many mature liberal democracies has become dichotomized between those who favour a continuation of a globalizing agenda (including open borders and dense webs of international cooperation) and those seeking a return to more closed, homogeneous, and self-sufficient national communities.[4] It is telling that during the French presidential campaign in the spring of 2017, one of Marine Le Pen's fiercest criticisms of her competitor, the centrist Emmanuel Macron, was that he was a "globalizer" who failed to put France's interests first. In the acrimonious television debate between the two front-runners — which French commentators unanimously declared as the most uncivil exchange between two presidential candidates in living memory — each sunk low to secure their base, with Macron describing the far-right Le Pen as a "hate-filled" liar who would bring "civil war" to France, and Le Pen characterizing her rival as a "smirking banker" who was bent on "butchering" the country.[5]

These episodes suggest that the causal relationship between polarization and democracy is complex and goes both ways: while electoral processes reveal divided opinion, they have also intensified polarization through the bitter language and imagery that they have unleashed. Brendan Cox, whose wife and former MP Jo Cox was murdered by a right-wing extremist, believes the referendum on British membership in the European Union was the moment when politicians crossed the line between showcasing passion to showcasing hate. "As soon as you tolerate hate as part of your discourse, it's very hard to put the pieces together again." During Britain's June 2017 general election, Cox devoted himself to campaigning for a change in the narrative of division dominating politics in his country, and succeeded in persuading the leaders of all the major political parties to pause their "regular programming" for an hour in order to visit an organization working to bring communities together.

The November 2016 presidential election in the United States was another high-water mark for hate-filled and uncivilized political discourse, both at traditional campaign rallies and on social media. While it is tempting to conclude that all election campaigns are raucous, the National Institute for Civil Discourse in the United States found a marked increase — even just in the period between 2012 and 2016 — in the use of bigoted and inflammatory speech, which started during the Republican primaries and carried over into the autumn run for the White House. The institute's executive director, Carolyn Lukensmeyer, maintains that while there are structural issues (including the party system) that foster division in the U.S., the particular *intensity* of the uncivilized language in 2016 was a function of the campaign itself and the individuals central to it.[6] The willingness of figures such as Donald Trump to use phrases such as "liar" or "lock her up" in reference to his opponent, and to identify subgroups of the population and characterize them in derogatory ways, legitimized divisive language and moved it from the fringes into the mainstream. As the writer Jonathan Rauch aptly puts it, Trump has not just crossed a line — in terms of standards of public conduct and discourse — but seems to have "erased a line."[7]

Those skeptical of the impact of Trump's language have often reacted with the following refrain: "Well, he is simply saying out loud what many are privately thinking." This is no doubt true, but it misses the point — in two crucial ways. First, views that are uttered "out in the open" can serve to license broader patterns of behaviour. As the philosopher Suzy Killmister explains, extremist language "has the power to alter the relations in which citizens stand to one another." Public expressions of bigotry or scapegoating affect "who is welcome in a community . . . and against whom violence can be inflicted."[8] Second, leadership carries with it responsibilities; while views expressed by an "ordinary citizen" at a dinner party may have limited impact, public figures have the potential to shape the actions of a huge number of followers. Hence, those who have suggested that Trump's words shouldn't garner so much attention, and that he often doesn't "really" mean what he says, are legitimizing a dangerous decline in expectations about the conduct of public officials.

Many political analysts, by contrast, have pointed to the strategic purpose of Donald Trump's language — namely, to actively leverage and sow division. As I illustrated in *The Return of History*, Trump-the-candidate preyed upon the disenchantment of those who had either experienced or perceived a decline in their living standards and/or social status, and depicted them as the innocent victims of a cast of villains produced by globalization: Mexican immigrants, Muslim refugees, and Chinese trade imbalances. Little wonder, then, that we awoke the day after the election not only to a

Trump victory but also to a deeply fractured society. Support for the Democratic candidate Hillary
Clinton, who won a greater share of the popular
vote, was concentrated in cities along the coastlines
of the United States; Trump, by contrast, soared to
victory on the backs of rural America and small
towns. While Barack Obama had partially transcended that division by bringing unprecedented
numbers out to vote for the Democrats, Clinton
could not mobilize beyond her base. Trump's campaign skilfully captured those parts of the country that had been badly hit by globalization's
pressure to outsource and find efficiencies, including Pennsylvania, Michigan, and Wisconsin. Had
Clinton been able to marginally increase her share
of the vote and win those three states — which had
all previously voted Democrat — she would have
become president. But this victory would not itself
have addressed the clashing worldviews and institutional deadlock that mark contemporary U.S. liberal democracy. She too would have presided over
a divided country.

Any hope that the forty-fifth U.S. President would
seek to bring Americans together, and govern on
behalf of all of them, was crushed by his inaugural
address on January 20, 2017. Trump-the-President

conjured up a grim dystopia, where once-hardworking Americans had been betrayed by the "establishment" in the country's capital, leading to poverty, "rusted-out factories," gangs, and widespread crime. In pledging to end this "American carnage," Trump proclaimed that his inauguration marked the day when "the people became the rulers of this nation again." But as his first months of office have shown, his governing agenda is aimed squarely at one slice of that "people," as he systematically attempts to reverse key planks of the Obama administration and continues to demonize key segments of American society — most notably the mainstream media, whom he decries as producers of "fake news," and migrants and refugees, whom he depicts as criminals and "infiltrators."[9]

The first few weeks and months of the new U.S. administration also seem to confirm Fukuyama's observation that Trump has taken an "à la carte" approach to the political system that triumphed at the end of the Cold War. While the president "gets the democracy part" — the adoring crowds at his rallies who stand for "the people" — he doesn't "get the liberal part" — the rules and institutions that are designed to constrain the exercise of power and ensure good and wise governance.[10] After disparaging the "so-called judge" who issued a nationwide halt to the new administration's immigration restrictions for citizens of seven mainly Muslim countries, Trump has continued to complain about the alleged political agenda of members of the federal U.S. judiciary. Even Trump's own nominee to the Supreme Court, Neil Gorsuch, is reported to have criticized the president's comments as "demoralizing."[11]

From where we stand today, it is difficult to predict the trajectory of liberal democracy. As I explained in *The Return of History*, its historical development was full of fits and starts; the diffusion of democracy in one era was followed by regress in another. Some argue that the very fact that liberal democracy is no longer viewed as "the only game in town" is a serious warning sign.[12] If alternative political systems come to have global appeal, contradicting Fukuyama's end-of-history thesis, there could come a point at which liberal democracy experiences a fundamental crisis of legitimacy. Others predict that the body-blow levelled at liberal democracy by the populist challenge could prompt a productive response: liberal democracy will bounce back in a more robust and appealing form. Roula Khalaf, deputy editor of the *Financial*

Times and a seasoned observer of the Middle East, presented this more positive scenario in the run-up to the French presidential elections. Drawing on the idea of "fertile regression" — coined by the Algerian sociologist Lahouari Addi in reference to reversals of democratization in North Africa — Khalaf suggests that the populist moment could prove to be a temporary setback. By reaching positions of power, she speculates, populists will demonstrate their inability to govern and their ideology will quickly lose its appeal: "Maybe the quicker the populists govern the faster they will self-destruct."[13]

This kind of optimism could play a productive role in "populist-proofing" liberal democracy, provided it doesn't breed further complacency. Indeed, a central aim of *The Return of History* was to shake liberal democrats out of their post–Cold War over-confidence. By assuming that our political system could have no rival, and could withstand any crisis, we failed to address — and through explicit policy choices continued to reinforce — deepening inequality and disengagement from the institutions of representative democracy. Is 2016 the year that, to borrow David Runciman's metaphor, liberal democrats — having looked down at the abyss — pull back from the edge of the cliff?[14]

In order for today's regression to become "fertile," citizens of liberal democracies, especially in the United States, need to do more than express disdain for particular policies — as unpalatable or dangerous as those policies may appear. They also need to understand and respond to the ways in which populists such as Donald Trump can more generally undermine liberal democracy's foundations. In his analysis of President Trump's early tenure, Jonathan Rauch concludes that it is difficult to pinpoint a "turn" to authoritarianism through a particular action, especially since some of these behaviours, such as the sweeping use of presidential power or attempted circumvention of judicial processes, have also been undertaken by previous occupants of the Oval Office. "Authoritarianism lies not in any individual presidential action but in the pattern of actions" that emerge over time. Moreover, Rauch writes, it depends "not just on the action itself but on how everyone else responds to it."[15]

As a result of the Trump victory, some observers already see a "course correction" in the United States. Ordinary citizens have become politicized — in some cases for the first time — and the institutions that make up America's intricate system of checks and balances, particularly local and national courts, are acting out the script proposed by the Founding Fathers. Civil society organizations that play a watchdog function, such as the American Civil Liberties Union, have seen a surge in donations and increased support for their activities. Yascha Mounk's new organization, After Trump, is reinforcing these efforts by using crowd-sourcing to monitor potential illiberal actions by the Trump administration. But he also hints at a concern I raised in my final Massey Lecture: the tendency for liberal democracy's defence to rest on critique and negative arguments. For the populist challenge to be temporary, individual citizens, activists, and elites also need to make the positive case for how liberal democracy can empower and deliver "good government." In addition, they need to paint "a positive vision of what politics can be after Trump."[16]

I suggested in *The Return of History* that a central element of liberal democracy's regeneration must be the tackling — head on — of unsustainable levels of economic inequality. Predatory capitalism and high degrees of economic and social stratification, I suggested, were not inevitable features of our system but the product of conscious policy choices.

Some readers and listeners disagreed passionately with that premise. They protested that liberal democracy has always had profound deformities at its very core that produce what C. B. Macpherson memorably called "possessive individualism."[17] In other words, excessive economic competition and inequality, and the breakdown in social cohesion are "what you sign up for" when you embrace liberal democracy. This critique of my book and lectures is in many ways the hardest-hitting argument, and I will continue to contemplate and grapple with it in the months and years ahead.

Macpherson's *The Real World of Democracy*, based on his 1964 Massey Lectures, was the first politics book I encountered, as a wide-eyed undergraduate in Political Science 101. I looked at it again just before I delivered my own first Massey Lecture in Winnipeg, and I was stunned by the enduring relevance of his observations and worries about the state of liberal democracy.[18] Macpherson identified capitalism as the key culprit in the crisis facing liberal democracy in his era, and his political project, delivered over a lifetime, was to try and "rescue" the political values of liberalism from their close association with capitalist market relations. Despite sharing some features of Macpherson's vision and intuition, I have argued that predatory capitalism and "possessive individualism" are not the only form that liberal democracy's economic system can take. Other historical periods have delivered, and other democratic jurisdictions around the world currently deliver, high levels of growth and prosperity with lower levels of economic inequality and better social outcomes.

In claiming the possibility of a different version of liberal democracy, and that the twenty-first century populist challenges may prove "fertile," I open myself to the charge (already expressed by some) that I am engaged in a futile exercise — that the circle cannot be squared. But I was reminded of the importance of seeing liberalism in a broader context, beyond its particular modern and "neo-liberal" economic form, when re-reading the man widely regarded as the founding father of capitalism, the late eighteenth-century economist Adam Smith. In spite of his reputation as a heartless advocate of laissez-faire economics, Smith voiced concern about the capacity for extreme economic inequality to distort citizens' "sympathies" and undermine their ability to identify with those less well off. He believed this, in turn, would corrupt the common "moral sentiments" necessary for a healthy society.[19] The contemporary research of behavioural psychologists that I profiled in *The Return of History* builds directly on Smith's observation, by demonstrating empirically how high levels of inequality can alter states of mind and interpersonal relations. Any effort to reinvigorate twenty-first century liberal democracy needs to disrupt the vicious circle of stratification created by the historically high levels of economic inequality and address the deeper erosion of our common moral sentiments.

A TROUBLED RELATIONSHIP

I began my Massey Lectures with a nostalgic look back at the jubilant days following the fall of the Berlin Wall, and the historic shift in relations it facilitated between East and West. By the same token, one of the most palpable signs of history's return has been the rapid deterioration of the West's relationship with post-Soviet Russia and the revival of Cold War–era rhetoric.

Nonetheless, one of the core arguments I advanced in *The Return of History* is that we are not necessarily experiencing Cold War 2.0. History never fully repeats itself. There are significant differences between the ideological confrontation between rival systems that dominated the decades after the Second World War, and the geopolitical competition we witness today in particular regions of the world. Most importantly, the status and might of the two key players — Russia and the United States — are nowhere near as evenly matched as they were during the original Cold War. To begin with, there remains a huge imbalance in material power in favour of the United States, which constrains the degree to which Russia could ever mount what writer Tony Wood calls a "frontal challenge to the West." In addition, President Putin's particular brand of authoritarianism lacks universal appeal: it is designed as a domestic rather than "export product."[20]

Here, however, I'd like to sound two cautionary notes about the current state of Russia-West relations.

First, while we may not be living in a new Cold War, Western and Russian leaders could still create one. In other words, it could become a self-fulfilling prophecy. The highly regarded analyst of U.S.-Russian relations Robert Legvold believes the key danger today lies in the fact that both American and Russian officials are mired in the blame game. They are fixated on the negative essence of the other, rather than the broader set of relations between the two countries and the costs of letting them deteriorate further. As a result, they are too quick to conclude that the relationship between Russia and the West can only be transactional — based on a series of one-off agreements — rather than one that both looks for and builds on some common ground.[21] These common interests include, for example, the United States and Russia exercising joint leadership over an increasingly multi-polar nuclear world, where more states have nuclear capability, as well as the need to cooperatively manage the power transition in Asia and potential conflict between Japan and China. The two countries also have a shared interest — even if they can't yet articulate it — in working to promote stable political change in and around the Middle East and the Caucasus, and in cooperating over security and economic development of the Arctic.

The second note of caution is directed solely at the West, and concerns the tendency to overestimate Russia's potential to "win" decisively in today's geopolitical competition. As Wood rightly observes, there is a tendency within Western policy-making circles to conflate how much raw power Russia actually has by pointing to the diplomatic and military results President Putin has managed to achieve by strategically deploying it.[22] Recent experience shows that he plays the cards he has been dealt to maximum effect, thus enabling Russia to "punch well above its weight." This should remind us that success in international politics derives not only from capacity but also from will: while Russia has a much smaller military, its willingness to deploy it decisively in Syria has allowed it to shift the direction of the conflict in its favour. But it is worth noting that Russia's use of military force is often a function of its inability to advance its interests in other ways — for example, through diplomatic persuasion or economic pressure.

The transition from the Obama to the Trump presidency has yet to provide a clear and consistent indication of how the United States intends to manage its troubled relationship with Russia. Trump-the-candidate frequently voiced his admiration for Putin's decisive style of leadership, and the president's choice for secretary of state, Rex Tillerson, initially promised a more "business-like" approach to the bilateral relationship, based on shared interests. On the other hand, members of the administration appear to have heeded the warnings of prominent Republican members of the U.S. Senate, including John McCain, who continue to advocate a tough stance against Russia, particularly in relation to its actions in Ukraine.

Moscow has undoubtedly upped the ante. In the autumn of 2016, credible evidence emerged of Russian interference in the electoral processes of Western countries, including the United States. Officials from the CIA, FBI, and National Security Agency have since issued a report declaring that Russian hackers accessed the servers of both of the main political parties and released damaging information about the Democratic Party. To be sure, foreign meddling in democratic elections is not a new phenomenon. The old KGB was instructed to employ "active measures" during the re-election campaign of Ronald Reagan in 1982, which included efforts to discredit the incumbent president as a pawn of military lobbyists. The U.S. also worked actively during the Cold War to overthrow regimes hostile to its interests (such as Cuba and Chile) and used both cash and propaganda to sway elections away from leftist parties in Italy, Indonesia, and Nicaragua.[23] But the digital era is proving particularly conducive to the game of undermining democratic processes, and its powerful tools are available to both state and non-state actors.

If the allegations that Russian interference is

government-sponsored prove to be well-founded (which at the time of writing has yet to be definitively proven), then the question of Putin's motives becomes all the more pertinent. On the face of it, the goal appears to be straightforward: President Putin made no secret of his disdain for Hillary Clinton and admiration for Donald Trump. Aiding the latter's victory was a way for the Russian leader to elevate a counterpart in Washington that would be ready to acknowledge Moscow's legitimate interests. The claims that have surfaced about contacts between the Kremlin and key members of Trump's campaign team — including former National Security Advisor Michael Flynn — give added weight to the story that Putin was seeking to reverse the punitive policies against Russia that marked the late Obama years (including economic sanctions) and to establish a more transactional relationship with the United States.

But there is another possible motive, which extends beyond the specifics of the Putin-Trump relationship and cuts to the vulnerability of contemporary liberal democracies. The hacking into party servers and disruption of democratic processes may also be designed to sow seeds of doubt about the robustness of liberal democratic institutions themselves. The wave of cyber-attacks on Emmanuel Macron's campaign in April 2017 coincided with a period in which dominant political parties in France were coming apart at the seams and overall trust in government was at historic lows. Some analysts thus speculate that the hacking was designed to accentuate the crisis of confidence and propose the "Russian model"—the strong state—as the solution.[24]

CRACKS — OR DEEP HOLES? — IN THE LIBERAL INTERNATIONAL ORDER

The costs of a worsening relationship between Russia and the West have already proven to be significant. One of the biggest casualties, as I suggested in *The Return of History*, has been the functioning of the collective security system of the United Nations, which depends on cooperation between major powers and a search for common ground. The final battle over Syria's largest city, Aleppo, which raged from July to December 2016, vividly demonstrated the impact of the Security Council's failure to discharge its responsibilities under the United Nations Charter—not just on high-politics as they play out in New York, but also on the fate of civilian populations.

Although the civil war in Syria had been raging and metastasizing for years, it commenced one of its grimmest chapters in the summer of 2016, when the long stalemate between government and oppositions forces was finally broken and Syrian government troops closed the rebels' last supply line into Aleppo (with the help of Russian airstrikes). This produced one of the longest sieges in the history of modern warfare — despite a series of counter-offensives by the opposition to break the stranglehold — and by many accounts the bloodiest battles of an already vicious civil war. Roughly 31,000 people died during the siege (one-tenth of all casualties thus far in the war), through the combined effects of explosions, shelling, barrel bombs and other aerial bombardment, field executions, and chemical attacks. While the UN's Commission of Inquiry for Syria continues to document instances of war crimes committed by both sides, its February 2017 report analyzed one particularly shocking attack by Syrian government forces on an aid convoy in the Aleppo countryside in September 2016, which killed more than a dozen aid workers and denied vital supplies to thousands of civilians in need. The

Commissioners condemned the attack — which included a grisly combination of helicopters loaded with barrel bombs, jet fighters, and the spraying of machine-gun fire — and concluded that the incident was "meticulously planned" as part of a broader policy of "starve-or-surrender" toward opposition-held areas. [25] Hospitals, schools, and marketplaces were also routinely hit during the siege, prompting the United Nations High Commissioner for Human Rights, Zeid Ra'ad Al Hussein, to characterize the abuses in Aleppo as constituting "crimes of historic proportions."[26] Those who managed to survive faced extortionately high prices for scarce food, medicines, and fuels, and endured medieval-like living conditions.

In December 2016, in the face of the almost complete collapse of rebel forces, the Syrian government initiated a campaign that would ultimately result in its triumphant recapturing of the city. On December 13, a ceasefire was announced, and the evacuation of populations from opposition areas of the city was organized and communicated. Yet the plan unfolded in fits and starts, with three failed attempts, sending frightened residents back to their homes and UN offices receiving credible reports of scores of civilians — suspected of being rebel sympathizers — being killed by summary execution.[27] On December 16, in his last press conference as UN secretary general, Ban Ki-moon summed up this spectacle of twenty-first century barbarism by declaring, "Aleppo is now a synonym for hell." Finally, on a cold day in the week before Christmas, the evacuation of the population of rebel-held Eastern Aleppo was completed, in a process that some critics have called an illegal instance of forced displacement.

The sordid episode of the Aleppo siege and evacuation all took place under the watchful eye of the UN Security Council. As the body designated with the primary responsibility for managing international peace and security, the Council has faced intensifying criticism, going back to the autumn of 2011, for its failure to produce a robust response to the documented commission of international crimes that have taken place in Syria, the flow of refugees into neighbouring states, and the ever-widening regional instability produced by the war. Permanent members of the Council, most notably Russia and China, have reverted to the old Cold War practice of vetoing resolutions designed to address the Syrian crisis, often describing the tabled draft resolutions as politically motivated or designed to give victory to one side in the war. The reasons behind the lack of cooperation and mutual recrimination, which are broader than the Syrian crisis itself, cannot be fully rehearsed here. But in short, they stem partly from the impact of past military interventions by both the U.S. and Russia — and the suspicions they have aroused; mistakes and miscalculations in each side's foreign policies in the Middle East; and a general breakdown in consensus with respect to the legitimacy of third-party involvement in internal unrest and civil war in another state.

But even when assessed against the low expectations that had been set by five years of unproductive bickering and name-calling in the Council, the inability of the permanent members to mount an effective response to the siege was a colossal abdication of responsibility. Veteran UN observer Richard Gowan referred to the vain attempts by Western members of the Security Council to lift the siege of Aleppo as "end times diplomacy" — desperate measures to try to alter an impending outcome (in this case, the fall of Aleppo). They were also a sign that cooperation to address peace and security challenges had all but collapsed.[28] When it became clear that Russia's verbal support for a ceasefire in the halls of the UN in New York was a smokescreen for its actions on the ground in Syria — where it saw an opportunity for a military victory that would avoid the need to compromise with the West over the political terms of a peaceful settlement — the only weapon that seemed to be left in the arsenal of U.S., British, and French diplomats was moral condemnation. In the tense Security Council debate that took place on December 13, in the midst of intense fighting in Aleppo, U.S. Permanent Representative Samantha Power rhetorically asked whether the Assad regime and its supporters, Russia and Iran, were "truly incapable of shame." But her Russian counterpart, Vitaly Churkin, shrugged off the critique as hypocritical American grandstanding. "She gave her speech," he retorted, "as if she were Mother Teresa herself."[29]

The frequent public clashes in the Security Council chamber revealed the uncomfortable truth that, ultimately, Russia and Western powers had conflicting objectives. And this is a reality that even the UN Charter cannot fix. In December 2014, bilateral negotiations between Moscow and Washington had led to Security Council Resolution 2254, which outlined a ceasefire and parallel political process to end the Syrian conflict. Western governments believed the resolution would produce a political outcome that would decrease Assad's influence in Syria — even if it would not eliminate it (as some had wanted at the start of the war). But Moscow's later support for the Syrian government's drive for Aleppo seemed to erase that possibility. As Gowan explains in intriguing detail, members of the outgoing Obama administration, including Samantha Power, confronted a two-part defeat: they were not only fearful of the fall of Aleppo, but of an incoming U.S. government that would be pro-Moscow and even more likely to negotiate an end to the war on Russia's terms — something Obama-era officials had worked painstakingly to avoid. Hence their embrace of "end times" diplomatic measures.[30]

The broader worry, however, is that the failure to find common ground and to fashion diplomatic solutions in Syria will spread beyond this particular "hard case" to crises in other parts of the globe where there is a similar call for the Security Council to manage peace and security. Even just four years ago, the contagion appeared to be limited: the Council still managed to pass resolutions and mount responses to instability in countries such as Mali and the Central African Republic.

But there are more recent signs that the deep mistrust is now infecting almost every item on the Council's agenda, as it did sixty years ago during the height of the Cold War. The UN's new chief, António Guterres, is encountering more limited political support for some of the organization's more ambitious normative agendas, such as the protection of civilians or human rights promotion. In the new international climate, the secretary general's greatest contribution may be the more traditional one envisaged in the original UN Charter: using his "good offices" to mediate between parties to a dispute.

The breakdown in cooperation among the major powers, which limits the capacity of institutions such as the United Nations to prevent or to help resolve conflict, appears all the more consequential if we consider the projections about peace and security in the next decades. According to the World Bank, two billion of the world's people now live in countries where development outcomes — and particularly the Sustainable Development Goals — are negatively affected by state fragility, conflict, and violence. And by the year 2030, the share of the global poor living in fragile and conflict-affected areas will reach a staggering 46 percent (up from

17 percent today).[31] Indeed, as I noted in *The Return of History*, violent conflict has spiked since 2010 and its impact on civilian populations has increased in terms of lethality. Conflicts currently drive 80 percent of all humanitarian needs worldwide, and in several cases — including South Sudan, Yemen, Somalia, and Nigeria — war is creating extensive famine.[32] Given the projections about proportions of conflict-affected populations, these human-made disasters are likely to intensify.

What makes the challenging diplomatic landscape different from earlier periods is that one of the key architects of the post-war international order, the United States, appears decidedly ambivalent about the value and purpose of that order. Washington has announced the U.S. withdrawal from the UN Population Fund, and President Trump and his advisors have given strong indications that they will significantly cut contributions to the UN budget. Historically minded observers of the UN, like David Bosco, remind us that "we've been here before": Republican politicians have long questioned the effectiveness of the United Nations, condemned its "bloated" bureaucracy, and derided its embrace of non-democratic regimes. However, Trump's disdain for multilateralism is both broader and deeper than what Bosco refers to as "garden variety Republican skepticism."[33] It extends to regional trade agreements like NAFTA, the World Trade Organization, and even NATO — the pillar of the transatlantic relationship. And it is underpinned by a short-term and transactional approach to solving global problems — one that is framed through the prism of winners and losers, rather than recognizing the virtue of compromise and mutual restraint in the name of a more equitable and more durable solution.

It was a telling sign of the divisions within the transatlantic alliance that at the summit of NATO leaders in late May 2017, Donald Trump came with a hard-hitting speech dedicated to chastising his fellow alliance members for falling short in their financial contributions, while German Chancellor Angela Merkel arrived with a chunk of the Berlin Wall to symbolize the alliance's long history in protecting and expanding liberal democracy. It is clear that the idea of "the West," which shaped the expectations of policy-makers and diplomats for more than five decades and which celebrated triumph at the end of the Cold War, is experiencing a serious crisis of identity and joint purpose — just as the generation that gave it meaning is fading away. But it is also facing a very different global distribution of power and an unstable and unpredictable world that is part of its own making. As C. B. Macpherson wrote at the start of his Massey Lectures, "Liberal-democratic nations can no longer expect to run the world, nor can they expect that the world will run to them."[34] The 1989 victory of Western liberal democracy is starting to look more and more like ancient history.

NOTES

CHAPTER 1: THE RETURN OF HISTORY

1. Timothy Garton Ash, *The Magic Lantern: The Revolution of 1989 Witnessed in Warsaw, Budapest, Berlin and Prague* (London, U.K.: Random House, 1990), p. 62.

2. Francis Fukuyama, "The End of History," *National Interest* (Summer 1989).

3. *An Agenda for Peace,* Report of the Secretary General, UN doc. A/47/277, 17 June 1992.

4. Francis Fukuyama, "The End of History," *National Interest* (Summer 1989).

5. See, for example, one of the earliest theorists of the sovereign state: Jean Bodin, *Les six livres de la République (The Six Bookes of a Commonweale),* edited by Christiane Frémont, Marie-Dominique Couzinet and Henri Rochais (Paris: Librairie Arthème Fayard, 1986), Book I, Chapters 8 and 10.

6. James Madison, Federalist Paper No. 10, "The Same Subject Continued: The Union as a Safeguard Against Domestic Faction and Insurrection," November 23, 1787. Available at: https://www.congress.gov/resources/display/content/The+Federalist+Papers#TheFederalistPapers-10

7. John Dunn, *Setting the People Free: The Story of Democracy* (London, U.K.: Atlantic Books, 2005).

8. Jean-Jacques Rousseau, *The Social Contract*, edited by Maurice Cranston (New York: Penguin Classics, 1968), Book I, Chapter 6.

9. Christian Reus-Smit, *The Moral Purpose of the State* (Princeton, NJ: Princeton University Press, 1999), p. 128.

10. Lynn Festa, "Humanity without Feathers," *Humanity: An International Journal of Human Rights, Humanitarianism, and Development*, Vol. 1, No. 1 (2010), pp. 3–27.

11. Jonathan Israel, *A Revolution of the Mind: Radical Enlightenment and the Intellectual Origins of Modern Democracy* (Princeton, NJ: Princeton University Press, 2010).

12. Lynn Festa, "Humanity without Feathers," *Humanity: An International Journal of Human Rights, Humanitarianism, and Development*, Vol. 1, No. 1 (2010), pp. 3–27.

13. The analysis here uses Our World in Data information, compiled at the University of Oxford. Available at https://ourworldindata.org/democratisation/

14. Robert Kagan, "Is Democracy in Decline?: The Weight of Geopolitics," *Journal of Democracy*, Vol. 26, No. 1 (2015), p. 23.

15. Ibid., p. 23.

16. Samuel P. Huntington, *The Third Wave: Democratization in the Late Twentieth Century* (Norman, OK: University of Oklahoma Press, 1991).

17. John Dunn, *Setting the People Free: The Story of Democracy* (London, U.K.: Atlantic Books, 2005).

18. Samuel P. Huntington, *The Third Wave: Democratization in the Late Twentieth Century* (Norman, OK: University of Oklahoma Press, 1991).

19. Robert Kagan, "Is Democracy in Decline?: The Weight of Geopolitics," *Journal of Democracy*, Vol. 26, No. 1 (2015), p. 27.

20. Francis Fukuyama, "The End of History," *National Interest* (Summer 1989).

21. Eliane Glaser, "Bring Back Ideology," *Guardian*, 21 March 2014.

22. Walter Russell Mead, "The Return of Geopolitics," *Foreign Affairs*, May/June 2014.

23. The number of displaced is the highest since the records tracking displacement began. See United Nations High Commissioner for Refugees, "Global Trends 2015," available at http://www.unhcr.org/news/latest/2016/6/5763b65a4/global-forced-displacement-hits-record-high.html

24. Timothy Garton Ash, "Europe's Walls Are Going Back Up — It's Like 1989 In Reverse," *Guardian*, 29 November 2015.

25. Francis Fukuyama, "At the 'End of History' Still Stands Democracy," *Wall Street Journal*, 6 June 2014.

26. *Freedom in the World 2016*. Full report available at https://freedomhouse.org/report/freedom-world/freedom-world-2016

27. Larry Diamond, "Facing Up to the Democratic Recession," *Journal of Democracy*, Vol. 26, No. 1 (January 2015), pp. 141–155.

28. Michelle Shephard, "The Daesh Files: Database Provides Snapshot of Recruits," *Toronto Star*, 30 May 2016. Available at https://www.thestar.com/news/atkinsonseries/generation911/2016/05/30/the-daesh-files-database-provides-snapshot-of-recruits.html

29. Fareed Zakaria, "The Rise of Illiberal Democracy," *Foreign Affairs*, Vol. 76, No. 6 (1997), pp. 22–43.

30. Ibid., p. 40.

31. Sidney Verba, "Fairness, Equality, and Democracy: Three Big Words," *Social Research*, Vol. 73, No. 2 (2006), pp. 499–540.

32. OECD, *Focus on Inequality and Growth*, December 2014.

33. Thomas Piketty, *Capital in the Twenty-First Century*, translated by Arthur Goldhammer (Cambridge, MA: The Belknap Press of Harvard University Press, 2014).

34. Institute for International Strategic Studies, *Armed Conflict Survey 2015*. Available at: https://www.iiss.org/en/topics/armed-conflict-survey/armed-conflict-survey-2015-46e5

35. Eric Melander, "Organized Violence in the World 2015: An Assessment by the Uppsala Conflict Data Program," Uppsala, 2015. Available at: http://www.pcr.uu.se/data/overview_ucdp_data/

36. "Civilians Under Fire," *Interaction*, Policy Brief, February 2016. Available at http://www.interaction.org

37. Walter Russell Mead, "The Return of Geopolitics," *Foreign Affairs*, May/June 2014. Available at https://www.foreignaffairs.com/articles/china/2014-04-17/return-geopolitics

38. Ibid.

39. William McCants, *The ISIS Apocalypse: The History, Strategy and Doomsday Vision of the Islamic State* (New York: St. Martin's Press, 2015).

40. Aatish Taseer, "The Return of History," *International New York Times*, 12–13 December 2015.

41. Francis Fukuyama, "At the 'End of History' Still Stands Democracy," *Wall Street Journal*, 6 June 2014. Available at: http://www.wsj.com/articles/at-the-end-of-history-still-stands-democracy-1402080661

42. Robert Kagan, "Is Democracy in Decline?: The Weight of Geopolitics," *Journal of Democracy*, Vol. 26, No. 1 (2015), p. 23.

43. This story is recounted by Timothy Garton Ash in "1989!," *New York Review of Books*, October 2009.

44. Mary Elise Sarotte, *1989: The Struggle to Create Post-Cold War Europe* (Princeton, NJ: Princeton University Press, 2009).

45. Michael Meyer, *The Year that Changed the World: The Untold Story Behind the Fall of the Berlin Wall* (New York: Simon and Schuster, 2009).

46. David Runciman, *The Confidence Trap: A History of Democracy in Crisis from World War I to the Present* (Princeton, NJ: Princeton University Press, 2014).

CHAPTER 2: THE RETURN OF BARBARISM

1. "'Our Generation is Gone'—The Islamic State's Targeting of Iraqi Minorities in Ninewa," *Bearing Witness* Trip Report, U.S. Holocaust Memorial Museum and Simon-Skjodt Center for the Prevention of Genocide, November 2015.

2. *The Global Terrorism Index 2015*, Institute for Economics and Peace. Available at http://economicsandpeace.org/wp-content/uploads/2015/11/Global-Terrorism-Index-2015.pdf

3.   Sheri Berman, "In Political Development, No Gain Without Pain," *Foreign Affairs*, January/February 2013.

4.   *The Iraq Inquiry*, July 2016. Full report available at http://www. iraqinquiry.org.uk.

5.   Report of the United Nations Office of the High Commissioner for Human Rights on the human rights situation in Iraq in light of abuses committed by the so-called Islamic State in Iraq and the Levant and associated groups, A/HRC/28/18, 13 March 2015.

6.   Hugo Slim, *Killing Civilians: Method, Madness and Morality in War* (London: Hurst, 2007).

7.   Richard Tuck, *The Rights of War and Peace: Political Theory and the International Order from Grotius to Kant* (Oxford, U.K.: Oxford University Press, 1999).

8.   John Fabian Witt, "Two Conceptions of Suffering in War," in Austrian Sarat, ed., *Knowing the Suffering of Others* (Tuscaloosa: University of Alabama Press, 2014), pp. 129–157.

9.   Hugo Slim, "Civilians, Distinction and the Compassionate View of War," in Marc Weller, Haidi Willmot, and Ralph Mamiya, eds., *The Protection of Civilians in International Law* (Oxford, U.K.: Oxford University Press, 2015).

10. John Fabian Witt, *Lincoln's Code: The Laws of War in American History* (New York: Free Press, 2012).

11. Graeme Wood, "What ISIS Really Wants," *The Atlantic*, 15 March 2015. Available at: http://www.theatlantic.com/magazine/archive/2015/03/what-isis-really-wants/384980/

12. Bernard Haykel, cited in Ibid.

13. James Meek, "After the Vote," *London Review of Books*, Vol. 37, No. 24 (December 2015).

14. Graeme Wood, "What ISIS Really Wants," *The Atlantic*, 15 March 2015. http://www.theatlantic.com/magazine/archive/2015/03/what-isis-really-wants/384980/

15. Margaret Coker, "How Islamic State's Win in Ramadi Reveals New Weapons, Tactical Sophistication and Prowess," *Wall Street Journal*, 25 May 2015.

16. Rukmini Callimachi, "To Maintain Supply of Sex Slaves, ISIS Pushes Birth Control," *New York Times*, 12 March 2016.

17. Plan of Action to Prevent Violent Extremism, Report of the United Nations Secretary General, UN doc. A/70/674, 24 December 2015.

18. David Malet, *Foreign Fighters: Transnational Identity in Civil Conflicts* (New York: Oxford University Press, 2013).

19. Olivier Roy, "What Is the Driving Force Behind Jihadi Terrorism?" Paper presented to the Bundeskriminalamt Autumn Conference, Mainz, Germany, 18–19 November 2015.

20. See *The Iraq Inquiry*, at http://www.iraqinquiry.org.uk.

21. Adam Hanieh, "A Brief History of ISIS," *Jacobin*, 3 December 2015. Available at: https://www.jacobinmag.com/2015/12/isis-syria-iraq-war-al-qaeda-arab-spring/

22. Hugo Slim, "Civilians, Distinction and the Compassionate View of War," in Marc Weller, Haidi Willmot, and Ralph Mamiya, eds., *The Protection of Civilians in International Law* (Oxford, U.K.: Oxford University Press, 2015).

23. International Committee of the Red Cross, "Interpretive Guidance on the Notion of Direct Participation in Hostilities under International Humanitarian Law," (Geneva, 2009).

24. "Attacks on Ghouta: Analysis of Alleged Use of Chemical Weapons in Syria," *Human Rights Watch*, 10 September 2013.

25. "United Nations Mission to Investigate Allegations of the Use of Chemical Weapons in the Syrian Arab Republic — Report on the Alleged Use of Chemical Weapons in the Ghouta Area of Damascus on 21 August 2013." UN doc A/67/997, 16 September 2013. Available at http://www.un.org/zh/focus/northafrica/cwinvestigation.pdf

26. Secretary-General's remarks to the Security Council on the report of the United Nations Missions to Investigate Allegations of the Use of Chemical Weapons on the incident that occurred on 21 August 2013 in the Ghouta area of Damascus, 16 September 2013. Available at: http://www.un.org/sg/statements/index.asp?nid=7083

27. "Syria/Syrian Chemical Programme — National Executive Summary of Declassified Intelligence," Paris, France, 3 September 2013. Available at: http://www.diplomatie.gouv.fr/en/IMG/pdf/Syrian_Chemical_Programme.pdf

28. "Syria Chemical Attack: What We Know," BBC News, 24 September 2013. Available at: http://www.bbc.com/news/world-middle-east-23927399

29. Cited in George H. Cassar, *Hell in Flanders: Canadians at the Second Battle of Ypres* (Toronto: Dundurn, 2010).

30. "One Humanity: Shared Responsibility." Report of the Secretary-General for the World Humanitarian Summit (A/70/709), para 23.

31. Helen Durham, "Atrocities in conflict mean we need the Geneva Conventions more than ever," *Guardian*, 5 May 2016.

32. Hugo Slim, "Civilians, Distinction and the Compassionate View of War," in Marc Weller, Haidi Willmot, and Ralph Mamiya, eds.,

The Protection of Civilians in International Law (Oxford, U.K.: Oxford University Press, 2015).

33. Anna Reid, *Leningrad: Tragedy of a City Under Siege, 1941–1944* (London, U.K.: Bloomsbury, 2011).

CHAPTER 3: THE RETURN OF MASS FLIGHT

1. http://www.theguardian.com/world/2015/dec/31/alan-kurdi-death-canada-refugee-policy-syria-boy-beach-turkey-photo?CMP=fb_gu

2. http://www.theguardian.com/world/2015/sep/03/refugee-crisis-friends-and-family-fill-in-gaps-behind-harrowing-images

3. http://www.theguardian.com/world/2015/dec/31/alan-kurdi-death-canada-refugee-policy-syria-boy-beach-turkey-photo?CMP=fb_gu

4. http://www.ctvnews.ca/world/they-were-all-dead-abdullah-kurdi-describes-losing-his-family-at-sea-1.2546299

5. http://www.npr.org/sections/thetwo-way/2015/11/28/457697276/relatives-of-drowned-syrian-boy-will-move-to-canada

6. *UNHCR Global Trends: Forced Displacement in 2015.* Available at https://s3.amazonaws.com/unhcrsharedmedia/2016/2016-06-20-global-trends/2016-06-14-Global-Trends-2015.pdf

7. http://missingmigrants.iom.int

8. Frank Dikötter, *The Cultural Revolution: A People's History, 1962–1976* (London, U.K.: Bloomsbury, 2016).

9. María-Teresa Gil-Bazo, "Asylum as a General Principle of International Law," *International Journal of Refugee Law*, Vol. 27, No. 1 (2015), pp. 20–22.

10. Ibid.

11. Emma Haddad, *The Refugee in International Society: Between Sovereigns* (Cambridge, U.K.: Cambridge University Press, 2008), pp. 51–53.

12. María-Teresa Gil-Bazo, "Asylum as a General Principle of International Law," *International Journal of Refugee Law*, Vol. 27, No. 1 (2015), p. 23.

13. Marjoleine Zieck, "The 1956 Hungarian Refugee Emergency, an Early and Instructive Case of Resettlement," *Amsterdam Law Forum*, Vol. 5 No. 2 (2013), pp. 45–63.

14. Gary Sheffield, *A Short History of the First World War*, (London, U.K.: Oneworld, 2014). See also the historian Hew Strachan's discussion of the 1914 Belgian migration on the BBC Radio program, *Start the Week*. Available at http://www.bbc.co.uk/programmes/b07bb89x

15. See Anna Holian and G. Daniel Cohen, "Introduction to Special Issue: The Refugee in the Postwar World, 1945–1960," *Journal of Refugee Studies*, Vol. 25, No. 3 (2012), pp. 313–25

16. For a history of UNHCR, see Gil Loescher, "'UNHCR and Forced Migration," in Elena Fiddian-Qasmiyeh, Gil Loescher, Katy Long, and Nando Sigona, eds., *The Oxford Handbook of Refugee and Forced Migration Studies* (Oxford, U.K.: Oxford University Press, 2014).

17. Ibid.

18. http://www.historylearningsite.co.uk/vietnam-war/vietnamese-boat-people/

19. http://www.grida.no/graphicslib/detail/refugees-and-displaced-people-from-the-former-yugoslavia-since-1991_0c5a

20. *UNHCR Global Trends: Forced Displacement in 2015*. Available at https://s3.amazonaws.com/unhcrsharedmedia/2016/2016-06-20-global-trends/2016-06-14-Global-Trends-2015.pdf

21. Ibid.

22. The list of top five was as follows: Turkey (2.5 million), Pakistan (1.6 million), Lebanon (1.1 million), Iran (979,400), Ethiopia (736,100), and Jordan (664,100).

23. Jodi Kantor and Catrin Einhorn, "Refugees Encounter a Foreign Word: Welcome," *New York Times*, 1 July 2016. Available at http://www.nytimes.com/2016/07/01/world/americas/canada-syrian-refugees.html?_r=0

24. http://www.zeit.de/politik/deutschland/2015-11/anti-immigrant-violence-germany

25. Standard Eurobarometer 84. Available at http://ec.europa.eu/COMMFrontOffice/PublicOpinion/index.cfm/Survey/getSurveyDetail/instruments/STANDARD/surveyKy/2098

26. For an overview of the agreement, see http://www.bbc.com/news/world-europe-35854413

27. http://www.marina.difesa.it/EN/operations/Pagine/MareNostrum.aspx

28. See, for example, the British House of Lords published report on Operation Sophia, available at http://www.publications.parliament.uk/pa/ld201516/ldselect/ldeucom/144/14404.htm#_idTextAnchor005

29. Patrick Kingsley, "More than 700 migrants feared dead in three Mediterranean sinkings," *Guardian*, 29 May 2016. Available at

https://www.theguardian.com/world/2016/may/29/700-migrants-feared-dead-mediterranean-says-un-refugees

30. *Obstacle Course to Europe: A Policy-Made Humanitarian Crisis at EU Borders*, Médecins Sans Frontières, December 2015. Available at http://www.msf.org/sites/msf.org/files/msf_obstacle_course_to_europe.pdf

31. For an overview of the phenomenon of "mixed migration," see Nicholas Van Hear, Rebecca Brubaker and Thais Bessa, "Managing Mobility for Human Development: The Growing Salience of Mixed Migration," *Human Development Research Paper 2009/20*. United Nations Development Program. Available at https://mpra.ub.uni-muenchen.de/19202/1/MPRA_paper_19202.pdf

32. http://www.wired.com/2015/12/smartphone-syrian-refugee-crisis/

33. http://www.independent.ie/business/technology/news/how-tech-firms-are-helping-to-solve-the-refugee-crisis-34262301.html

34. http://news.psu.edu/story/350156/2015/03/26/research/ist-researchers-explore-technology-use-syrian-refugee-camp

35. http://europe.newsweek.com/five-ways-technology-helping-refugee-crisis-333741

36. Thomas Grammeltoft-Hansen, *Access to Asylum: International Refugee Law and the Globalisation of Migration Control* (Cambridge, U.K.: Cambridge University Press, 2011).

37. Ruth Wodak, *The Politics of Fear: What Right-Wing Populist Discourses Mean* (Thousand Oaks, CA: Sage Publications, 2015).

38. Joanne van Selm, "Resettlement," in Elena Fiddian-Qasmiyeh, Gil Loescher, Katy Long, and Nando Sigona, eds., *The Oxford*

Handbook of Refugee and Forced Migration Studies (Oxford, U.K.: Oxford University Press, 2014), p. 514.

39. Eiko Thielemann, *Does Policy Matter? On Governments' Attempts to Control Unwanted Migration*. IIIS Discussion Paper No. 9 (2003). Available at http://papers.ssrn.com/sol3/papers.cfm?abstract_id=495631

40. Michael Ignatieff, *The Rights Revolution*, 2nd Edition (Toronto: House of Anansi Press, 2007).

41. See the discussion of this risk in *The United States and the Syrian Refugee Crisis: A Plan of Action*, Shorenstein Center on Media, Politics, and Public Policy, Harvard University, January 2016. Available at http://shorensteincenter.org/united-states-syrian-refugee-crisis-plan-action/

42. http://migrationpolicycentre.eu/docs/policy_brief/P.B.2015-12.pdf?utm_source=MPC+Newsletter&utm_campaign=5d651e0cf8-New_MPC_Policy_Brief_12_22_2015&utm_medium=email&utm_term=0_5739ea1f8b-5d651e0cf8-40570957

43. Laura Hammond, "'Voluntary' Repatriation and Reintegration," in Elena Fiddian-Qasmiyeh, Gil Loescher, Katy Long, and Nando Sigona, eds., *The Oxford Handbook of Refugee and Forced Migration Studies* (Oxford, U.K.: Oxford University Press, 2014).

44. Seyla Benhabib, *The Rights of Others: Aliens, Residents, and Citizens* (Cambridge, U.K.: Cambridge University Press, 2004), p. 87.

45. For an example of the former, see Michael Walzer, *Spheres of Justice: A Defense of Pluralism and Equality* (New York: Basic Books, 1984), and for an example of the latter, see Joseph Carens, "Aliens and Citizens: The Case for Open Borders," *The Review of Politics*, Vol. 49, No. 2 (1987), pp. 251–73.

46. Garrett Hardin, "Lifeboat Ethics: The Case against Helping the Poor," *Psychology Today*, Vol. 8, No. 4 (1974). Available at http://web.ntpu.edu.tw/~language/course/research/lifeboat.pdf

47. http://www.utilitarian.net/singer/by/199704--.htm

48. Anna Badkhen, "The New Reorder," *Foreign Policy*, Vol. 216 (January/February 2016).

49. Alexander Betts, *Survival Migration: Failed Governance and the Crisis of Displacement* (Ithaca, NY: Cornell University Press, 2013).

50. Seyla Benhabib, *The Rights of Others: Aliens, Residents, and Citizens* (Cambridge, U.K.: Cambridge University Press, 2004), p. 221.

CHAPTER 4: THE RETURN OF COLD WAR

1. Louis Charbonneau, "Russia: Yanukovych asked Putin to Use Force to Save Ukraine," Reuters, 3 March 2014. Available at http://www.reuters.com/article/us-ukraine-crisis-un-idUSBREA2224720140304

2. For an examination of the rationale deployed by the U.S. and USSR during the Cold War, see Thomas M. Franck and Edward Weisband, *Word Politics: Verbal Strategy Among the Superpowers* (Oxford, U.K.: Oxford University Press, 1972).

3. Melvyn Leffler, *For the Soul of Mankind: The United States, the Soviet Union, and the Cold War* (New York: Hill and Wang, 2007).

4. Chrystia Freeland, *Sale of the Century: Russia's Wild Ride from Communism to Capitalism* (New York: Crown Business, 2000).

5. http://foreignpolicy.com/2014/03/04/welcome-to-cold-war-ii/

6. http://www.theguardian.com/world/2014/nov/19/new-cold-war-back-to-bad-old-days-russia-west-putin-ukraine

7. George F. Kennan, "The Long Telegram," February 1946. The Telegram was subsequently revised and published under a pseudonym and became widely known as the "X Article." "The Sources of Soviet Conduct," *Foreign Affairs,* Vol. 25, No. 4 (1947), pp. 566–82.

8. Strobe Talbott, "The Making of Vladimir Putin," *Politico Magazine,* 19 April 2014.

9. Liudas Zdanavičius and Matthew Czekaj, eds., *Russia's Zapad 2013 Military Exercise: Lessons for Baltic Regional Security* (Jamestown Foundation, 2015). Available at http://www.jamestown.org/uploads/media/Zapad_2013_-_Full_online_final.pdf

10. http://www.europeanleadershipnetwork.org/medialibrary/2014/11/09/6375e3da/Dangerous%20Brinkmanship.pdf

11. Office of the United Nations High Commissioner for Human Rights, *Report on the Human Rights Situation in Ukraine, 16 November 2015 to 15 February 2016.* Available at http://www.ohchr.org/Documents/Countries/UA/Ukraine_13th_HRMMU_Report_3March2016.pdf

12. Somini Sengupta, "Russian Foreign Minister Defends Airstrikes in Syria," *New York Times,* 1 October 2015. Available at http://www.nytimes.com/2015/10/02/world/europe/russia-airstrikes-syria-assad.html

13. "Taking Sides: Major Split in the UNSC after Syria Veto," *Russia Today,* 5 February 2012. Available at https://www.rt.com/news/lavrov-clinton-syria-resolution-517/

14. http://www.syriahr.com/en/2016/03/31/russian-warplanes-kill-5081-civilians-40-of-them-were-civilians/

15. John Lewis Gaddis, *Strategies of Containment* (Oxford, U.K.: Oxford University Press, 1982), Chapter Two.

16. http://www.energypost.eu/case-nord-stream-2/

17. http://www.fiia.fi/en/publication/571/dividing_the_eu_with_energy/

18. Edward Lucas, *The New Cold War: Putin's Russia and the Threat to the West*, 3rd edition (New York: Palgrave Macmillan, 2014); and Lucas Kello, "The Meaning of the Cyber Revolution: Perils to Theory and Statecraft," *International Security*, Vol. 38, No. 2 (Fall 2013), pp. 7–40.

19. https://www.fbi.gov/news/stories/2011/october/russian_103111/russian_103111

20. http://www.reuters.com/article/us-usa-russia-putin-idUSKCN0PE0CO20150704

21. John Lewis Gaddis, *We Now Know: Rethinking Cold War History* (Oxford, U.K.: Oxford University Press, 1997), p. 291.

22. Ibid., p. 152.

23. Halford J. Mackinder, "The Geographical Pivot of History" in *Democratic Ideals and Reality* (New York: Norton and Company, 1962).

24. Walter Russell Mead, "The Return of Geopolitics," *Foreign Affairs*, Vol. 93, No. 3 (May/June 2014).

25. Alexis de Tocqueville, *Democracy in America*, ed. J. P. Mayer, trans. George Lawrence (New York: Doubleday, 1969), pp. 412–13.

26. Edward Lucas, *The New Cold War: Putin's Russia and the Threat to the West,* 3rd edition (New York: Palgrave Macmillan, 2014).

27. James Stavridis, "Are We Entering a New Cold War? It's Not a Strong Russia We Should Fear, But a Weak One," *Foreign Policy,* 16 February 2016. Available at http://foreignpolicy.com/2016/02/17/are-we-entering-a-new-cold-war-russia-europe/

28. Robert Legvold, "Managing the New Cold War: What Moscow and Washington Can Learn from the Last One," *Foreign Affairs,* Vol. 93, No. 4 (2014). Available at https://www.foreignaffairs.com/articles/united-states/2014-06-16/managing-new-cold-war

29. Andrew Kuchins, "Crimea One Year On: Where Does Russia Go Now?" *Center for Strategic and International Studies,* Vol. 18 (March 2015).

30. James Stavridis, "Are We Entering a New Cold War? It's Not a Strong Russia We Should Fear, But a Weak One," *Foreign Policy,* 16 February 2016. Available at http://foreignpolicy.com/2016/02/17/are-we-entering-a-new-cold-war-russia-europe/

31. Michael McFaul, "Putin the (Not So) Great," *Politico Magazine,* 4 August 2014.

32. Sergey Karaganov, "Europe and Russia: Preventing a New Cold War," *Russia in Global Affairs,* No. 2 (April/June 2014). Available at http://eng.globalaffairs.ru/number/Europe-and-Russia-Preventing-a-New-Cold-War-16701

33. http://www.ecfr.eu/article/commentary_in_search_of_russias_elusive_repression_strategy_6021. The legislation that outlaws these activities appears in Articles 280 and 282 of the Criminal Code of the Russian Federation.

34. http://news.bbc.co.uk/2/hi/europe/7124585.stm

35. https://www.amnesty.org/en/press-releases/2007/11/russian-federation-systematic-repression-eve-elections-20071128/

36. http://www.theguardian.com/world/2012/mar/05/russian-election-skewed-putin-favour

37. http://www.osce.org/odihr/elections/88661

38. http://www.forbes.com/sites/paulroderickgregory/2016/03/14/putin-changes-september-election-rules-to-prop-up-his-united-russia-party/#7e6b61c958a2

39. Edward Lucas, *The New Cold War: Putin's Russia and the Threat to the West*, 3rd edition (New York: Palgrave Macmillan, 2014).

40. http://www.nytimes.com/2016/01/22/world/europe/alexander-litvinenko-poisoning-inquiry-britain.html?_r=0

41. http://www.themoscowtimes.com/article/502258.html

42. http://www.theatlantic.com/international/archive/2015/04/how-the-media-became-putins-most-powerful-weapon/391062/

43. Edward Lucas, *The New Cold War: Putin's Russia and the Threat to the West*, 3rd edition (New York: Palgrave Macmillan, 2014).

44. Maya Atwal and Edwin Bacon, "The Youth Movement Nashi: Contentious Politics, Civil Society, and Party Politics," *East European Politics*, Vol. 28, No. 3 (2012), pp. 256–66.

45. Robert Kagan, "The End of the End of History", *The New Republic*, 23 April 2008.

46. Edward Lucas, *The New Cold War: Putin's Russia and the Threat to the West*, 3rd edition (New York: Palgrave Macmillan, 2014).

47. https://www.wilsoncenter.org/publication/putin-and-the-russian-tradition-illiberal-democratic#sthash.3t29Kguf.dpuf

48. http://www.theguardian.com/world/datablog/2015/jul/23/vladimir-putins-approval-rating-at-record-levels

49. Sergey Lavrov, "The Present and the Future of Global Politics," *Russia in Global Affairs*, No. 2, April/June 2007. Available at http://eng.globalaffairs.ru/print/number/n_8554

50. Fareed Zakaria, *The Future of Freedom: Illiberal Democracy at Home and Abroad* (New York: W. W. Norton, 2001).

51. Edward Lucas, *The New Cold War: Putin's Russia and the Threat to the West*, 3rd edition (New York: Palgrave Macmillan, 2014), p. 6.

52. Vladislav Surkov, "Nationalization of the Future" (2006), cited in Andrey Okara, "Sovereign Democracy: A New Russian Idea or a PR Project?" *Russia in Global Affairs*, No. 3, 2007. Available at http://eng.globalaffairs.ru/number/n_9123

53. Ivan Krastev, "'Sovereign Democracy,' Russian Style," *Open Democracy*, 16 November 2006. Available at https://www.opendemocracy.net/globalization-institutions_government/sovereign_democracy_4104.jsp

54. Edward Lucas, *The New Cold War: Putin's Russia and the Threat to the West*, 3rd edition (New York: Palgrave Macmillan, 2014), pp. 156–57.

55. Leonid Polyakov, "Sovereign Democracy as a Concept for Russia," *Russia Beyond the Headlines*, 24 October 2007. Available at http://rbth.com/articles/2007/10/25/sovereign democracy_as_a_concept_for_russia.html

56. Robert Kagan, "The End of the End of History", *The New Republic*, 23 April 2008.

57. http://www.theguardian.com/commentisfree/2014/dec/08/russia-europe-right-putin-front-national-eu

58. http://www.kormany.hu/en/the-prime-minister/the-prime-minister-s-speeches/prime-minister-viktor-orban-s-speech-at-the-25th-balvanyos-summer-free-university-and-student-camp

59. http://www.independent.co.uk/news/world/europe/greece-crisis-alexis-tsipras-woos-vladimir-putin-as-greeks-rush-for-their-savings-10333104.html

60. http://www.nytimes.com/2014/05/21/opinion/bittner-putin-mr-putins-far-right-friends.html?_r=0

61. Samuel Charap and Jeremy Shapiro, "How to Avoid a New Cold War," *Current History* (October 2014), pp. 265–71.

62. For a strong statement of this view, see John Mearsheimer, "Why the Ukraine Crisis is the West's Fault: Liberal Delusions that Provoked Putin," *Foreign Affairs*, Vol. 93, No. 5 (2014).

63. Robert Kagan, "The End of the End of History", *The New Republic*, 23 April 2008.

64. George F. Kennan, cited in Gaddis, *Strategies of Containment*, p. 35.

CHAPTER 5: THE RETURN OF INEQUALITY

1. George F. Kennan, "The Long Telegram," February 1946.

2. The figures are based on U.S. Census Data. See the research conducted by the Carsey Institute at http://carseyinstitute.unh.edu/publication/IB-Same-Day-Child-Poverty-2012

3. Joseph E. Stiglitz, *The Price of Inequality: How Today's Divided Society Endangers Our Future* (W. W. Norton, 2012); and Thomas

Piketty, *Capital in the Twenty-First Century*, translated by Arthur Goldhammer (Cambridge, MA: The Belknap Press of Harvard University Press, 2014).

4. George F. Kennan, "The Long Telegram," February 1946.

5. Branko Milanović, *Global Inequality: A New Approach for the Age of Globalization* (Cambridge, MA: Harvard University Press, 2016).

6. Thomas Piketty, *Capital in the Twenty-First Century*, translated by Arthur Goldhammer (Cambridge, MA: The Belknap Press of Harvard University Press, 2014), pp. 41–42.

7. Ibid, pp. 35–36.

8. Göran Therborn, *The Killing Fields of Inequality* (Cambridge, U.K.: Polity Press, 2013).

9. Joseph E. Stiglitz, *Rewriting the Rules of the American Economy: An Agenda for Growth and Shared Prosperity* (London, U.K.: W. W. Norton & Company, 2015).

10. Facundo Alvaredo, Anthony B. Atkinson, Thomas Piketty, Emmanuel Saez, and Gabriel Zucman, *The World Wealth and Income Database*. Available at http://www.wid.world/

11. Chrystia Freeland, *Plutocrats: The Rise of the New Global Super-Rich and the Fall of Everyone Else* (New York: Penguin, 2012).

12. OECD, *Focus on Inequality and Growth*, December 2014.

13. Keith Banting and John Myles, eds., *Inequality and the Fading of Redistributive Politics* (Vancouver, B.C.: University of British Columbia Press, 2013).

14. Thomas Lemieux and W. Craig Riddell, "Who are Canada's Top 1%?" *Institute for Research on Public Policy*, 9 July 2015. Available at http://irpp.org/research-studies/aots5-riddell-lemieux/?mc_cid=98dd3664a8&mc_eid=6e34c36680

15. https://www.thestar.com/news/gta/2015/02/27/toronto-now-canadas-inequality-capital-united-way-study-shows.html

16. Available at http://3cities.neighbourhoodchange.ca

17. Benjamin Disraeli, *Sybil, or the Nations*, Oxford World Classics paperback edition (Oxford: Oxford University Press, 1998), p. 66.

18. Thomas Piketty, *Capital in the Twenty-First Century*, translated by Arthur Goldhammer (Cambridge, MA: The Belknap Press of Harvard University Press, 2014), p. 8.

19. Paul Krugman, "Why We're In A New Gilded Age," *New York Review of Books*, 8 May 2014. Available at: http://www.nybooks.com/articles/2014/05/08/thomas-piketty-new-gilded-age/

20. Branko Milanović, *Global Inequality: A New Approach for the Age of Globalization* (Cambridge, MA: Harvard University Press, 2016).

21. Cited in Christian Schweiger, *The EU and the Global Financial Crisis: New Varieties of Capitalism* (Cheltenham, U.K.: Edward Elgar Publishing, 2014), p. 96.

22. Joseph E. Stiglitz, *The Great Divide* (London, U.K.: Allen Lane, 2015).

23. Joseph E. Stiglitz and Linda J. Bilmes, "The Book of Jobs," *Vanity Fair*, 6 December 2011. Available at: http://www.vanityfair.com/news/2012/01/stiglitz-depression-201201

24. See, for example, Andrew Berg and Jonathan Ostry, "Inequality and Unsustainable Growth: Two Sides of the Same Coin?" International Monetary Fund Staff Discussion Note No. 11/08, April 2011; and International Monetary Fund, "Fiscal Policy and Income Inequality," Policy Paper, 23 January 2014. Available at http://www.imf.org/external/np/pp/eng/2014/012314.pdf

25. OECD, "How's Life," 23 October 2015. Available at http://www.oecd.org/std/how-s-life-23089679.htm

26. Richard Wilkinson and Kate Pickett, *The Spirit Level: Why More Equal Societies Almost Always Do Better* (London: Allen Lane, 2009).

27. Branko Milanović, *Global Inequality: A New Approach for the Age of Globalization* (Cambridge, MA: Harvard University Press, 2016).

28. Joseph E. Stiglitz, *The Price of Inequality: How Today's Divided Society Endangers Our Future* (W. W. Norton, 2012), p. 384.

29. See, for example, Tom Englehardt, "5 Signs America is Devolving into a Plutocracy," *Salon,* 22 March 2015. Available at http://www.salon.com/2015/03/22/5_signs_america_is_devolving_into_a_plutocracy_partner/

30. Michael Brenner, "Plutocracy in America," *Huffington Post,* 1 April 2013. Available at http://www.huffingtonpost.com/michael-brenner/plutocracy-in-america_b_2992965.html

31. Martin Gilens, *Affluence and Influence: Economic Inequality and Political Power in America* (Princeton, NJ: Princeton University Press, 2014).

32. Steve Fraser, *The Age of Acquiescence: The Life and Death of American Resistance to Organized Wealth and Power* (New York: Little, Brown, 2015).

33. See Media Reform Coalition, "The Media's Attack on Corbyn," 26 November 2015. Available at http://www.mediareform.org.uk/press-ethics-and-regulation/the-medias-attack-on-corbyn-research-shows-barrage-of-negative-coverage

34. Martin Kettle, "For Labour the Choice Is Stark: Purity or Power," *Guardian,* 25 June 2015.

35. Paul Myerscough, "Corbyn in the Media," *London Review of Books*, Vol. 37, No. 2 (October 2015), pp. 8–9.

36. Joseph E. Stiglitz, *The Price of Inequality: How Today's Divided Society Endangers Our Future* (W. W. Norton, 2012).

37. Thomas Rainsborough, "The Putney Debates: The Debate on the Franchise (1647)," in *Divine Right and Democracy*, ed. David Wooton (Harmondsworth: Penguin, 1986), pp. 285–317.

38. Marshall Steinbaum, "Should the Middle Class Fear the World's Poor?" *Boston Review*, 11 May 2016.

39. The earliest explanation of loss aversion can be found in Daniel Kahneman and Amos Tversky, "Prospect Theory: An Analysis of Decision Under Risk," *Econometrica*, Vol. 47 (1979), pp. 263–91.

40. H. G. Wells, *The Shape of Things to Come* (London, U.K.: Penguin Classics, 2005), Chapter 14.

41. David Runciman, "The Confidence Trap," *Foreign Policy*, 17 October 2013. Available at http://foreignpolicy.com/2013/10/17/the-confidence-trap/. See also his full-length monograph, *The Confidence Trap: A History of Democracy in Crisis from World War I to the Present*.

42. Ibid.

43. Ibid.

44. David Runciman, *The Confidence Trap: A History of Democracy in Crisis from World War I to the Present* (Princeton, NJ: Princeton University Press, 2013), p. 29.

45. *Churchill By Himself: The Definitive Collection of Quotations*, Richard Langworth, ed. (New York: Public Affairs, 2008), p. 574.

46. Paul K. Piff, "Wealth and the Inflated Self: Class, Entitlement, and Narcissism," *Personality and Social Psychology Bulletin*, Vol. 40,

No. 1 (2014), pp. 34–43; and Paul K. Piff et al., "Higher Social Class Predicts Increased Unethical Behavior," *Proceedings of the National Academy of Sciences of the USA*, Vol. 109, No. 11 (March 2012), pp. 4086–91.

47. Michael W. Kraus, Stéphan Côté, and Dacher Keltner, "Social Class, Contextualism, and Empathetic Accuracy," *Psychological Science*, Vol. 21 (2010), pp. 1716–23.

48. Paul K. Piff, "Wealth and the Inflated Self: Class, Entitlement, and Narcissism," *Personality and Social Psychology Bulletin*, Vol. 40, No. 1 (2014).

49. See Piff's Ted Talk, "Does Money Make You Mean?" originally broadcast on 20 December 2013. Available at https://tedsummaries.com/2014/09/05/paul-piff-does-money-make-you-mean/

50. Elizabeth Anderson, "What Is the Point of Equality?" *Ethics*, Vol. 9, No. 2 (1999).

51. Paul Mason, "Thomas Piketty's Capital," *Guardian*, 28 April 2014. Available at https://www.theguardian.com/books/2014/apr/28/thomas-piketty-capital-surprise-bestseller

AFTERWORD

1. Freedom House, *Freedom in the World 2017: Populists and Autocrats; The Dual Threat to Global Democracy*. Full report available at https://freedomhouse.org/report/freedom-world/freedom-world-2017

2. Freedom House, *Nations in Transit 2017: The False Promise of Populism*. Full report available at https://freedomhouse.org/report/nations-transit/nations-transit-2017

3. Roberto Stefan Foa and Yascha Mounk, "The Danger of Deconsolidation: The Democratic Disconnect," *Journal of Democracy*, Vol. 27, No. 3 (July 2016), pp. 5–17.

4. Francis Fukuyama, "US against the World? Trump's America and the New Global Order," *Financial Times*, 11 November 2016.

5. Angelique Chrisafis, "French Election: Macron Hailed as Winner of Bruising Le Pen TV Debate," *Guardian*, 4 May 2017.

6. Interview with Carolyn Lukensmeyer, CBC News, 21 October 2016. Available at http://www.cbc.ca/player/play/791109699872/

7. Jonathan Rauch, "Containing Trump," *The Atlantic*, March 2017. Available at https://www.theatlantic.com/magazine/archive/2017/03/containing-trump/513854/

8. Justin W., "Philosophers on the 2016 US Presidential Race," *Daily Nous*, 14 March 2016. Available at http://dailynous.com/2016/03/14/philosophers-on-the-2016-u-s-presidential-race/

9. Michael Gerson, "Trump's 110th-Day Speech May Have Been the Most Hate-Filled in Modern History," *Washington Post*, 1 May 2017.

10. Francis Fukuyama, "US against the World? Trump's America and the New Global Order," *Financial Times*, 11 November 2016.

11. Abby Phillip, Robert Barnes, and Ed O'Keefe, "Supreme Court Nominee Gorsuch Says Trump's Attacks on the Judiciary Are 'Demoralizing,'" *Washington Post*, 9 February 2017.

12. Roberto Stefan Foa and Yascha Mounk, "The Danger of Deconsolidation: The Democratic Disconnect," *Journal of Democracy*, Vol. 27, No. 3 (July 2016), pp. 5–17.

13. Roula Khalaf, "Could Populism Represent a Fertile Regression?" *Financial Times*, 4 May 2017.

14. David Runciman, "The Confidence Trap," *Foreign Policy*, 17 October 2013. Available at http://foreignpolicy.com/2013/10/17/the-confidence-trap/

15. Jonathan Rauch, "Containing Trump," *The Atlantic*, March 2017. Available at https://www.theatlantic.com/magazine/archive/2017/03/containing-trump/513854/

16. Yascha Mounk, cited in ibid.

17. C. B. Macpherson, *The Political Theory of Possessive Individualism: From Hobbes to Locke* (Oxford: Oxford University Press, 1962).

18. C. B. Macpherson, *The Real World of Democracy* (Toronto: House of Anansi Press, 1965).

19. Dennis C. Rasmussen, "Adam Smith on What Is Wrong with Economic Inequality," *American Political Science Review*, Vol. 110, No. 2 (May 2016), pp. 342–52.

20. Tony Wood, "Eat Your Spinach," *London Review of Books*, Vol. 39, No. 5 (March 2017), pp. 9–12.

21. Robert Legvold, *Return to Cold War*. London: Polity, 2016.

22. Tony Wood, "Eat Your Spinach," *London Review of Books*, Vol. 39, No. 5 (March 2017), pp. 9–12.

23. Evan Osnos, David Remnick, and Joshua Yaffa, "Trump, Putin and the New Cold War," *The New Yorker*, 6 March 2017. Available at http://www.newyorker.com/magazine/2017/03/06/trump-putin-and-the-new-cold-war

24. Uri Friedman, "Russia's Interference in the U.S. Elections Was Just the Beginning," *The Atlantic,* 26 April 2017.

25. Report of the Independent International Commission on the Syrian Arab Republic, UN doc. A/HRC/34/64, 2 February 2017. Available at https://documents-dds-ny.un.org/doc/UNDOC/GEN/G17/026/63/PDF/G1702663.pdf?OpenElement

26. "'Crimes of Historic Proportions' Being Committed in Aleppo, UN Rights Chief Warns," UN News Centre, 21 October 2016. Available at http://www.un.org/apps/news/story.asp?NewsID=55364#.WSgvtTOB0fA

27. "Syria: Aleppo Terror and Slaughter Must Be Halted," Press Release, Office of the High Commissioner for Human Rights, 13 December 2016.

28. Richard Gowan, "End Times Diplomacy at the UN?" *Columbia Journal of International Affairs* (forthcoming, summer 2017). Available at https://jia.sipa.columbia.edu/online-articles/end-times-diplomacy-un

29. The transcript of the debate can be found at UN doc., S/PV.7834, 13 December 2016.

30. Richard Gowan, "End Times Diplomacy at the UN?" *Columbia Journal of International Affairs* (forthcoming, summer 2017). Available at https://jia.sipa.columbia.edu/online-articles/end-times-diplomacy-un

31. Overview available at http://www.worldbank.org/en/topic/fragilityconflictviolence

32. International Crisis Group, "Instruments of Pain: Conflict and Famine", 13 April 2017. Available at https://www.crisisgroup.org/global/instruments-pain-conflict-and-famine

33. David Bosco, "We've Been Here Before: The Durability of Multilateralism," *Columbia Journal of International Affairs*, 13 April 2017. Available at https://jia.sipa.columbia.edu/online-articles/durability-multilateralism

34. C. B. Macpheron, *The Real World of Democracy* (Toronto: House of Anansi Press, 1965), p. 3.

ACKNOWLEDGEMENTS

The initial idea for *The Return of History* was developed through conversations with my long-time friend Greg Kelly, producer of CBC Radio's *Ideas*. He also pointed me in the direction of various pernicious effects of economic inequality, including the findings of the behavioural psychologists at Berkeley. Greg is one of a kind — and I wish there were more of his kind. His creativity, quirky humour, and kindness are enriching for all who know and work with him. Above all, I have Greg to thank for giving me the privilege of delivering the Massey Lectures.

The CBC's Philip Coulter was a great source of inspiration as the ideas for the lectures and book evolved. Philip is a true polyglot, and his enthusiasm for drawing the connections between past and present is contagious. Janie Yoon, at House of Anansi Press, also helped me to see more possibilities for drawing out the book's central argument. And as an editor, she is by a wide margin the best and most diligent I have worked with: conscientious and appropriately demanding — yet always supportive. There are moments I suspect she worried we wouldn't make it to the finishing line, but she never showed it! As the publishing world changes, Janie is a rare but precious asset.

Joao Labareda and Rutger Birnie, doctoral researchers at the European University Institute in Florence, were much more than research assistants: they were my intellectual companions over the past year. Both of them understood — sometimes better than I — what *The Return of History* needed to convey, and both helped me to improve the messages with evidence and wider context. They also managed to pick up the random threads I dropped (often late at night over email), and enabled me to weave them into the expanding tapestry. I only hope I have done justice to their hard work and ideas. To them, *grazie mille*.

Martina Selmi, my fantastically efficient and cheerful assistant at the EUI, has seen me through an incredibly intense year by managing my academic responsibilities, my role at the United

Nations, and the writing of this book. She carefully guarded my "writing days" and supported me in ways too numerous to elaborate.

My greatest thanks are reserved for my family. My children, Ellie and Max, have had to share me far too often this year. They have also had to keep the door to the home office closed and tolerate my domination of the iMac. I now look forward to showing them Mummy's final product. But I owe the greatest debt to my husband, Frank. There were many evenings when a cup of tea — or glass of wine! — would suddenly appear on the desk. But Frank also kept the rest of our lives ticking along. The phrase "I couldn't have done it without you" is overused, but couldn't be more appropriate. He makes the impossible seem possible. Above all, he keeps me smiling.

JW
Florence, Italy
July 2016

INDEX

(THE CBC MASSEY LECTURES SERIES)

LOVE THE MASSEY LECTURES? THERE'S AN APP FOR THAT!

Available for free on the iTunes App Store, the award-winning Massey Lectures iPad App immerses users in the Massey universe. Winner of the Silver Cannes Lion Award and a Best Online Design, the app brings together, for the first time, the full text of the CBC Massey Lectures with the audio recordings of the live lectures, and contains free bonus content, including discussions with the authors, video interviews, and more.

Uncover the rich legacy and history of the CBC Massey Lectures series, from 1961 to today. Learn more about selected Massey authors, their lives, their achievements, and their impact. Explore the complex web of themes within the Massey universe, and hear unique thoughts and insights from the lecturers. And contribute to the conversation yourself.

Download at bit.ly/MasseysApp

MASSEY LECTURES   ANANSI

The Massey Lectures iPad App was conceived, designed, and developed by Critical Mass, a global digital marketing agency.